Prayers
for
Saints

Rupert
Bristow

Prayers for Saints

**A biography and prayer for over 670 saints
in the Anglican, Catholic and Celtic traditions**

Augsburg Books

MINNEAPOLIS

For Kevin for his active encouragement of this project
For Sarah for her practical support

PRAYERS FOR SAINTS
A biography and prayer for over 670 saints in the Anglican, Catholic and Celtic traditions

Cover image: Emily Drake
Cover design: Emily Drake

Print ISBN: 978-1-5064-6018-5

Contents

About the author

Rupert Bristow, a Reader in Trinity Benefice, Folkestone, is the author of six books of prayers and was Director of Education for Canterbury Diocese from 1995 until his retirement in 2008. He has taught on VSO, was the second Director of the UK Council for Overseas Student Affairs, and then Dean of Student Services at London South Bank University. He has also been a specialist adviser to a House of Commons Select Committee, edited and written for various educational publications and chaired Kent SACRE (Standing Advisory Council for Religious Education). He is an Honorary Fellow of Canterbury Christ Church University.

Foreword

'Greet one another with a holy kiss. All the saints greet you.'
(2 Corinthians 13:12)

St Paul starts his first letter to the Corinthians, 'To the church of God that is in Corinth, to those who are sanctified in Christ Jesus, called to be saints . . .'

He frequently calls the Christian community from which he is writing, or to which he is writing, 'the saints'.

If we are to follow Christ, we are called to be saints. As such we join the great company of men and women through Christian history who make up the body of Christ, who are holy as he who called us is holy (see 1 Peter 1:15).

Rupert Bristow holds up for our instruction and as an example to us one or more of the saints for every day of the year. Most have been called saints by at least part of the universal Church in one way or another. All can encourage us in our Christian pilgrimage.

And to help us deeper into the mystery of their faithful following of Christ, we are also given a prayer, to bring us as it were to our knees. That will help move us from just thinking into direct communication with almighty God, without whose grace we cannot follow Christ.

The way of discipleship is not easy. We need the encouragement of the Church. That means the living, local Christian community. But it also means all the saints who have gone before us and now enjoy the fullness of the vision, who know God as they have always been known, who now see face to face what we see only through a cloud darkly.

The Collect for All Saints' Day is well worth pondering and seriously praying:

> Almighty God, you have knit together your elect in one communion and fellowship in the mystical body of your Son Christ our Lord: grant us grace so to follow your blessed saints in all virtuous and godly living, that we may come to those inexpressible joys that you have prepared for those who truly love you; through Jesus Christ our Lord. Amen

May the example of the saints inspire you and their fellowship in Christ encourage you! And may almighty God bless you!

The Very Reverend Dr John Hall
Dean of Westminster

Introduction

I came to write this book when I thought it might be good to read and pray about a 'saint' on a daily basis and I found that there was no one book to turn to for a comprehensive set of prayers for the saints, so I thought I would try to write one. Initially I read about saints on a day by day basis and based a prayer on what I had learnt, but Kevin Mayhew saw the need for the prayer and story to be combined and the book then took shape in earnest, as well as taking longer in practice!

I am of course indebted to those (many) books that have been compiled on the lives of the saints, on which I have drawn for the back stories and which are listed in the bibliography. As for the prayers, any resemblance to existing prayers is coincidental and may just stem from the fact that those prayers have been inspired by the same person, the same 'saint'.

In this book the term 'saint' is shorthand for a person who has shown their Christian witness in a special way, often through miracles and martyrdom, but for other reasons too. They include those in some traditions, such as the Roman Catholic Church, who have technically been raised to the status of 'saints', as well as those who, in the Church of England for example, which no longer confers the status of 'saint', nevertheless have feast days or lesser festivals dedicated to them in their Church calendars, for which prayers can be found in *Common Worship*. In all cases the date in brackets is the date of death, as far as is known.

Because in writing this book I rapidly realised that the number of 'saints' is almost limitless, I have made choices along the way which may upset some. I wanted to ensure that there is at least one saint included for every day of the calendar year, but on days when many saints are commemorated I have not necessarily featured them all. In some of these cases, where evidence seems a bit thin on the life of the person, I have tended to omit. So, if I have left out your own personal, or local, favourite saint, I plead guilty and apologise! There is always the internet to fill any gaps.

At the same time, I have tried to honour most, if not all, of the saints of the main Christian traditions and hope that I have not erred and strayed too much in this regard.

As to use, the CD Rom allows individual pages to be printed or downloaded for any one day or saint, for a group, a service, or inclusion in intercessions. I will personally turn to this book as I originally thought I might and hope others will find it useful on that basis too. It has been a long and rewarding task – and I trust it may become what John Bell has usefully termed 'a common demanding task' for many individuals and groups of Christians to read and pray about some astonishing people who have kept the flame of faith alive over the centuries. Lest we forget . . .

Rupert Bristow

January

1 January

Almachus (Telemachus), monk and martyr (c 400)

Almachus was a monk who came to Rome from the east and who made every effort to put an end to gladiatorial combats. This included running into the arena to try to separate the contestants. He was immediately set upon by either the gladiators or the spectators and was killed. As a result it is said that Emperor Honorius abolished such shows and Almachus became revered as a martyr.

We give thanks for the stand your servant Almachus took in order to bring an end to gladiatorial contests in ancient Rome, for which he himself suffered death in the arena. May he be blessed and remembered for the abolition of such shows shortly afterwards as we commemorate him today. Amen

2 January

Basil the Great (379) and Gregory of Nazianzus (389), bishops and teachers of the faith

Basil and Gregory were friends who joined forces to promote and defend the divinity of Christ as proclaimed in the Nicene Creed. This was at a time when the doctrine of the Trinity was under threat from both the Church and the State because of the rise of Arianism, which denied Christ's divinity. Basil was the more forceful and combative of the two and Gregory the more prayerful and ascetic. However, Basil needed Gregory's brilliant oratory to further the cause and their joint eloquence and persuasiveness carried the day at the first Council of Constantinople in 381, which ratified the text of the Creed in the East used to this day.

We look back with awe and gratitude to the early fathers, Basil and Gregory, friends and defenders of the divinity of your Son. We are blessed that Gregory's prayer and oratory combined with Basil's commitment and will to distil and establish the Creed we say today, by which we express the faith we are happy to call Christianity. Amen

Munchin, abbot (seventh century)

Often referred to as 'the Wise', Munchin is peripherally associated with Limerick and is claimed as that city's patron and first bishop. Also known as 'the little monk', Munchin began a tradition of prayer and study marking a golden period of Irish Christianity and Celtic monastic life.

Lord, at a time when we celebrate the coming of the Magi to seek out the newborn King, may we also give thanks for the life and prayer of Munchin the Wise. We praise you for his example of prayer and study in his beloved Limerick, heralding a golden period of Irish Christianity and Celtic monastic life. Amen

Seraphim of Sarov, monk and spiritual guide (1833)

Born at Kursk in Russia, the son of a builder, Seraphim took his name when he entered the monastery of Sarov, where he was ordained priest in 1793. Saddened by his abbot's death a year later, he became a hermit and lived as a solitary for thirty years. Known for his visions and spirituality, he was much sought after as a spiritual guide. He used the 'Jesus Prayer' as the heart of his devotions and advocated to all Christians the need to have an increasing communion with the person of Jesus.

May we seek always the will to pray and pray and pray again, as Seraphim showed us in his life and spiritual service, joy and humility, healing and wholeness. And may he always be revered as an icon of Orthodox spirituality. Amen

Vedanayagam Samuel Azariah, bishop and evangelist (1945)

Born in 1874 in a south Indian village, Samuel was brought up in a Christian family, his father being a village priest and his mother being fully acquainted with the Scriptures. As a YMCA evangelist and then secretary of the YMCA in South India, he saw the need for indigenous leaders and was himself ordained priest at the age of 35 and then bishop. An ardent ecumenist, he combined his passion for improving the educational standards of Indian clergy with a strong belief in the importance to mission of a united Church. His vision of a united Church of South India became a reality just two years after his death.

Lord, we give thanks for the pioneering work of your servant Samuel Azariah in setting in motion the drive towards church unity in South India. May we learn from his prophetic words and true discipleship in furthering your vision and spreading your word. Amen

3 January

Morris Williams (Nicander), priest and poet (1874)

Born at Caernarfon in 1809, Morris Williams was apprenticed to a carpenter, then educated at King's School, Chester, and Jesus College, Oxford, graduating and being ordained in 1835. Serving his curacy at Holywell and Amlwch and being appointed rector of Llanrhuddlad in 1859, he undertook major work in revising the Book of Common Prayer in Welsh and was a pioneer of the Tractarian movement in the Diocese of Bangor. Usually known by his bardic name of Nicander, he used his poetic gifts as a contribution to the movement and also had a collection of his poems published in 1843, which were adapted into hymns and had a profound effect on Welsh Anglicanism.

Gifting God, may we recognise and learn from the literary and academic gifts of Morris Williams, known as Nicander, who laboured to bring your word to the people of Wales. Let the legacy of his hymns, poems and prayers be acknowledged in the liturgy of Welsh-speaking Anglicanism today. Amen

Genevieve, Patroness of Paris (c 500)

Born at Nanterre around 420, Genevieve took the veil at the age of about 15, moving to Paris on the death of her parents. There she devoted her life to prayer, austerity and charitable works, supported by Germanus of Auxerre. She demonstrated her bravery in making a dangerous sortie when Paris was besieged, in search of provisions. She is also said to have warded off attacks by Attila and the Huns through prayer and fasting, leading to their decision to change their route and head for Orleans instead. After her death a number of miracles were attributed to her.

Heavenly Father, who inspired and blessed your servant Genevieve with a life of prayer and austerity, we thank you that she repaid your trust in all her interventions to save others. May she be remembered for her miracles and daring. Amen

4 January

Elizabeth Seton, laywoman and foundress (1821)

Born in New York in 1774, Elizabeth (née Bayley) was born of a devout and well-off Episcopalian family and was to become the first native-born saint in the USA. Left a widow after nine years of marriage and five children, Elizabeth joined the Roman Catholic Church two years after the death of her husband and set up a small religious community in Emmitsburg, USA, to care for children of the poor and to teach in parish schools. This order grew into the American Sisters of Charity, based on the rule of Vincent de Paul. She overcame the pressures she faced, both external and internal, through faith, charm and determination.

We rejoice at the faith and witness of Elizabeth Seton, who, after difficult years as a young widow, devoted her life to establishing, leading and fostering a small religious community to care for the children of the poor. In wrestling with our own difficulties, may we take our inspiration from Elizabeth's capacity to cope with her own and build something wonderful for you, Sovereign Lord. Amen

5 January

Simeon the Stylite, hermit (459)

The son of a shepherd, Simeon was born on Cicilia on the Syrian border. From his youth he subjected himself to various austerities, including fasting. After a vision he entered a monastery and lived in a number of hermitages and monasteries for twenty years before setting himself up on a series of pillars, the last one sixty feet high, at Telanissus, where he spent the last twenty years of his life. He attracted many visitors and sightseers including emperors. As well as his practical preaching and teaching, his was a unique witness to the need for penance and prayer.

God of height and depth, may we look up to Simeon in word and deed, in his example of discipline and faithfulness. Let the pillar on which he dwelt be a beacon of hope and an abiding witness to the need for prayer and penitence. Amen

6 January

Peter of Canterbury, abbot (607)

Made the first Abbot of SS Peter and Paul (later Augustine's Abbey), Peter is reputably the monk who was sent by Augustine to take the news to Pope Gregory the Great about the outcomes of his mission, in particular the Anglo-Saxon conversions. He also brought back Gregory's responses to Augustine's queries. Buried inappropriately after perishing in the English Channel on another mission for Augustine, his body was later taken to a more suitable resting place in Boulogne after the appearance of a mysterious light over his grave.

Today we give thanks for Peter of Canterbury, abbot and emissary between Augustine and Gregory, first Abbot of St Augustine's. May his memory not be lost, just as his body was given a proper resting place after being rescued from the unsuitable grave near where he drowned. Amen

7 January

Raymund of Penafort, Dominican friar and canonist (1275)

Born at Penafort in Catalonia, Raymund was educated at Barcelona and Bologna and joined the Dominican friars in 1222, already a respected academic and preacher. He was called to Rome in 1230 and was commissioned by Gregory 9th to bring together the conciliar and papal decrees in a collection which became the standard work for canon lawyers. Becoming Master-General of the Dominicans in 1238, he then devoted himself to the conversion of Jews and Muslims, encouraging Thomas Aquinas in his work. He may also have been involved in the founding of the Mercedarian order.

Lord, we thank you for the literary works undertaken by Raymund and his encouragement of others, including Thomas Aquinas, in his long and varied ministry. We acknowledge his tireless work of conversion amongst those of other faiths and his disciplined practice of contemplation, preaching and administering the sacrament of penance. Amen

8 January

Gudula, laywoman (seventh century)

The daughter of Count Witger and Amalberga, who was the niece of Emperor Pepin, Gudula was brought up in the convent of Nivelles and educated by her cousin, Gertrude of Nivelles. She then lived with her parents at Ham, in Brabant, spending her time in religious devotion, fasting and good works for her neighbours. The great church of Sainte-Gudule in Brussels is dedicated to her and she is known as the Patron of Brussels.

Merciful God, may we look at the life and devotion of Gudula and admire her good works for neighbours, honoured in the name of a church in Brussels. Even though we know little of her life, let us remember her legacy and be glad. Amen

9 January

Adrian (Hadrian) of Canterbury, abbot (710)

African by birth, Adrian was a monk who became Abbot of Nerida, near Naples. He was twice offered the archbishopric of Canterbury in successive vacancies but declined, suggesting the name of Theodore, a Greek monk, on the second occasion. This suggestion was accepted by the pope, who nevertheless asked Adrian to accompany Theodore to Canterbury. There Theodore soon appointed him Abbot of SS Peter and Paul (later Augustine's Abbey). Adrian, a learned scholar himself, founded an important monastic school in Canterbury where a number of future abbots and bishops were educated. He was a great support to Theodore in particular, whom he outlived.

Father of all, let us rejoice in the modesty and learning of Adrian, who turned down preferment, but faithfully followed Theodore to Canterbury. We give thanks for his scholarship and pastoral wisdom, as Abbot of St Augustine's. Amen

10 January

William Laud, Archbishop of Canterbury (1645)

Born at Reading, the son of a master tailor, William Laud was educated at St John's College, Oxford, becoming a Fellow in 1593 and receiving holy orders in 1601. After a period as President of St John's he was appointed Dean of Gloucester, where he moved the communion table to the east of the choir, putting him in direct conflict with the Puritans. Charles 1st appointed him Archbishop of Canterbury in 1633 with a view to countering the Puritan movement. As the Puritans' stock rose he became increasingly under attack for his High Church views from the Puritans, who impeached him in 1640, leading to his imprisonment in the Tower of London and beheading in 1645.

God of righteousness and majesty, we look on the life and death of William Laud in gratitude for his order and discipline in the face of diversity of practice. May we learn from his love of liturgy and have respect for the way he faced his execution at the hands of his parliamentary opponents. Amen

11 January

Mary Slessor, missionary (1915)

Born at Aberdeen in 1848, Mary Slessor grew up in a Presbyterian working-class family in Dundee, where she was captivated by the stories of missions in Africa. Accepted as a teacher on a mission in Calabar, Nigeria, she flourished in that role, learning the local language and endearing herself to the people with whom she worked. She adopted unwanted children and shared her skills in trade and mediation of disputes, settling with the Okoyong people for the rest of her life.

Lord of all, may we honour and cherish the life and work of Mary Slessor, who tirelessly ministered to the people of Nigeria. Let us learn from the way she identified with the people she served, took the trouble to learn their ways and language, and encouraged them into your kingdom of love, tenderness and mercy. Amen

12 January

Aelred of Hexham, Abbot of Rievaulx (1167)

Born at Hexham in 1109, Aelred was the son of a parish priest. After being taken into the service of King David of Scotland for some years, he entered the Cistercian order at Rievaulx. In 1143 he became Abbot of Revesby and then returned to Rievaulx as abbot there. Known for both energy and gentleness, Aelred was also influential through his writings, which included *Our Spiritual Friendship* and *Mirror of Charity*. During his time as Abbot of Rievaulx the number of monks rose to six hundred.

God of love, we give thanks for the life and ministry of Aelred, the qualities of friendship and spirituality he showed in word and deed, and the pain he endured in carrying out his ministry. May his dedicated service and love of your Son as friend and Saviour be a model to us in our faith journey. Amen

Benedict Biscop, abbot (c 690)

Born of a noble Northumbrian family in 628, Biscop went into the service of King Oswy of Northumbria until 653, when he felt called to become a monk, travelling twice to Rome, first with Wilfrid and then with Aldfrith, the son of Oswy. On his way home he became a monk at the Benedictine house at Lering and took the name Benedict, returning from his third trip to Rome with Theodore, newly appointed as Archbishop of Canterbury, who made him Abbot of St Augustine's for a short time. In 674 he established his own foundation at Wearmouth and in 682 founded the monastery at Jarrow. His love of books and his encouragement of singing in the Roman fashion helped ensure the primacy of Roman over Celtic practice in the north of England. Bede was one of his pupils.

Founding Father, today we celebrate the life of Benedict Biscop, founder and first Abbot of Wearmouth, a lover of libraries who never missed an opportunity of obtaining books for the benefit of his pupils, including Bede. We especially remember the important part he played in the development of the Church in northern England and give thanks. Amen

13 January

Kentigern (Mungo), bishop (612) – *see under 14 January*

Hilary, Bishop of Poitiers and teacher (367)

Born into a prosperous pagan family in Poitiers in about 315, Hilary received an excellent education, became an orator, married and had a daughter, Alfra. Baptised at the age of 30 after much personal study, he was elected Bishop of Poitiers in 350 and became the outstanding opponent of Arianism in the West, which caused his banishment to Phrygia by the Arian Emperor Constantus 2nd. He continued the struggle in his writings, such as *On the Trinity* and was known as the 'Athanasius of the West' and returned to Gaul, influencing, among others, Martin of Tours. He was proclaimed a 'doctor of the Church' in 1851.

Father, Son and Holy Spirit, who blessed your defender and advocate, Hilary, for his staunch and persistent loyalty to the true faith, may we have the same determination in the face of threats to the core Christian beliefs. Despite exile and decrees against him, we celebrate the triumph of 'the Athanasius of the West' as we remember him today and in the name given to the university term starting at this time. Amen

George Fox, founder of the Society of Friends (Quakers) (1691)

Born at Fenny Drayton in Leicestershire in 1624, he became an apprentice shoemaker before giving up his ties with family and friends and travelling in search of enlightenment. In 1646 he abandoned any church attendance, following instead the 'Inner Light of the Living Christ' and going on to found 'The Friends of the Truth'. They became known as the Quakers because of the movements they often made as they welcomed God into the soul. George Fox sometimes landed in gaol because of his insistence on preaching anywhere and his widespread travelling and organisational flair ensured the continuation of the Quakers worldwide after his death in 1691.

God of light and life, we thank you that your servant George Fox discerned the 'inner light of Christ' and through the Friends of the Truth gave us the long legacy of the Quakers. May we admire his insight, inspiration, peaceful intent and organisational ability. Amen

14 January

Kentigern (Mungo), bishop (612)
– commemorated in some traditions on 13 January

Said to be a native of Lothian, the grandson of a British prince and educated by Serf at Culross, Kentigern was a monk of the Irish tradition. A founder of the church in Glasgow and missioner to Cumbria, he was driven by persecution into Wales, founding the monastery at Llanelwy before returning to Scotland, living in Dumfries and Glasgow, where he died and was buried.

Unfailing God, we honour the faithfulness of Mungo, who followed your call from Scotland to Wales and back to his beloved Strathclyde, where he continued his work of evangelism. We thank you for the anchor of hope he gave to others which secured his own ministry. Amen

15 January

Paul the Hermit (c 347)

Widely regarded as the first Christian hermit, Paul went into the Theban desert as a young man initially to escape the persecution under Decius, but remained there for the rest of his life, living to a great age. Antony of Egypt is said to have visited towards the end of his life, in recognition of his holiness, and eventually buried him, with the help of two lions, wrapping him in the cloak of Athanasius.

We give thanks for the life of Paul, the first Christian hermit, beloved of Antony and protected by palm trees, whose body was buried with the help of lions. An example of faith and devotion, may he be an inspiration to us even today. Amen

16 January

Fursey, abbot (c 650)

Born in Ireland and becoming a monk there, Fursey travelled to East Anglia as a 'pilgrim for Christ'. King Sigebert gave him the fort of Cnobheresburg (Burgh Castle, Suffolk) to establish a monastery with his companions. After the pagan King Penda defeated and killed Sigebert in battle, Fursey went to France, founding a monastery at Lagry-sur-Marne, near Paris. Bede records his experience of visions of good and evil and of the afterlife during trances.

May the words and works of Fursey, first in Ireland, then in England and France, inspire us on our faith journey. May his visions of the world of both good and evil spirits give us strength to deal with the evil spirits of today. Amen

17 January

Antony of Egypt, hermit and abbot (356)

Born in Coma (in Egypt) in about 251, Antony heeded the call at the age of 20 to sell all his possessions, give the money to the poor and go to live in the desert, where he combined severe austerity and putting the love of God before all else. He survived by making mats and gradually attracted like-minded disciples, as well as visitors coming to consult him. His simple rule of personal discipline and prayer had a profound effect throughout the Christian world, which looked to the 'desert fathers' for inspiration in living a holy and spiritual life. Antony was staunch in his opposition to Arianism, which caused him to visit Alexandria to engage in the debate.

God of space and silence, we give thanks for the desert father, Antony, and his example of selfless and possessionless living. May his life as a hermit, fleeing from the world yet praying for this world, help us to restore a proper balance between doing and being, between fellowship and solitude. Amen

Charles Gore, bishop and founder of the Community of the Resurrection (1932)

Born in 1835, Charles Gore was an Oxford don educated at Harrow and Balliol College who was an Anglo-Catholic who helped reconcile the Church to certain aspects of biblical criticism and discovery. He was also keen to bring catholic principles to bear on social problems and was known as a formidable preacher. He founded and led the Community of the Resurrection which was eventually located at Mirfield. In 1902 he was appointed Bishop of Worcester and went on to become Bishop of Birmingham and then Oxford.

Lord of all, who gave us the breadth of Church we enjoy today, may we show our grateful thanks today for the life and work of Charles Gore and the community he founded. True to Church and Bible, great preacher and interpreter of your Word, may his awareness of social issues influence our own faith journey. Amen

18 January

Ulfrid, martyr (1028)

An Englishman, Ulfrid, along with Sigfrid and others, helped evangelise Sweden. Initial success in his mission came to a halt when his attacks on idolatry and actual destruction of a statue of Thor were met with hostility by onlookers, who lynched him and threw his body into a marsh.

God of great deeds, we remember today the zealous efforts of Ulfrid to bring the good news to Sweden. May the actions which precipitated his death be seen as a brave episode in the mission of many people in that land. Amen

19 January

Wulfstan, Bishop of Worcester (1095)

Born about 1009 of Anglo-Saxon parents at Itchington in Warwickshire, Wulfstan was educated at the Abbeys of Evesham and Peterborough. After being ordained priest he spent twenty-five years in the monastery at Worcester before being appointed, rather against his will, Bishop of Worcester in 1062. He proved to be an excellent administrator and pastor and is regarded as the first English bishop to have made systematic visitations of his diocese. He encouraged the building of churches and the use of stone, rather than wooden, altars and carefully nurtured Church and State through the transition from Saxon to Norman rule.

Lord God, today we remember your humble servant, Wulfstan, called from his life of prayer to be Bishop of Worcester. We give thanks for his powerful preaching and pastoral sensitivity and especially acknowledge his careful nurturing of Church and State during the changes from Saxon to Norman rule. Amen

20 January

Sebastian, martyr (288)

Sebastian was a captain of the imperial guard in Rome under Diocletian, who was unaware that he was a Christian. On discovering this Diocletian ordered his death by arrows, but these failed to kill him, so he was beaten to death by clubs. He was buried on the Appian Way close to the basilica which today bears his name. His emblem is an arrow.

Forgiving God, you gave your servant Sebastian the courage to assist those under Roman persecution and the fortitude to resist the Emperor's arrows himself. May we emulate his frankness of speech and strength of character in living our faith. Amen

Richard Rolle of Hampole, spiritual writer (1349)

Born in about 1300 at Thornton in Yorkshire, Richard Rolle broke off his education at Oxford University and began to live as a hermit from the age of 18. He eventually moved his hermitage close to the Cistercian convent at Hampole, where he wrote extensively on mysticism and asceticism. He wrote mainly in Italian and his writings were influential for hundreds of years after his death.

Serene Lord, may we aspire to the highest degree of love identified by the mystic Richard Rolle so that we might also love Jesus, think Jesus, dream Jesus in a song of praise and love. Today we ask with him that our souls are comforted in our praise and love of you. Amen

21 January

Agnes, child martyr at Rome (304)

One of the most famous of Roman martyrs, Agnes was a girl of about 13 who refused to consider marriage, preferring to dedicate her life to Christ, which caused dissension in her family and attracted threats, whereupon she chose martyrdom by allowing her throat to be pierced with a sword. She is often depicted in Renaissance paintings and late medieval stained glass and from early times, in sixth century Ravenna, her emblem being a lamb.

Merciful Father, on this day we remember your gentle virgin martyr, Agnes, at once fearless and faithful to you, in the face of cruelty and awful provocation. For one so young, her example speaks to those more mature in age as a model of steadfastness and sacrificial dedication to you, for which we give you our thanks. Amen

22 January

Vincent of Saragossa, deacon, first martyr of Spain (304)

A victim of the persecutions under Diocletian and Maximian, Vincent was the most celebrated of early Spanish martyrs. Trained by Valerius, Bishop of Saragossa, Vincent was a deacon who was imprisoned for his faith and, refusing to make sacrifices to idols, was subjected to torture on a gridiron, from which he died. His fame spread through a poem by Prudentius recounting his martyrdom.

Enduring God, as we celebrate the life and martyrdom of Vincent of Saragossa, we especially remember his eloquence in defence of his bishop and his church. In the torment he experienced in the face of persecution and torture we can see that true Christian endurance is a gift of God, both holy and religious. Amen

23 January

John the Almsgiver (c 620)

Born about 560 at Amathus in Cyprus, John lived with his wife and family for much of his life in Cyprus or Egypt, becoming Patriarch of Alexandria, where he championed orthodoxy against the monophysite heresy. Known for his virtuous lifestyle, charitable works and alms-giving, he helped the poor both practically and in introducing the regulations of weights and measures. He settled disputes and helped refugees, finally retiring to Cyprus.

God of great gifts, we thank you for your servant John, who served you with great humility and his other 'masters', the poor, with great generosity. As we celebrate his hospitality for strangers and championing the needy, let us also recognise his respect for the liturgy and the sanctuary. Amen

24 January

Francis de Sales, Bishop of Geneva, teacher of the faith (1622)

Born at Château de Sales near Annecy in 1567, Francis studied at Paris and Padua and, despite his father's opposition, was ordained priest in 1593. Skilled at countering the influence of Calvinism, Francis became Bishop of Geneva in 1602, proving an able administrator and writing a number of influential works, including his *Treatise of the Love of God* and *Introduction to the Devout Life*. Among the friends he influenced was Jane Frances Chantel, who founded the order of the Visitation.

Lord God, we remember this day your servant Francis, who preached with great love and understanding, patience and gentleness. May his devotion to you and his guidance on the devotional life be helpful to us in our own prayers and meditation. Amen

25 January

The Conversion of Paul

The book of the Acts of the Apostles recounts the turning of the zealous anti-Christian, Saul, into the Apostle Paul, from the Damascus Road conversion through to the tireless journeying and preaching of his later ministry. The process took some time for Saul to become Paul as he came to comprehend the full implications of his call to preach, to Jews and Gentiles, the saving power of Jesus, the son of God. Celebrated since the sixth century, the feast became universal in the twelfth century.

Transforming God, we celebrate on this day the conversion of Paul, from persecutor to believer, the start of a process leading to his great work of preaching, organising and converting. Loved by Christ, despised by many, may we follow his example of virtue and faithfulness. Amen

26 January

Timothy and Titus (first century), companions of Paul

Timothy was born in Lystra in Asia Minor, the son of a Greek father and Jewish mother, while Titus was wholly Greek. Described by Paul as 'partners and fellow-workers in God's service', they both had epistles addressed to them and Paul entrusted Timothy with the oversight of the Christians at Ephesus, where he was regarded as their first bishop. Titus was assigned by Paul to the Christians of Crete and he became the first bishop of the Cretan city of Gortyna. Timothy was reputedly battered to death for opposing the observance of a heathen festival, while Titus is said to have died in Crete after a mission to Dalmatia.

> **God of discipleship, we thank you for the life and work of two faithful companions of Paul, Timothy and Titus, who responded to your call and worked in partnership to sustain devotion and faithfulness to the gospel, by their action and example. Through your grace they helped to lay the foundation of your Church. Amen**

27 January

Angela of Brescia (Angela Merici), foundress of the Ursuline nuns (1540)

Born at Desenzano near Lake Garda in 1474 and orphaned while young, Angela Merici became a Franciscan tertiary and devoted herself to the education of poor girls from the village, with such conspicuous success that in 1516 she was invited to do similar work in Brescia. She and a number of companions formed themselves into what was to become the Company of Ursula (Ursuline nuns), an order which only received formal recognition in 1565, after her death. This was the first teaching order of women to be established.

> **God of understanding, let your servant Angela, who founded the oldest teaching order of the Roman Catholic Church, be a beacon of education and learning in the Church. May her background as orphan and teacher inspire us today, as she inspired others in her lifetime, to embark on something which endures. Amen**

28 January

Thomas Aquinas, priest, philosopher and teacher of the faith (1274)

Born at Rocca Secca, near Aquino, into a noble family around 1225, Thomas was educated at Monte Cassino and Naples, where he joined the Dominican friars in 1244, despite strenuous efforts by his family (including kidnapping) to prevent his doing so. He was a student under Albert the Great and went on to have a glittering career of teaching, preaching and writing, in Paris and various cities in Italy, ending up in Naples. It was said of him that 'his wonderful learning owes far less to his genius than to the effectiveness of his prayer'. He died at the age of 49, leaving his great work *Summa Theologica* unpublished.

> **Lord of all, we celebrate today a man of learning and prayer, Thomas Aquinas, universal teacher and 'Angelic doctor' of letters. We give thanks for his gifts of teaching and theological wisdom and for his ability to communicate your Word through homilies and hymns. Amen**

29 January

Gildas, abbot (c 570)

Born about 500, probably near the Clyde, Gildas studied under Illtyd at Llaniltud in South Wales. Well educated, with a wide biblical knowledge and known as 'the Wise', he was a leading figure in Welsh monastic life. He was a man of decided views and moral indignation, both of which characterise his famous work entitled *Concerning the Ruin and Conquest of Britain*, in which he criticises contemporary leaders and seeks to learn lessons from history. He had considerable influence on the development of the Irish Church and ended his days in Brittany.

> **God of light and learning, we remember today your servant Gildas, who wrote of the errors of those in Britain who had allowed the invaders to triumph. Let us recognise his courage and insight and vow to understand the lessons of the past. Amen**

30 January

Charles, king and martyr (1649)

The second son of King James 1st, Charles was born in 1600. On the death of his elder brother, when he was 12, he became the heir apparent and succeeded to the throne in 1625. Faced with an antagonistic Parliament and the rise of religious puritanism, he became dismissive of Parliament and sought to impose high church principles and practices throughout the kingdom. The result was civil war, which led to his imprisonment, trial and execution in 1649. He was proud till the end, but his faith was never in doubt.

Almighty God, we remember today a temporal king, whose pride helped to bring about his martyrdom, but whose faith was undoubted. Help us to avoid the strife between Christians which led to his death and to discern your will and judgement in accepting difference, but withstanding relativism. Amen

31 January

Aidan or Maedoc, Bishop of Ferns (632)

Born in Connacht, Aidan was educated in Leicester and then studied in Wales, possibly under David. On return to Ireland he established a monastic community at Ferns in County Wexford, becoming the first bishop there, going on to found monasteries at Drumlane and Rossinver. He was known for his generosity and kindness and a number of miracles are attributed to him.

Generous Lord, you gave us Aidan, who founded a monastic community in Wexford, after studying with your servant, David, in Wales. We remember his kindness and generosity and thank you for the miracles he performed in your name. Amen

Charles Mackenzie of Central Africa, bishop and missionary (1862)

Charles Mackenzie was a man with a simple, practical faith who was made bishop in Cape Town in 1861 in order to lead a mission on behalf of the Universities Mission to Central Africa, formed in response to an appeal by David Livingstone. The mission, progressing up the Zambesi towards Lake Nyassa, encountered opposition to the preaching of the gospel and their efforts to free slaves and Charles fell ill and died only a year into the mission.

> **God of integrity, we offer our thanks and praise for the life of Charles Mackenzie, outspoken missionary and full of grace. May his love of poetry and truth inspire our souls too, in our search for the Holy Spirit in our lives and in our living. Amen**

John Bosco, priest, founder of the Salesian teaching order (1888)

Born in Piedmont, in 1815, to a peasant family, John was brought up by his mother in extreme poverty. Entering a seminary in 1831, he was ordained priest in 1841 and spent the rest of his life in the Turin area, pioneering new educational methods of teaching and training boys and young men. His admiration for Francis de Sales led to his naming his helpers 'Salesians'. This religious community grew quickly and became established in several countries in John's lifetime. His work with homeless youth and his emphasis on the importance of vocational training were taken up by political leaders as a model approach to educational provision for these groups.

> **Forgiving God, we look on the life and works of John Bosco with gratitude and respect. In his encouragement of young men who had strayed into bad ways, he showed the loving kindness and mercy your Son demonstrated in his life. May we learn from his example in coping with aggression. Amen**

February

1 February

Brigid, Abbess of Kildare (c 525)

Thought to have been born about five miles from Kildare, with parents of humble origin, and baptised by Patrick, Brigid became a nun at an early age and proved to be a woman of compassion with a strong character who founded the community of dedicated women at Kildare, the first of its kind in Ireland. She had great affinity with the world of nature and through her prayers, miracles and charitable works is said to have greatly influenced the development of the Irish Church, leading to her being regarded, with Patrick, as the Patron Saint of Ireland.

> **Creator God, we thank you for the example of Brigid, in her love of the birds of the air and the beasts of the field. As founder of a religious community at Kildare, you set her on the road toward the establishment of your Church throughout Ireland. Baptised by Patrick and buried next to Patrick, she is remembered today as a witness to your presence in that island. Amen**

2 February

Theophane Vénard, martyr (1861)

Born at Saint-Loup-sur-Thouet in 1829, the son of a schoolteacher, Theophane entered the seminary of Poitiers diocese before joining the Society of the Foreign Missions in Paris. Ordained priest in 1852, he was sent shortly afterwards to Vietnam. There he was subjected to persecution in various places, latterly in Hanoi. Going into hiding did not save him and he was arrested, held in a bamboo cage and then beheaded, still professing his faith. His experience and letters influenced Thérèse of Lisieux, who was inspired to volunteer to go to the Carmelite nunnery in Hanoi.

> **Transforming God, on this day we celebrate the life and martyrdom of your servant Theophane Vénard, who inspired Thérèse of Lisieux and whose persecution and death were a powerful witness to the Christian faith in Vietnam. Amen**

3 February

Laurence of Canterbury, bishop (619)

One of Augustine's companions in his mission to England in 596-7, Laurence was chosen to go back to Rome to inform Gregory of progress and to seek answers to various questions about organisational strategy. He succeeded Augustine as Archbishop in c 604 and, despite setbacks in relations with British bishops, he was fortified by a vision of St Peter, which led to the conversion of Eadbald, the son of Ethelbert, and enabled the Church to continue to expand.

> **Heavenly Father, we bring to you our remembrance of Laurence of Canterbury, companion and successor of Augustine. Strengthened by a vision of Peter, may his vision and hope give us hope and confidence in our own lives and faith journeys. Amen**

Anskar, Archbishop of Hamburg, missionary in Denmark and Sweden (865)

Born near Amiens in Picardy into a noble family, Anskar was educated at the nearby monastery of Corbie, becoming a monk at the young age of 13, moving to Corvey in Westphalia and then on an evangelising mission to Denmark and to Sweden, where he is said to have built the first Christian church. He was appointed the first Bishop of Hamburg in 832 and after Viking attacks, Bishop of Bremen too. He resumed his work in Scandinavia, founding schools, preaching and ministering to the poor and seeking to mitigate the effects of the Viking slave trade.

> **Empowering God, you gave your servant Anskar great responsibility over your Church in Denmark, Norway and Sweden. We celebrate today his energy and sacrificial way of life, together with his dedication to the poor, to education and to the transforming power of preaching. Amen**

As recorded in the Acts of the Apostles, Paul, Barnabas and Peter paved the way for other missionaries over the centuries to spread the good news of the Gospels throughout the Roman Empire and to barbarians following the fall of Rome. Many were martyred in the process, but this did not prevent their successors from continuing their work, bringing Christianity to the pagans of northern and eastern Europe too.

God of vocations, today we celebrate the saints and martyrs of Europe who followed in the steps of Paul and Peter to spread the faith far and wide. May faithful people continue to proclaim the kingdom of God with the same energy and commitment as those who have gone before. Amen

4 February

Gilbert of Sempringen, founder of the Gilbertine order (1189)

Born in Sempringen, the son of a Norman knight and an Anglo-Saxon mother, in 1083, Gilbert was considered unfit for knightly duties because of a physical deformity from birth. However, he became a cleric, studied in France, was ordained priest in 1131, then returned to set up a school and also a religious community of lay sisters and brothers, in the Benedictine tradition. His order spread, Gilbert as Master continuing his austere way of life and travelling from house to house. His support of Thomas Becket incurred the displeasure of Henry 2nd but he survived this and other challenges to his authority before his death at the great age of 106.

Lord of all, we thank you that your servant Gilbert overcame physical deformity to encourage and establish communities of women and men across the land. Through his example, leadership and pastoral persistence your Church has been blessed by Gilbert's long life of witness and inspiration. Amen

Manche Masemola, martyr (1928)

As a young woman born and brought up near Pietersburg in South Africa, Manche and her cousin joined baptism preparation classes in 1927. Each time she went she was beaten afterwards by her parents and even attacked with a spear. Finally her mother took away her clothes and she had to run away naked, before she was found and beaten to death. As she had previously predicted to her priest, she was 'baptised in her own blood'.

God of the oppressed, we remember today the short life of Manche Masemola, torn between love of family and commitment to her faith. A victim of the times and society in which she lived, may she remain an inspiration and a witness to the power of the one true faith. Amen

Andrew Corsini, Bishop of Fiesole (1373)

Born into a Florentine family in 1302, Andrew led a dissolute life as a youth but underwent a change of heart and became a Carmelite friar in Florence in 1318. After further study in Paris he became prior of his community, preaching to great effect and showing his ability to settle quarrels. Made Bishop of Fiesole, initially against his will, he adopted an austere lifestyle seeking out the poor and ministering to them, as well as continuing his mediation work, often between rich and poor.

God of forgiveness, we thank you for the example of your servant Andrew Corsini, dissolute in youth, austere in faith. May his example of ministry to the poor, reconciliation of disputes, and healing of the sick and distressed inspire us in our lives and work today. Amen

Phileas, Bishop of Thmuis and martyr (306)

A man of distinction and learning, Phileas was baptised a Christian in adult life, becoming bishop of his own city and being arrested soon after his consecration in Alexandria, where he was imprisoned as part of the Diocletian persecution of Christians in 303. From prison he wrote moving accounts in his letters of the suffering of Alexandrian Christians and, refusing to deny his faith and make sacrifices to idols, he engaged in debate with the prefect interrogating him, eloquently professing his beliefs, before being beheaded, together with Philoromus, a Christian official.

> **Lord of suffering and sacrifice, we recognise today the distinction and learning of Phileas, who refused to bend his beliefs to the will of the Roman authorities in Alexandria. His resistance, even to death, was a true witness of faith as someone who observed torture among Christians in his care and was martyred for his own beliefs. Amen**

5 February

Agatha, virgin and martyr (third century)

Born and brought up at Catania in Sicily, Agatha is said to have been a wealthy girl who was pursued relentlessly by the consul, Quintinian, but who dedicated her virginity to Christ. When she was rejected she was tortured, humiliated and maimed, but her spirits were upheld by a vision of St Peter. She finally died of her maltreatment.

> **God of mercy, we remember today the fortitude of Agatha and her suffering on the instruction of Quintinian the consul. May her courage and faith, strengthened by a vision of Peter, ring out as loudly and shine as brightly across the centuries, even to today. Amen**

6 February

The Martyrs of Japan (1597 and 1622)

These martyrs suffered under the persecution of the ruler Hideyoshi, fifty years after the arrival of Francis Xavier, Japan's first Christian apostle. Paul Miki and twenty-five others were horribly mutilated then crucified close to Nagasaki, marking the beginning of thirty-five years of persecution, resulting in further martyrs, notably Charles Spinola and fifty-five others, who were beheaded and burned in 1622.

Lord of justice, may we never forget the martyrs of Japan, inspired by Francis Xavier and crucified in terrible fashion, professing their faith. Let us recall especially the twenty-five men and women who died with Paul Miki at Nagasaki in 1597 and those martyred with Charles Spinola in 1622. Amen

Dorothy, virgin and martyr (c 303)

Thought to have been a maiden of Caesarea in Cappadocia, Dorothy was a victim of the Diocletian persecution of Christians. She converted those sent to persuade her to give up her faith and was condemned to death. On the way to be beheaded, a lawyer named Theophilus mocked her and asked to be sent flowers and fruit from heaven. He too was converted when a child appeared bearing such gifts.

God of marvellous works, we remember your servant Dorothy, whose persecution and martyrdom brought people to faith and who inspired the gifts of heavenly fruit and flowers, an inspiration to us even to this day. Amen

Photius, bishop and patriarch (c 891)

Born in Constantinople, Photius was an able man of great learning who initially pursued a career in public service in the imperial court, including the post of secretary of state. He was a layman, but in 858 he was chosen by Michael 3rd to take the place of the banished Ignatius as patriarch. Until 879 there was conflict with successive popes over the appointment, which was finally ratified in that year by Pope John 8th. He was at the forefront of the Eastern Church's disagreements with Rome, but everyone acknowledged his blameless personal life and prodigious academic talents, which led to a number of important writings, including *Bibliotheca*.

Lord God, you showered gifts of learning and scholarship on Photius as layman and patriarch. We remember today his talents of translation, theological argument and upholder of Eastern Orthodox Christianity. Amen

7 February

Romuald of Ravenna, Benedictine abbot (c 1027) – *see under 19 June*

Theodore 'the General' (fourth century)

Not to be confused with another fourth century martyr, Theodore 'the Recruit', Theodore 'the General' is thought to have been martyred in Pontus for his opposition to paganism and, along with George and Demetrius, was one of the great soldier saints of the Eastern Church. He is featured in mosaics at St Mark's and in the windows of Chartres.

> **Lord of might and right, we give thanks today for one of the soldier saints of the East, Theodore 'the General', who was resolute in opposing paganism. May his martyrdom be honoured and his steadfastness of faith be an inspiration. Amen**

8 February

Cuthman, shepherd and hermit (eighth century)

Born near Bosham about 681, Cuthman is said to have been a shepherd in south-west England who, on his father's death, made his way to Steyning in Sussex, pulling his mother all the way on a handcart. On arrival he built a hut for his mother, as well as a church with the help of his neighbours. There he lived and ministered as a hermit.

> **God of justice and mercy, we thank you for the humble service of Cuthman, shepherd and hermit, who sacrificially cared for his mother while engaged in his priestly ministry. We also remember him for the church he built and the monastery that was established there. Amen**

Elfleda, Abbess of Whitby (714)

The daughter of King Oswiu of Northumbria and Enfleda, Elfleda was committed to the religious life by her parents in the event of victory over

Penda, the pagan King of Mercia. Accordingly, after the battle of Winwaed in 654, she was entrusted to Hilda, Abbess of Hartlepool. Moving on to Whitby, Enfleda and Elfreda became successive abbesses. She was on friendly terms with both Cuthbert and Wilfrid, proving her mediation skills in the synod of the River Nidd in 705.

Holy Lord, today we record our gratitude for your servant Elfleda, who faithfully served under Hilda at Whitby and then as an abbess in her own right. As mediator and counsellor, we acknowledge her skills of reconciliation, much needed then as now. Amen

9 February

Teilo, bishop (sixth century)

Thought to have been born at Penally, near Tenby, Teilo studied under Dyfrig and Paul Aurelian before travelling to Brittany. On his return to Wales the centre of his ministry was at Llandeilo Fawr in Carmarthenshire, though Teilo was claimed by Llandaff Cathedral, where his body is buried, as their second bishop.

Immanent God, help us to understand and appreciate the ministry of Teilo, alongside St David, in the development of the faith in Wales and Brittany. Through pilgrimage in his life and through miracles at Llandaff, may his life continue to be a source of inspiration today. Amen

Apollonia, deaconess of Alexandria and martyr (249)

During an outbreak of violence against Christians in Alexandria, the mob struck and killed her and others, attacking Apollonia with blows to the jaw and knocking her teeth out. They lit bonfires and threatened to burn her alive if she did not renounce her faith. Before they could do this she said a short prayer and then walked into the flames of her own accord and died. Because of the nature of the attack on her, her name is sometimes invoked by those suffering toothache.

God who strengthens, we look on the life and death of Apollonia and admire her courage and sacrifice in the face of the mob. May we be strengthened by the example of her steadfastness of faith and act of sacrifice. Amen

10 February

Scholastica, sister of Benedict, Abbess of Plombariola (c 543)

Born at Nurzia, sister (and probably the twin) of Benedict, Scholastica dedicated herself to God at an early age, but remained in her parents' home for some time. After Benedict moved to Monte Cassino she settled at Plombariola nearby, founding and governing a nunnery under his direction on spiritual matters. The two used to meet once a year in a house a little way from his monastery. At their last meeting Scholastica begged him to stay longer but he would not, the only thing preventing him from leaving that night being a violent thunderstorm. She died three days later, her body being laid to rest in the tomb prepared for himself.

Heavenly Father, we thank you for the life and example of Scholastica, sister of Benedict, who founded a nunnery and met up with her brother annually to further their spiritual development. May we too seek every opportunity, by prayer and discussion, to deepen our spiritual life. Amen

11 February

Benedict of Aniane, abbot (821)

Born into a noble family, Benedict served at court until, aged 20, he experienced a conversion and became a monk at Saint-Seine, near Dijon. In about 780 he formed a very austere community by the River Aniane in Languedoc, but unhappy at their community life he adopted the Rule of St Benedict and was at the forefront of monastic reform, restoring the whole of the kingdom of the Franks to the Benedictine Rule and issuing a code of regulations binding on all houses. Maintaining a rigorous austerity throughout his life, Benedict of Aniane permanently influenced Benedictine life, especially in terms of his emphasis on the daily monastic office, and on teaching and writing rather than manual work. He ended his days at the monastery built for him to oversee this work by Emperor Louis 1st, at Cornelimünster, near Aachen.

Almighty God, may we recall and admire the ministry of Benedict of Aniane, who did so much to reform and renew the Rule of St Benedict. We thank you for his emphasis on liturgy, on teaching and writing, and on community monasticism where art and learning flourished. Amen

Caedmon, monk of Whitby (680)

A herdsman from the Whitby area, Caedmon discovered and developed a gift of poetry and song. Becoming a monk at Whitby, he composed poems about creation and many other biblical stories in the vernacular. These must have had a considerable impact in promoting Christianity amongst people who largely could neither read nor write and did not understand Latin.

God of Creation, we remember your servant Caedmon, herdsman, poet and monk, who set your Word to verse and song. We partly owe the tradition of Christian songs and poetry to his special gifts and spiritual soul, which we honour today. Amen

Gregory 2nd, pope (731)

Born in Rome, Gregory was a subdeacon under Pope Sergius and then became treasurer and librarian, accompanying Pope Constantine, as a deacon, to assist in settling doctrinal disputes. He was chosen as Constantine's successor and proved to be an active and effective apostolic ruler, rebuilding churches, establishing new monasteries and hospitals and zealously guarding the independence of Rome from all quarters. He showed his interest in the Anglo-Saxons by encouraging Boniface, consecrating him bishop and sending him on a mission.

God of firm foundations, we give thanks for the wisdom and energy of Gregory 2nd in rebuilding old churches and establishing new hospitals and monasteries. We remember him also for his encouragement and direction of Boniface, whom he consecrated bishop, giving him his important mission. Amen

12 February

Ethilwald, monk and Bishop of Lindisfarne (740)

A Northumbrian disciple of Cuthbert, Ethilwald became prior and then abbot at Melrose. When Edfrith, scribe of the Lindisfarne Gospels, died, Ethilwald succeeded him as Bishop of Lindisfarne, respecting the tradition and known for his sanctity. He commissioned the hermit Billfrith to make the precious cover of the Gospels, now sadly lost.

Lord of the Isles, we celebrate today the life and work of Ethilwald, a disciple of Cuthbert. We thank you especially for his ministry as Bishop of Lindisfarne and his reputation for sanctity. Amen

13 February

Catherine dei Ricci, Dominican nun and visionary (1590)

Born at Florence in 1522, of a wealthy family, Catherine entered a Dominican convent at Prato in Tuscany, which had been founded in 1535 under Savaranola's influence. After a period as novice-mistress, she became sub-prioress and in 1552 prioress. Her ability as an administrator and in nursing the sick was admired by Philip Neri and Charles Borromeo among others, but her real claim to fame arose from her weekly visions and ecstasies, during which she relived Christ's passion and which were accompanied by the impression of the stigmata. She was also a very powerful influence on reform in the Church.

God of power and might, you gave your servant Catherine dei Ricci the gift of empowering ecstasies reliving Christ's passion. We also remember today her zeal for reform in your Church and her careful and efficient work as prioress of the Dominican convent at Prato in Tuscany. Amen

Ermengild, Queen of Mercia, Abbess of Ely (c 700)

The daughter of Erconbert, King of Kent, and Sexburga, Ermengild married Wulfhere, who was King of Penda, and converted him to Christianity, bringing up two children. After Wulfhere's death she joined the convent founded by her mother at Minster-in-Sheppey and succeeded her when Sexburga moved to Ely, founded by Sexburga's sister, Ethedreda, where later on Ermengild also became abbess on Sexburga's death.

> **Lord of all, on this day we remember Ermengild, daughter of the King of Kent, who became a nun at Minster-in-Sheppey, before becoming Abbess of Ely. We thank you for this your servant, who provided continuity in royal abbesses and brought honour to her vocation. Amen**

14 February

Cyril and Methodius, apostles to the Slavs, Patrons of Europe (869 and 885)

Cyril (also known as Constantine) and his brother Methodius were born in Salonika, educated in Constantinople and invited in 867 to go to Moravia to reform the Church on Byzantine lines. Known as 'the apostles of the Southern Slavs', they were enthusiastic in translating some of the Scriptures into Slavonic, Cyril inventing an alphabet for the purpose, Cyrillic, which bears his name. They were diplomatic but firm in various controversies and after Cyril died while in Rome Methodius, the older of the two, continued his missionary and translation work. Together with Benedict, they are known as 'Patrons of Europe'.

> **Lord of faithfulness and companionship, today we remember and celebrate the brothers Cyril and Methodius, apostles to the Slavs, patriotic and scholarly. We rejoice in the Cyrillic language and translation work which they achieved and the ecumenism they fostered. Amen**

Valentine, martyr at Rome (c 269)

Valentine is thought to have been a priest or bishop martyred in Rome under Emperor Claudius. There is nothing in the Valentine legend to give rise to the custom of choosing a partner and sending 'valentines' on 14 February. It is more likely to be based on the old idea that birds begin to pair on that date or even linked with the pagan Lupercalia festival. For Christians the day marks a further confirmation of an all-loving God who blesses those who love one another, as Jesus asked his disciples to do.

God of love, we thank you for the life and faith of your servant, Valentine, who, as witness to his love for you, died a martyr at Rome. In our love for you and our love for each other, may we be inspired in faith and fidelity. Amen

15 February

Sigfrid, bishop, apostle of Sweden (c 1045)

Thought to have been a priest from York, Sigfrid was sent by King Ethelred to evangelise Norway and Sweden. He made his centre of operations Vaxjo in southern Sweden, consecrating bishops for East and West Gothland and evangelising more remote areas himself. Among those he converted was King Olaf and he is much revered throughout Scandinavia.

God of courage and commitment, we bring before you today the life and work of Sigfrid, called by you from York to minister to the Swedes. Let us remember his bravery, his organisational skills, his success in conversion, and his loyalty to your calling. Amen

Thomas Bray, founder of the SPCK and the SPG (1730)

Born at Marton in Shropshire in 1656 and educated at Oxford, Thomas Bray was chosen after ordination to work with the Church in Maryland, USA, by the Bishop of London. In the delay before he went there he managed to organise a system of free parochial libraries for Maryland, a model he later instituted in England, in the form of the 'Society for the

Promotion of Christian Knowledge' (SPCK), founded in 1668. After a spell in Maryland he returned to England and also founded the 'Society for the Propagation of the Gospel'.

> **Lord of learning, we remember on this day your servant Thomas Bray, organiser of the Church in Maryland and also founder of the Society for the Promotion of Christian Knowledge and the Society for the Propagation of the Gospel. We give thanks that, through his work, countless generations of Christians have come to the faith and deepened their faith. Amen**

16 February

Elias and companions, martyrs

These five Christians travelled from Egypt in solidarity with their brethren who had been sentenced to forced labour in the quarries of Cilicia because of their faith. On seeking to enter Caesarea they were challenged and asked to give their names and home towns. They chose to give the biblical names of Elias, Jeremiah, Isaiah, Samuel and Daniel and their home town as Jerusalem, being the 'city of heaven'. Refusing to impart any further information, even under torture, they were beheaded.

> **Lord of service and sacrifice, we remember today your five servants who showed solidarity with their fellow Christians. May we honour and admire their willingness to witness to their faith in adopting the names of biblical prophets when confronted by heathen authorities and suffering martyrdom as a consequence. Amen**

17 February

Finan of Lindisfarne, bishop (661)

An Irish monk from Iona, Finan succeeded Aidan as Bishop of Lindisfarne and was like him in character and approach, continuing his missionary work south of the Humber. He worked closely with Oswiu, King of

Northumbria, upheld the Celtic traditions, built the wooden church at Lindisfarne and rebuilt the monastery at Whitby. His converts included Penda, King of the Angles, and Sigebert, King of the East Saxons.

God of holiness and wholeness, as we remember Finan today, we give thanks for the Iona community from which he came to succeed Aidan as Bishop of Lindisfarne. As a zealous defender of Celtic tradition, learned and prudent, may he be a beacon of steadfastness, a warning against flexibility. Amen

Janani Luwum, Archbishop of Uganda, martyr (1977)

Born in 1922 at Acholi in Uganda, Janani Luwum spent his childhood and youth tending goats, but soon demonstrated his readiness to learn and quickly became a teacher. He was converted to Christianity and was ordained in 1965, becoming Bishop of North Uganda in 1969 and then Archbishop of Uganda in 1974. During Idi Amin's rule the Church became critical of his government and he and two government ministers were found dead at the scene of a car accident in 1977, apparently the victims of Amin's revenge.

God of mercy, today we remember your servant and martyr, Janani Luwum, whose witness in the face of tyranny in Uganda led to his martyrdom. We thank you, Lord, for his enthusiasm for the good news of Jesus and for his outspokenness against evil. Amen

18 February

Colman of Lindisfarne, bishop (676)

A monk of Iona, Colman succeeded Finan as Bishop of Lindisfarne, at a time when the dispute over the correct date of Easter was at its height. At the Synod of Whitby in 663/4, convened to resolve the issue and chaired by King Oswiu of Northumbria, Colman put forward the Celtic case and Wilfrid advanced the arguments of Rome. While neither side could prove their claims historically, the king was swayed in favour of the Roman usage and Colman resigned and retired first to Iona and then to Ireland, where he founded a monastery. As a bishop and pastor Colman was held in high esteem and known for his frugality of living.

God of mediation, on this day we praise you for the ministry and devotion of Colman of Lindisfarne, whose community flourished under his authority. May we recognise the pain he felt when he lost the argument over the accepted date of Easter, but rejoice in his firmness of purpose. Amen

19 February

Thomas Burgess, bishop, teacher of the faith (1837)

Born at Odiham in Hampshire in 1756, Thomas Burgess was ordained in 1784, rising to prebendary at Durham Cathedral ten years later. Appointed Bishop of St David's in 1803, he embarked on the reform of his diocese by bringing improvements to the preparation and training for ministry of the clergy. This led to the establishment of St David's College, Lampeter, in 1822. Although an Englishman, he envisaged the revival of the Eisteddfod and the resurgence of the literary and cultural movement in Wales, before his move to Salisbury in 1825.

Gentle Lord, we celebrate today the life of Thomas Burgess, pastor and scholar, who founded St David's College, Lampeter. May we admire his efforts of championing Welsh language and culture and seek to emulate his love of community. Amen

20 February

Wulfric of Haselbury, priest and hermit (c 1154)

Born at Compton Martin in Somerset, near Bristol, Wulfric trained to be a priest and began his ministry at Deverill, near Warminster. He was known as a 'hunting parson', especially with hawks and dogs, but a chance conversation with a beggar led him to lead a more austere life. After ministering as a parish priest at Compton Martin in 1125 he became an anchorite at Haselbury Plucknett, about twenty miles from Exeter, supported by the Cluniac monks of Montacute. His fasting and gift of prophesy were legendary and he was consulted by kings and queens. He was also skilled in bookbinding and making other items for the use of churches.

God of insight, we give thanks today for the gift of prophecy, holiness and second sight shown by your servant Wulfric of Haselbury. May his example of solitude, fasting and penitence bring admiration and emulation today in equal measure. Amen

Saints, martyrs and missionaries of Africa

Over the centuries there have been many who have witnessed to the good news of Jesus throughout the continent of Africa. These include the early saints and martyrs of North Africa, notably Perpetua and her companions, Augustine of Hippo and his mother Monica; also the nineteenth century missionaries to Central and Southern Africa, such as Mary Slessor and James Hannington; as well as martyrs like Charles Mackenzie, Bernard Mizeki and Charles Lwanga and compatriots in Uganda; not forgetting twentieth-century figures including Charles de Foucauld and Janani Luwum and those in our own time who have made a stand by word or deed.

Lord God, Father of all, let us today celebrate and commemorate the martyrs of Africa over the ages, from Perpetua and Augustine of Hippo, to Charles de Foucauld and Janani Luwum in the recent era. May this properly reflect the richness of belief in a continent where Christianity flourishes partly because of these martyrs. Amen

21 February

Peter Damian, theologian and reformer (1072)

Born in Ravenna and orphaned when young, Peter Damian was left in the charge of one brother who oppressed him and another who arranged a good education for him. Such was his progress that he became a teacher at

Ravenna and, already leading an austere life, he joined the community of hermits founded by Romuald at Fonte Avellana, where he initially suffered a breakdown of health. However, he recovered and entered into all the monastic activities, including study, manual labour and translating manuscripts as well as prayer. In 1043 he became abbot and though strict with himself was kind to his monks and to penitents. He was made Bishop of Ostia in 1057 and later returned to his monastery at Fonte Avellana where he made wooden spoons, as well as continuing to compose hymns and poems.

God of grace, we remember your servant Peter Damian, who looked back to the example of the desert fathers. We acknowledge his severity and his outspokenness, his scholarship and his gift of hymn-writing, and give thanks. Amen

22 February

Margaret of Cortona, Franciscan penitent (c 1297)

Born at Lavinio, the handsome daughter of a Tuscan peasant, Margaret became the mistress of a knight from Montepulciano and bore him a son. When her lover was murdered and she saw his decaying body she gave up all her goods, begged her father's forgiveness and returned home with her son. She then led an increasingly austere life and enrolled herself as a Franciscan tertiary, making a living and doing charitable works until her son grew up. She became more and more of a recluse, but her prayer ministry grew and her fame spread as visitors came from far and wide to seek her counsel and witness her miraculous powers.

Lord of forgiveness, we remember today the penitence and works of Margaret of Cortona, who gave so much back in prayer, seclusion and self-denial after years of self-indulgence. We give thanks for her conversions and counsel in the midst of her mortifications and austerity. Amen

23 February

Polycarp, Bishop of Smyrna, martyr (c 155)

A disciple of John the Apostle, Polycarp was Bishop of Smyrna for over forty years and became one of the most influential Christian figures in Roman Asia. He defended Orthodox Christian belief against the Gnostics and earnestly sought to establish a uniform date for Easter in discussion with Anicetus, Bishop of Rome, but without success. Soon after returning to Smyrna, at the great age of 86, he was arrested as part of the persecution, taken to the proconsul in the city and asked to renounce his religion, which he refused to do, saying 'How can I blaspheme my king and saviour?', and was ordered to be burnt alive. The tradition started that a Eucharist was held at his burial place outside the city every Easter.

God of hope, on this day we thank you for the life and martyrdom of Polycarp, Bishop of Smyrna, who in his life as in his death witnessed to the faith which drove him to great deeds. We remember him for his efforts to bring in a common date for Easter, for his hymns and writing, and for a brave testimony to faith at the point of death. Amen

Mildburga, abbess (715)

Mildburga was the daughter of Merewald, King of Mercia, and Ermenburga, Princess of Kent. Her sisters were Mildred and Mildgyth. Merewald founded the nunnery at Wenlock and Mildburga became its second abbess. She is said to have had miraculous healing powers and lived and died in a particularly saintly way. Cures were ascribed to her relics and to her likely grave.

God of grace and love, may we rejoice in the life and healing powers of Mildburga, Abbess of Wenlock, who lived and died in a conspicuously saintly way. We thank you that churches were named after her and that cures followed the discovery of her relics. Amen

24 February

Montanus and Lucius, martyrs (259)

Montanus and Lucius were among a number of African martyrs, some of whom were clergy under Cyprian, who had been executed earlier. Wrongly arrested for involvement in a revolt against the procurator at Carthage, eight of them were kept in prison on restricted rations. Montanus, who experienced a series of visions, coped better than Lucius with the debilitating regime and lack of food. After several months those in holy orders were condemned to death and Lucius was the first to die, Montanus protesting and proclaiming the good news out loud till he too was beheaded.

God of resilience and strength, on this day we remember two of your servants, Montanus and Lucius, who endured imprisonment and approached their deaths while confessing their faith to all around; Lucius through silent witness and Montanus through courageous evangelism, even while being led to execution. We salute their faith and fortitude. Amen

25 February

Ethelbert of Kent, first Christian king among the English (616)

Married to Bertha, a Christian Frankish princess, Ethelbert had not converted when he welcomed Augustine and his companions on their arrival in Kent in 597. However, he did convert a few years later, while not compelling his subjects to follow suit. He gave the missionaries every assistance and encouragement in preaching the gospel and was instrumental in building the monastery of SS Peter and Paul at Canterbury and St Andrew's Cathedral in Rochester. Ethelbert was the most influential ruler of his time in southern England and he was the first Anglo-Saxon king to leave a code of laws.

God of power and might, let us remember with thanksgiving the life and witness of Ethelbert, first Christian king among the English, who welcomed St Augustine to these shores. Brought

to faith through the example of his wife, Bertha, may his encouragement in the spread of Christianity be for us an example and inspiration. Amen

26 February

Porphyry of Gaza, bishop (c 420)

Born at Salonika about 352, Porphyry spent years in the Egyptian desert and the Jordan valley before travelling to Jerusalem, where he made a living as a shoemaker, selling his property for the benefit of the poor. He became a priest at the age of 40 and in 396 was made Bishop of Gaza. His initial efforts to evangelise the heathen living there was set back by the brutal removal of temples and idols by the imperial troops. However, his more patient approach eventually succeeded in bringing Christianity to the region.

Lord God, hope of the poor, we look back today on the ministry of Porphyry, Bishop of Gaza, who at the end of the pagan era held fast to the faith. We thank you that by his example and his care for the poor and needy he pointed people to the Way, the Truth and the Life. Amen

27 February

Gabriel Possenti, passionist cleric (1862)

The younger son of the governor of Assisi, Gabriel studied at the Jesuit college at Spoleto. Always very theatrical with a love of clothes and dancing, Gabriel tried and failed to join a religious order. However, in a procession he became overwhelmed with the desire to become a religious, which he achieved when he joined the Passionist monastery at Morrovalle in 1856. He also felt called to be a priest, such was his commitment to prayer, penance and devotions to Mary, but he died before realising this ambition, at the age of 24.

Ever-living God, on this day we remember Gabriel Possenti, religious and passionist, who died young yet achieved much in a short but exemplary life. May we celebrate someone who was noted for his cheerfulness, in the midst of his prayer and penance. Amen

George Herbert, priest and poet (1633)

From an aristocratic Pembroke family, George Herbert studied at Westminster School and Cambridge, becoming a fellow of Trinity College and then Public Orator at the University. Seemingly destined for a career as a courtier, he became ordained and after a time with Nicholas Ferrar at Little Gidding, he was made deacon in 1626 and ordained priest in 1630. Now married, he became parish priest of Bemerton near Salisbury, where he wrote hymns and poetry which have stood the test of time. His pastoral care in the parish was said to be exemplary.

Sublime Lord, may we praise you, as George Herbert did, seven whole days, not one in seven. Today we give thanks for his life and work, as a conscientious country parson and a poet with the words of an angel, as contemporary today as when he put pen to paper. Amen

28 February

Oswald of Worcester, bishop (992)

From a Danish military family settled in England, Oswald was educated under his uncle, Odo of Canterbury, and was sent to learn monastic discipline at the Abbey of Fleury in France. Appointed Bishop of Worcester in 962, he set about reforming his own cathedral chapter, as well as establishing monasteries at Westbury-on-Trim and Ramsey. Through his connections with the king he acquired large tracts of land for his bishopric and monasteries, and in 972 he was made Archbishop of York as well. Oswald is said to have been gentle and kind and known for his sanctity.

Father of all, today may we celebrate the contribution of Oswald, Bishop of Worcester and York, who distinguished himself in his wise counsel of the king and his gift of administration. And let us not forget that he achieved all this while returning the love of his people through his gentleness and kindness. Amen

29 February

John Cassian, abbot (c 433) – *see under 23 July*

March

1 March

David (Dewi), Bishop of Menevia, Patron of Wales (c 601)

Said to have been the son of a Cardigan chieftain, Sant, and Non, David was a monk and a bishop who was noted for his ascetic, spiritual life and highly regarded for his generosity and compassion, especially towards the poor and the sick. He founded twelve monasteries, from Croyland to Pembrokeshire, including Menevia, now St David's. He was consecrated bishop in Jerusalem, following a pilgrimage, and took a major role at the Councils of Brefi in Cardigan and Caerlon, at the first of which he succeeded Dubricius as primate of Wales. His monasteries were strongly influenced by the regime adopted by the monks of the Egyptian desert. David became known as the Patron Saint of Wales from the twelfth century.

Almighty God, we give thanks today for the inspiration of your servant David, founder of monasteries and Patron Saint of Wales. May his example of kindness and compassion, simple living and persuasive preaching bring us to a right relationship with you, living, loving Lord. Amen

2 March

Chad, Bishop of Lichfield, missionary (672)

Born in Northumbria, Chad was the youngest of four brothers, all of whom became both monks and priests, all entering the monastery on Lindisfarne and taught by Aidan. He succeeded his brother Cedd as Abbot of Lastingham, founded by Cedd. During an uncertain period Chad was made Bishop of York, but he stepped down in favour of Wilfrid on the arrival of Theodore as Archbishop of Canterbury, who then appointed him as bishop to the Mercians, with the centre of the diocese at Lichfield. Chad travelled widely and frequently across his large diocese, initially on foot and then, at the request of Theodore, on horseback. He was loved for his wisdom and gentleness.

God of love and loyalty, we remember on this day the humility and commitment of your faithful servant Chad, who gave way to Wilfrid as Bishop of York, as commanded by Theodore. Yet we also celebrate his subsequent appointment as Bishop of Lichfield, carrying out his role with exemplary diligence and leaving a strong legacy for the future of that diocese. Amen

3 March

Non, mother of David of Wales (sixth century) – see under 5 March

Marinus of Caesarea, martyr (c 260)

Both noble and wealthy, Marinus had a successful career as a soldier and was about to be promoted to centurion when he was denounced as a Christian by a rival for the position. Under questioning by the magistrate, Marinus confessed that he was a Christian and refused to make sacrifices to idols. Asked whether he preferred the sword or the gospel he unhesitatingly chose the gospel book and was led out to be executed.

Lord of all, may we rejoice at the faith and firmness of Marinus, Roman soldier and Christian martyr, who was faced with preferment or loyalty to the gospel. We admire his choice, which led to his execution, but also to his elevation to your kingdom and we pray for his soul and example today. Amen

4 March

Adrian of May Island, abbot, and his companions, martyrs (ninth century)

A missionary bishop from Ireland, possibly of Hungarian descent, Adrian was killed, along with a large number of English companions, by Danes on the Isle of May in the Firth of Forth in 875. The Isle became a notable pilgrimage centre after David, King of Scotland, built a monastery there, initially inhabited by Benedictine monks from Reading and later by canons from St Andrews.

God of mercy, on this day we remember and give thanks for the sacrifice of Adrian, missionary bishop, and his companions, who ministered to Vikings, converting some, but succumbing to the raids of others. On their refuge, the Isle of May, where they were killed, a monastery was founded and we celebrate this as a place of pilgrimage. Amen

Casimir, Prince of Poland (1484)

Born in 1458, the third of thirteen children of Casimir 4th, King of Poland, Casimir was sent by his father to the Hungarian border with a large army expecting the disaffected Hungarian nobles to overthrow their king, Matthias Corvinus, and install Casimir and their king in his place. On the failure of this venture he refused to take up arms against another Christian country and his father banished him to a castle near Cracow. After a period as Viceroy of Poland he preferred a life of celibacy to marriage and, thanks to his early instruction by the Canon of Cracow, he proved in the period 1481-83 to be a ruler of justice, wisdom and firmness before his early death in 1484.

Almighty God, ruler of all, we remember today Casimir, Prince of Poland, pious and devout, who refused to fight against Christian countries, preferring a life of celibacy, devotion and austerity. May we emulate his desire to be just and firm in his faith. Amen

5 March

Non, mother of David of Wales (sixth century)
– commemorated in some traditions on 3 March

Non was the daughter of a chieftain from Pembrokeshire and may even have been a nun at Ty Gwyn near Whitesand Bay in Dyfed when she was seduced by the King of Ceredigion named Sant, leading to the birth of David of Wales. At some point in her life she was certainly a nun, either before she gave birth to David or after becoming a widow, and had connections with Altarnon in Cornwall as well as Finistère in Brittany, where she was buried.

Great Redeemer, on this day we celebrate the life of Non, the mother of David, Patron of Wales. Despite her violation by the King of Ceredigion, we thank you that she retained her modesty and her faith and brought into the world a man of God, noted for his wisdom and elegance. Amen

Kieran (Ciaran) of Saighir, bishop and monk (c 545)

Born in West Cork, Kieran travelled widely in Europe as a young man, getting baptised and ordained along the way. He returned to Ireland and settled at Saighir near Birr in County Offaly, initially as a hermit and later as abbot of a large monastery, also founding a convent with his mother as its abbess. It is reputed that he was consecrated bishop by Patrick.

Lord of time and space, today we give thanks for Kieran, hermit, abbot and bishop, who loved animals and was consecrated bishop by St Patrick. He lived and died a servant of Christ and his beloved Ireland. Amen

6 March

Colette, virgin and abbess (1447)

The daughter of a carpenter in Picardy, christened Nicolette Boylet, Colette, as she became known, joined the Franciscan third order after her parents died in 1398. Living alone in a hermitage lent by the Abbot of Corbie, she had a vision of Francis of Assisi calling her to reform the Poor Clare order of nuns. Despite opposition she was permitted to join the order and to embark on her reforms of existing convents and to establish new ones. Through the sheer power of her faith she achieved great things, founding convents throughout France, Flanders and Savoy.

God of tranquillity, on this day we commemorate the life and reforming work of Colette, Franciscan nun and reformer. We thank you for her dedication to prayer and solitude, the restoration of the Rule of Francis and Clare and the establishment of Poor Clare convents in France, Flanders and many other parts of the world. Amen

7 March

Perpetua, Felicity, and their companions, martyrs, at Carthage (203)

Perpetua, a young married noblewoman of Carthage with a babe in arms, wrote a moving account of much of what befell her, together with her slave Felicity, who was pregnant, and other slaves, as well as a priest. Most were catechumens and were baptised while under 'house arrest', before they were imprisoned. They were condemned as Christians by the Roman authorities, Perpetua experiencing visions of the ladder to heaven. She and Saturus record other visions of the fight between heaven and hell. Perpetua's baby was taken away from her and we learn from contemporary accounts that Perpetua and her companions were mauled to death by wild animals in the arena, showing great courage, news of which spread throughout the Christian community as an inspiration in the face of adversity.

Lord of hope, we thank you for the inspiration of your servants Perpetua, Felicity and their companions, who died at Carthage for their faith and remained strong in that faith even to death. We remember the distress of leaving young ones behind and of seeing companions torn to pieces by leopards, but wonder at the courage and beliefs shown in the face of unimaginable cruelty. Amen

8 March

Felix, apostle to the East Angles (647)

Born and educated in Burgundy, Felix was consecrated and sent by Honorius, Archbishop of Canterbury, to evangelise the East Angles after he had converted their king, Sigebert, who had now returned to his people. Newly consecrated as a bishop, Felix made Dunwich the centre of his new diocese, founding schools and monasteries, including Soham, where he was buried, from where his relics were translated to Ramsey Abbey. His seventeen years at the helm of his diocese were fruitful and Felix has given his name and patronage to the town of Felixstowe in Suffolk.

God of great generosity, we thank you for giving us your servant Felix, who was called from Burgundy to serve in East Anglia and to bring the faith to the subjects of King Sigebert, whom he had already converted. On this day we celebrate the blessings Felix brought, the monasteries he founded, including the one in Soham, and the establishment of his episcopal see at Dunwich, where he ruled for seventeen years. Amen

Edward King, Bishop of Lincoln (1910)

Born in 1829 in London, Edward King was a chaplain and then Principal of Cuddesdon Theological College and professor of theology at Oxford. In these capacities he greatly influenced generations of ordinands. In 1885 he was made Bishop of Lincoln and proved himself to be a pastorally aware and caring bishop to both clergy and laity, though his Catholic principles and theology attracted controversy. He was, however, widely revered for his holiness and wisdom.

Lord God, caring Saviour, we celebrate today the life and ministry of Edward King, revered for his holiness and pastoral awareness. We especially remember his abilities as teacher and theologian, together with his example as caring bishop to clergy and laity alike. Amen

Geoffrey Studdert Kennedy, priest, poet (1929)

Born in 1883, Studdert Kennedy became an important figure as a result of his work as an army chaplain during the First World War with soldiers who nicknamed him 'Woodbine Willie' because of the brand of cigarette he shared with them. A vicar in Worcester before the war, he became a much sought-after preacher and writer following the Great War and worked assiduously for the Christian Industrial Fellowship, dying at a relatively young age in 1929.

Father Almighty, give us happy insights and memories as we recall the life of Geoffrey Studdert Kennedy, chaplain and poet, beloved of soldiers alongside him in the horrors of the First World War. We give thanks for his frankness and authenticity as preacher and writer, as well as his warmth as a friend and comrade. Amen

John of God, founder of the Brothers Hospitaliers (1550)

A mercenary soldier, born in Portugal, who fought for Spain against the French and Turks, John repented of his ways at the age of 40 and converted to a life dedicated to the service of God and determined to work for the sick and the destitute, while earning his living as a wood-merchant. John of Avila helped him to focus his ministry. After his death his followers were organised into an order of hospitaliers know as the Brothers of St John of God or the Brothers Hospitaliers. He is patron of hospitals and the sick.

On this day we give thanks for John of God, who turned his life round from godless mercenary to champion of the poor. We remember him for his care for the physical and spiritual well-being of his patients and now revere him as patron of hospitals and the sick. Amen

9 March

Gregory of Nyssa, bishop and theologian (c 395)

Born at Caesarea in Cappadocia, Gregory was the younger brother of Basil and received a superb education, became a teacher of rhetoric and married Theosebeia. Persuaded to pursue a career in the Church by his namesake, Gregory of Nazianzus, he was made Bishop of Nyssa by his brother, Basil. After a difficult start to his episcopacy he came to the fore as a powerful opponent of Arianism and was acknowledged by the Council of Constantinople in 381 as 'a pillar of orthodoxy'. His influential writings include *On the Soul and the Resurrection* and *Against Fate* and he is held to be a spiritual writer of authority and depth.

Heavenly Father, we celebrate with grateful thanks the erudition and polemic abilities of Gregory of Nyssa, younger brother of

Basil the Great. We recognise his great defence of the fruits of the Council of Nicea and his support of orthodoxy over Arianism, as well as the richness and depth of his theology. Amen

Frances of Rome, laywoman and foundress (1440)

A daughter of Roman aristocracy, Frances was married in accordance with her parents' wishes to a rich young nobleman, Lorenzo Ponziano, having several children together. Ascetic and charitable by nature, she and others in her household sought to relieve the distress of Rome's poor. Following attacks on their property by invading forces and the loss of her children to illness, Frances founded a society of devout women known as the Oblates of Tor de' Specchi, entering the community after her husband's death and becoming its superior.

Lord of love, help us today to remember with gratitude the selfless commitment of Frances of Rome, who devoted herself to relieving the distress of the poor of Rome. We give thanks that as a widow she became superior of the community which she had founded and in which she died. Amen

10 March

Kessog, bishop and martyr (c 700)

Born at Cashel into Munster royalty, Kessog travelled to Scotland, became a monk and later a bishop in the Loch Lomond region, living on Monks' Island and carrying out missions to the Picts. A statue of Kessog took the place of a heap of stones, known as St Kessog's Cairn, which marked the spot where he is said to have been murdered, near Luss on Loch Lomondside.

We remember today the missionary bishop, Kessog, who lived in a cell on Monks' Island, Loch Lomond. We give thanks for his labours amongst the Picts, resulting in his martyrdom by assassin, and rejoice that his name is commemorated by churches dedicated to his name in different parts of Scotland. Amen

The forty martyrs of Sebastea (320)

Ordered to repudiate their religion under the edicts of Emperor Lucinius, forty soldiers of the 'thundering legion' refused, despite the punishment of death. As a result they were stripped naked and left exposed on a frozen lake outside the city of Sebastea in Armenia, with the offer of warm baths to those who co-operated and denied their faith. Only one succumbed to this offer and he was quickly replaced by another professing Christianity. The youngest and the last to die was Melito.

Generous and merciful Father, we give thanks today for the faithfulness of the forty martyrs of Sebastea, who suffered grievously under the persecution of the Emperor Lucinius for professing their faith. May their witness, having been stripped and left to freeze to death, inspire us today, as it inspired the other soldiers who observed and came to believe. Amen

11 March

Eulogius of Cordoba, theologian and martyr (859)

From a wealthy family living under Islamic rule, Eulogius was educated by priests, including Abbot Sperandeo. Well read and learned in the Scriptures, he often visited monasteries and hospitals, drawing up new monastic rules and reading the Scriptures to others. He kept a diary of the sufferings and persecution that followed anti-Muslim activity and attempted proselytism. Although chosen as the next Archbishop of Toledo, Eulogius did not live long enough to be consecrated, having been found to have given shelter to a Muslim girl, Leocretia, who had been converted. He was beheaded four days before she met the same fate.

Lord God, on this day we remember Eulogius of Cordoba, an example of a Christian who lived under Islamic occupation, and thank you for his devotion and steadfastness, in his writing and in his life. We celebrate his clear profession of faith when discovered to have helped a convert from Islam, for which he was beheaded, having shown himself to be indifferent to threats. Amen

12 March

Maximilian, martyr (295)

The son of a veteran in the Roman army, the 21 year-old Maximilian was obliged to join the army and was brought before a court and ordered to enrol as a soldier. He refused, declaring, 'My army is the army of God, and I cannot fight for this world.' Threatened with death if he did not comply Maximilian responded, 'I shall not die. When I leave this earth I shall live with Christ, my Lord.' He was sentenced accordingly and beheaded, an early example of a Christian conscientious objector.

God of peace, we thank you for the life and witness of your servant Maximilian, conscientious objector and martyr. We praise you for his courage and integrity in declaring that he would not be a soldier of this world because he was a soldier of God. Amen

Paul Aurelian (Paulinus), Bishop of Léon (sixth century)

Better known as St Pol, Paul Aurelian was the son of a chieftain in Wales and was educated at the monastery of St Illtyd, where he became a monk and a priest. Along with a dozen companions he travelled to Brittany, where they founded a number of churches. A powerful missioner in Finistère, he became bishop in a place now named after him, Saint-Pol-de-Léon, and ended his days in the monastery of Batz.

God of mission and mystery, on this day we celebrate the work of evangelism of Paul Aurelian, the British Celtic saint who came from Wales and went to Brittany and then to the Loire valley. Founder of churches and Bishop of Léon, his early feats of mission and ministry are remembered to this day. Amen

13 March

Gerald of Mayo, abbot (732)

An English monk at Lindisfarne, Gerald of Mayo travelled with Colman to Inishbofin in Galway. This community came to be known as Mayo and the Saxons, a famous centre of study which corresponded with Alcuin. He is also said to have founded the Abbeys of Tempul-Gerald and Teaghna-Saxon.

Lord of all, we celebrate today the Englishman Gerald, who became a monk at Lindisfarne and went to minister in Ireland with Colman. As abbot and founder of abbeys, may his name be remembered and his life and work honoured. Amen

Euphrasia, nun (410)

Born in Constantinople about 382, Euphrasia was taken by her widowed mother to live in Tabbenisi in Egypt at the age of 7. Although betrothed at the age of 5, she broke off her engagement when her mother died and spent the rest of her life with a community of dedicated women, giving away her property and living apart from the world. She showed herself to be diligent and patient, often taking on the most arduous jobs for the community and fasting for up to a week.

God of purity, today let us remember Euphrasia, a perfect example to us of humility, meekness and charity. We thank you for her gentleness and patience, and her dedication to her community in Egypt, by hard work and penance. Amen

14 March

Matilda (Maud), Queen of Germany (968)

Born in Westphalia, the daughter of Theodore, a Saxon count, Matilda married the German King Henry 'the Fowler'. Their children included Emperor Otto and Bruno, Archbishop of Cologne. A widow for over thirty years, Matilda suffered ill treatment from Otto, as well as at the hands of Henry 'the Quarrelsome'. Both complained about her generosity to the Church and to the poor, but among the people she was loved for her goodness and patience.

Extravagant Lord, we give thanks today for Matilda, wife of the German King Henry 1st and mother of Bruno, Archbishop of Cologne. We especially remember her generosity to the poor and to the Church in the face of the opposition of relatives during her long widowhood. Amen

15 March

Clement Hofbauer, priest (1820)

Born at Tasswitz in Moravia in 1751, the son of a Slavonic butcher, Clement was a baker's apprentice before going to work at a monastery in Klosterbruick. After a spell as a hermit he desired a more active life and went to Rome to be educated for the priesthood. Joining the Redemptorists, he went back to Vienna, but his efforts at founding a Redemptorist house there were thwarted, while he did open the house of St Benno in Warsaw, staying in Poland until 1808. Back in Vienna he fought hard against state control of religious and church affairs and established a new college in the city, as well as demonstrating care for the sick and concern for devout Protestants.

Lord of learning and wisdom, today we remember your student Clement Hofbauer who, without any advantages of birth and general education, was known for his wisdom in religious matters and social issues, founding a college in Vienna. We give thanks for his tireless care of the sick and for his sensitivity towards devout Protestants. Amen

Louise de Marillac, foundress (1660)

Born in Auvergne in 1591 into an aristocratic country family, Louise was educated by nuns at Poissy and married Antony Le Gras, an official of the royal court. After he died in 1625 she wanted to devote herself to God's service and sought the direction of Vincent de Paul. Recognising Louise's qualities, he chose her to train and organise the order; they co-founded the Sisters of Charity, whose sole purpose was to care for the sick poor in a very practical way. By the time she died forty such houses were operating, alongside care for people at home and shelter given to hundreds of women.

Merciful God, on this day let us remember with grateful thanks the life and work of Louise de Marillac, follower of Vincent de Paul and founder of the Sisters of Mercy. May her example of endurance, selfless devotion and ability to train others be long remembered and much admired. Amen

16 March

Boniface of Ross, bishop (eighth century)

Said to have come from Italy, Boniface is linked to two Christian sites in Scotland, Restenneth in Angus, where he baptised the Pictish King Nechtan in 710 and founded a monastery; and Rosemarkie on the Black Isle, where he re-founded a monastery. Famous for founding churches, his likely Italian origins were demonstrated by the dedication of these foundations to St Peter, implying an influence from Rome rather than from the Celtic West.

God of formation and foundation, we thank you today for the noble work of Boniface, founder of churches in Scotland. Seeking inspiration from Rome, and particularly from Peter, may his legacy be recognised and felt even until this day. Amen

Abraham Kidunaia, hermit (sixth century)

Born of wealthy and noble parents at Chidana in Mesopotamia, Abraham bowed to his parents' wishes that he should marry, but just before the wedding, in the middle of the marriage feast, he ran off to the desert. There his friends found him at prayer after searching for seventeen days. He then walled up the door of his cell, with only a small opening for food, living the austere life of a hermit for some fifty years, venturing out against his will at the request of the Bishop of Edessa, who made him a priest to encourage him to preach the faith to the pagan community about him. Despite being maltreated, his patience and holiness eventually led to baptisms before he retired once again to his cell.

Loving Lord, on this day we contemplate the solitary life of Abraham Kidunaia of Mesopotamia, his fifty years of penance and his call to priesthood. We give thanks that following his ordination he was able, through patience and prayer, to win over converts to the faith, as well as rescuing his orphan niece Mary from evil ways. Amen

17 March

Patrick, bishop, missionary, Patron of Ireland (c 460)

Born on the west coast of Britain, Patrick was the son of a deacon who was a town councillor and the grandson of a priest. Captured by Irish pirates while still a youth, he managed to escape after six years and went to the continent before finding his way back to his own family. There his faith grew and he travelled to Gaul to study and train as a priest under the influence of Martin of Tours. Returning to Ireland as Bishop of Armagh he proceeded to evangelise throughout the land, walking and facing opposition wherever he went, but establishing a monastic system which sustained the faith after his death.

Almighty and overarching God, today we praise your name for your gift of Patrick who, though abducted from his homeland into slavery in Ireland and managing to escape, nevertheless returned there as missionary and bishop. Through his supplications and deep pastoral care you gave him the skills to evangelise and become Patron of Ireland, securing the faith for future generations, for which we give you thanks. Amen

Joseph of Arimathea, disciple (first century)
– commemorated in some traditions on 31 July

A high-born Jew and a member of the Sanhedrin, Joseph kept his discipleship of Jesus secret but had not joined in the condemnation of him and, after Jesus' death, asked Pilate for the body and buried it in his own tomb, with the help of Nicodemus, then playing a significant part in the passion narrative, at some risk to himself. He is said to have come to Britain later and built a church at Glastonbury.

Lord of legend and loyalty, we give thanks today for the faithfulness of Joseph of Arimathea who, risking his position and riches, saw it as his duty to ask Pilate for the body of Jesus and arrange for his burial. We acknowledge his special association with Glastonbury, which inspired the building of a church and hermitage there. Amen

18 March

Cyril of Jerusalem, teacher of the faith (386)

Born in or near Jerusalem and educated there, Cyril was a priest who was given oversight of the instruction of catechumens. His most famous work, *Catecheses*, was written for this purpose. He was made bishop in about 349 but was exiled several times, having sold church goods to relieve the poor and fallen foul of Arians, especially the Arian Emperor Valens. However, he took a full part in the Council of Constantinople in 381, having been reinstated in his see by the Council of Seleucia.

Constant Lord, on this day we celebrate and give thanks for the life and work of Cyril of Jerusalem during a period of turbulence in your Church. Grant that we, like Cyril, are able to resist wrong paths in the faith and choose, through your grace, to remain true to the Trinity of Father, Son and Holy Spirit. Amen

Edward the Martyr, king (c 979)

Born about 962, the son of King Edgar and his first wife, Aethelflaed, Edward succeeded his father in 975. After only three years on the throne he was assassinated at Corfe Castle after a power struggle involving his half-brother and his stepmother Elfrida. Buried at Wareham and then translated to the church at Shaftesbury, Edward was venerated as a saint and martyr, a young man who had suffered an unjust death.

Almighty God, on this day we give thanks for the short life of Edward, son of Edgar, struck down at the hands of assassins after only three years as king. May we ponder on the miracles that followed and the eventual penance of those responsible for the murder. Amen

19 March

Joseph of Nazareth, foster-father of Christ and husband of the Blessed Virgin Mary (first century)
– commemorated in some traditions on 1 May

Descended from the great kings of the tribes of Judah, Joseph was a carpenter by trade and the foster-father of Jesus. According to the Gospels he was an 'upright man' who stood by Mary when she was with child, following an angelic vision. He ensured the escape of the Holy Family to Egypt before returning to Israel after Herod's death and proved to be a faithful guardian to Jesus and husband to Mary. It is not known when he died, but it was before the crucifixion.

> Trusting Lord, we offer praise and thanks to you on this day, as we remember your Son's guardian and protector, Joseph of Nazareth, alongside Mary, his wife. We remember Joseph as a holy man, faithful to the end, to whom we owe special thanks and honour for his selfless devotion and duty of care. Amen

20 March

Cuthbert, Bishop of Lindisfarne, missionary (687)
– commemorated in some traditions on 4 September

Born in the Scottish lowlands about 640 to a well-to-do Anglo-Saxon family, Cuthbert turned his mind at an early age to a godly life, assisted by his upbringing as a shepherd. A vision of heavenly lights and angels conducting the soul of Aidan to heaven convinced him of his vocation and a few years later he joined Melrose Abbey as a monk, becoming prior before undertaking a series of missionary journeys there, moving to be abbot at Lindisfarne and then bishop in 685. His travelling and preaching continued, interspersed with spells as a hermit on Farne Island, where he died.

We thank you on this day for the life of Cuthbert, inspired at the death of Aidan to heed your call. We remember his gifts of healing and prophecy which, together with his zeal for teaching, visiting and preaching, gave to Lindisfarne a special place in English Christianity, and Cuthbert a special place in your kingdom as his life came to an end on his beloved Farne Island. Amen

21 March

Thomas Cranmer, Archbishop of Canterbury, Reformation martyr (1556) – *in Wales, commemorated jointly with Hugh Latimer, Nicholas Ridley and Robert Ferrar*

Born in Aslockton in Nottinghamshire in 1489, Thomas Cranmer joined the diplomatic service from Cambridge University. He assisted Henry 8th in the annulment of the king's marriage to Catherine of Aragon and was made Archbishop of Canterbury in 1533 to give effect to this. A reformer, he worked closely with Thomas Cromwell and was the chief architect and author of the Book of Common Prayer of 1549 and 1552, together with the Ordinal of 1550 and the Thirty-nine Articles. Convicted of treason and heresy under Queen Mary's reign in 1553 and 1554 respectively, Thomas Cranmer initially signed recantations, but was condemned to die at the stake and made a final, bold statement of Protestant faith before he was burnt.

Today we offer our thanks for the great contribution of Thomas Cranmer, Archbishop of Canterbury and martyr, to the knowledge, understanding and practice of our faith. For the Book of Common Prayer, for the Ordinal and for the Thirty-nine Articles we owe him a debt of gratitude – and remember today his martyrdom and his bold final statement of faith at the stake. Amen

Nicholas of Flue, hermit and Patron Saint of Switzerland (1487)

Born at Flueli near Sachseln in Switzerland in 1417, Nicholas followed his father into the family farm, also joining a lay association known as the

Friends of God. He took an active part in public affairs, although unable to read or write, fought in two wars, during one of which he prevented the destruction of a nunnery, and was frequently consulted because of his wise judgement. In 1465 he withdrew from public life in protest over a decision of a local court and shortly afterwards, despite having a big family, he devoted the next twenty years to divine contemplation as a hermit, with the consent of his wife Dorothy. He made a crucial intervention when civil war was threatened and his proposed terms of settlement were accepted in full at the Compromise of Stans in 1481.

> Lord, you have shown us the gift of mediation, through your Son; on this day we recognise the skills and qualities of Nicholas of Flue, a wise hermit consulted by the great and good as well as the humble and lowly. We thank you for his counsel in the early days of the Swiss nation, when compromise and reconciliation were required and which he facilitated. Amen

22 March

Basil of Ancyra, priest (362)

A priest of Ancyra under Bishop Marcellus, Basil held out against the Arian bishops who banned him from holding ecclesiastical assemblies. He then railed against the sacrifices of the heathens when the Emperor Julian the Apostate re-established idolatry. He was dragged before the proconsul, tortured on the rack and imprisoned. Then he faced the Emperor, who had stopped in Ancyra en route to Antioch. He stood up to Julian, refusing to deny Christ and warning the Emperor that 'you are deceived – you have renounced Christ at a time when he conferred on you the empire. But he will deprive you of it, together with your life'. For this response Basil had his flesh removed piece by piece and then he was pierced with red-hot spikes and he died, praying constantly.

> We give thanks and praise for your faithful servant Basil of Ancyra, whose unswerving loyalty to the true faith was testament to his holy life and great fortitude in the face of torture and death. May we be inspired by his challenges to heathen authorities and committed to sharing your Word, whatever the consequences. Amen

23 March

Turibius, Archbishop of Lima (1606)

Born at Mayorga in Spain in 1538, Turibius was a professor of law at Salamanca University when he was appointed by Philip 2nd to be principal judge in the court of the Inquisition at Granada. Although a layman, he was then chosen to be Archbishop of Lima in Peru. Despite his protests, he was duly consecrated bishop and took up his post in 1581. In the face of huge distractions, corruption and oppression, Turibius took steps to correct abuses and administer discipline among clergy, together with building hospitals and religious houses. He showed the way as a pioneering missionary and reforming bishop, learning local dialects and travelling extensively throughout his vast diocese, showing concern for Indians and impoverished Spaniards alike.

> **On this day we look back and acknowledge the life and ministry of Turibius, Archbishop of Lima, during the early period of Spanish rule in South America. We give thanks especially for his advocacy on behalf of the poor, his reform of the Church and his intolerance of abuse and oppression, which inspired him to set up hospitals, religious houses and a training college. Amen**

Gwinear, Patron of Cornwall (sixth century)

Gwinear was the leader of a group of Welsh or Irish missionaries who landed in Cornwall at the mouth of the Hayle River. Some were killed by the local heathen ruler, Teudar, but the remainder persevered in evangelising the district of Gwinnear and Camborne, giving their names to Saint Ives and Portleven. He and Meriadoc continued their work in Brittany where, at Pluvigner, Gwinear is commemorated in the stained-glass window of the church.

> **Lord of all time, today we celebrate the life of Gwinear, Patron of Cornwall, who came from Wales and evangelised the district of Gwinnear and Camborne. We give thanks that he continued his ministry in Brittany, where he is also remembered and venerated. Amen**

24 March

Macartan, bishop (c 505)

Known as the 'strong man' of Saint Patrick, Macartan was one of the earliest Irish saints with a reputation as a miracle-worker. He established the church in Clogher and spread the good news in Fermanagh and Tyrone. A silver shrine and an eighth century manuscript of the Gospels are associated with his time at Clogher.

> **Glorious God, let us acknowledge with thanks the contribution of Marcatan to the Church in Ireland, as the strong right hand of Patrick, Patron Saint of Ireland. We remember him as bishop and miracle-worker who built up the early Christian life of Clogher diocese. Amen**

Oscar Romero, Archbishop of San Salvador, martyr (1980)

Born in a village in El Salvador in 1917, Oscar was known as a quiet and gentle priest and pastor. During a time of political trouble and social turmoil for his country he was chosen as its Archbishop as being a safe and neutral appointment. His increasingly critical and outspoken pronouncements in support of the demands of the poor and oppressed, and against violence, led to threats of assassination. He continued to preach in the same way and was shot and killed by a gunman while presiding at Mass.

> **Just Lord, we give thanks on this day for the life, ministry and martyrdom of Oscar Romero, Archbishop of San Salvador. May his example of speaking out against violence and his championing of the poor in seeking economic and social justice be an inspiration to Christians everywhere. Amen**

Walter Hilton of Thurgarton, Augustinian canon, mystic (1396)

Born in 1343, Walter Hilton studied Canon Law at Cambridge before spending time as a hermit and then becoming an Augustinian canon at

Thurgarton Priory, Nottinghamshire, about 1386. A respected spiritual guide who wrote in English and Latin, he translated several Latin devotional works. His principal work is *The Scale of Perfection* which describes the 'luminous darkness' of mortification, the transition from disordered self-love to love of God, and contemplation as 'awareness of grace and sensitivity to the Spirit'.

God of inspiration, we remember today the canon and mystic Walter Hilton of Thurgarton, writer, translator and theologian. We especially give thanks for his spiritual writings about the role of contemplation in raising awareness of grace and sensitivity to the Spirit. Amen

Hildelith, Abbess of Barking (c 712)

Hildelith succeeded Ethelburga, first Abbess of Barking and sister of Erhenwald, Bishop of London. She developed the buildings and ruled with firmness, enhancing the holiness of the community and experiencing visions. Aldhelm dedicated his treatise on virginity to her and Boniface praised her highly in his letters.

On this day we celebrate your servant Hildelith, successor to Ethelburga as Abbess of Barking. May her vision for the development of the monastic buildings, combined with her firmness and self-discipline, be a legacy of her gifts and ministry. Amen

25 March

The Annunciation of our Lord to the Blessed Virgin Mary

The feast marks the conception of Christ in the womb of Mary, the announcement of the coming of God made flesh in the person of his Son, Jesus Christ, as depicted in Luke's Gospel. This event began to be celebrated in the fourth century and is marked in the East and the West on the same day. This is the affirmation of the perfect humanity and perfect divinity of Jesus, with the emphasis on Mary as 'Mother of God', hence the term 'Lady Day', which was often used in England. It is now a Feast of our Lord, albeit giving his virgin mother due honour and veneration.

We celebrate today the announcement of the coming of God made flesh in the person of your Son, Jesus Christ, the Anointed One. May we rejoice at the conception of Christ in the womb of Mary and the affirmation of the bringing together of the perfect humanity and the complete divinity of Jesus. Amen

Alfwold, monk of Winchester and Bishop of Sherborne (1058)

At a time when self-indulgence was commonplace among clergy, Alfwold was known, as monk of Winchester and Bishop of Sherborne, for the austerity of his way of life, his habitual abstinence and use of plain wooden platters and bowls. He venerated Swithun and Cuthbert, in the image he had of Swithun in the church at Sherborne and in his visits to Cuthbert's shrine and singing of his antiphon.

On this day we thank you, Lord, for the life and ministry of your servant Alfwold, monk of Winchester and Bishop of Sherborne. We remember his ascetic habits at a time of self-indulgence and his devotion to Swithun and Cuthbert. Amen

Dismas, the good thief (c 30)

One of the two thieves executed with Jesus, Dismas (a name derived from the Greek for 'dying') was the one who recognised Jesus' innocence and admitted his own guilt, asking Jesus, 'Lord, remember me when you come into your kingdom,' to which Jesus replied, 'Truly, I say to you, today you will be with me in Paradise.' Dismas came to be regarded in the Middle Ages as the patron of prisoners and thieves.

Merciful Father, today we remember Dismas, who asked Christ on the cross, 'Lord, remember me when you come into your kingdom.' Known as the 'good thief', we rejoice that your Son recognised his repentance, giving hope to us all. Amen

26 March

Harriet Monsell, founder of the Community of St John the Baptist, Clewer (1883)

Born Harriet O'Brien into an Irish family, Harriet was married to a priest Charles Monsell, and after his death she worked in a penitentiary for fallen women at Clewer near Windsor. She became a religious in 1852 and then first superior of the Community of St John the Baptist, which grew under her oversight, with foundations at home and abroad. The community ran schools and hospitals, opened mission houses and cared for orphans. In 1875 she retired to a hermitage in Folkestone, where she died.

On this day we remember with gratitude the ministry of Harriet Monsell, a religious and subsequently first superior of the Community of St John the Baptist, Clewer. We celebrate the way she ran schools and hospitals and opened mission houses before retiring to a hermitage in Folkestone. Amen

Ludger (Luidger), Bishop of Munster, apostle of Saxony (809)

Born near Utrecht about 744, Ludger travelled to England as a young man, studying under Alcuin at York. Returning to Utrecht, he rebuilt the church at Deventer and preached throughout Frisia before a spell of two years in Monte Cassino. He returned to continue his missionary work in Frisia until he was entrusted by Charlemagne with evangelising the Saxons in Westphalia. He was based in Munster, where he was consecrated bishop and where he built a monastery for canons. He died at the Benedictine monastery at Werden, which he founded.

God of purpose, we give thanks today for the life and mission of Ludger, who served under Alcuin of York and evangelised the Frieslanders for some years. We remember his gentle persuasiveness and rebuilding of ruined churches, culminating in his consecration as Bishop of Munster and his foundation of the monastery at Werden. Amen

27 March

Rupert of Salzburg, missionary bishop (c 710)

Probably of Frankish origins, Rupert became Bishop of Worms and towards the end of the century went as a missionary to Regensburg in Bavaria and extended his activities over a wide area along the Danube. He made Salzburg his centre, founding the church and building a monastery and a nunnery known as the Mönchberg and Nonnberg respectively. It is said that he developed the saltmines nearby, giving rise to the name of Salzburg, and his emblem is a barrel of salt.

May we honour and give thanks for the life and ministry of your servant Rupert, Bishop of Worms and then Salzburg, from where he evangelised throughout the Danube area. We remember the way he brought light and salt to the places and people where his mission took him, in your name. Amen

28 March

Alkelda (Athilda), nun and martyr (c 800)

Probably a Saxon princess and nun, Alkelda was strangled to death by Viking women and buried in the church of which she was patron at Middleham in Yorkshire. She gave her name to the college set up later by Richard 3rd, at Middleham.

Lord of transformation, we remember today your faithful servant Alkelda, slain by Viking women, but in whose memory a college was built. May the learning that resulted be a consolation and lasting compensation for this loss of a good church woman to the forces of darkness. Amen

29 March

Jonah and Berikjesu, martyrs (327)

Jonah and Berikjesu were victims of persecution by Shapur 2nd in Persia. Arrested for giving encouragement to imprisoned Christians, they suffered torture and inducement to renounce their faith, but they held fast and refused to perform an act of idolatry. Berikjesu had burning pitch poured down his throat and Jonah was first dismembered, then crushed to death.

Faithful God, we thank you today for the lives and witness of Jonah and Berikjesu, martyrs in ancient Persia, persecuted for giving encouragement to imprisoned Christians. Steadfast to the last in refusing to perform acts of idolatry, may their death strengthen our resistance to false gods, our resolve to keep the faith. Amen

Gwynllyw (Woolos) and Gwladys, parents of Cadoc (sixth century)

Gwynllyw was a chieftain from south-east Wales and Gwladys one of twenty-four children of Brychan Brycheiniog. Their son, Cadoc, who became a leading figure among the monks of South Wales, converted them to a devout life. They settled at Stow Hill near Newport, Gwent, where they lived an austere life, but they eventually lived separate lives, encouraged by Cadoc. Gwynllyw built a church on the site in Newport where the cathedral, named after him, now stands.

Father Almighty, today we salute the parents of your servant Cadoc, converted from a life of armed violence by their son to live a life of austerity and devotion. May we always be open to learn from our offspring, with the help of your Son, our Saviour, Jesus Christ. Amen

30 March

John Climacus, monk and Abbot of Mount Sinai (649)

Born in Palestine, John married early and became a monk on the death of his wife. He spent much of his life as a hermit, living at Thole like the Egyptian monks. His second name, Climacus, meaning 'ladder', is derived from his great work, *The Ladder of Divine Ascent*, an influential treatise on monastic spirituality, translated into English in 1959. Towards the end of his life he was chosen as Abbot of Sinai, retiring eventually to his hermitage, where he died.

God of perfection, we remember with grateful thanks John Climacus, monk, hermit and Abbot of Mount Sinai, who lived a humble, obedient and holy life. May we be inspired by the fruits of his spirituality, *The Ladder of Divine Ascent*, a book which gave rise to great paintings as well as a pious rule of life. Amen

Osburga, Abbess of Coventry (c 1018)

Osburga was abbess of the nunnery at Coventry from its foundation by Cnut before he was recognised as King of England. Although little is known of her life, her shrine became a place where many miracles were said to have taken place, giving rise to requests from the clergy and people of Coventry for this feast day in her honour.

God of miracles, we thank you on this day for the memory of Osburga, Abbess of Coventry, whose shrine became the place of many miracles. May this recognition of her worth continue to encourage and inspire others in their healing ministry and mission. Amen

Leonard Murialdo, founder of the Congregation of St Joseph (1900)

Born and educated in Turin, Leonard Murialdo was ordained priest in 1851. He then committed himself to the education of working-class boys as director of the oratory of St Louis, encouraged by John Bosco. After a spell in Paris he returned to Turin as rector of a Christian college of technical training and further education, establishing its high reputation and founding the Congregation of St Joseph to ensure that this work and ministry became permanent.

God of virtue and mercy, may we honour and remember the name of Leonard Murialdo, who devoted himself to the education

of working class boys before becoming rector of a Christian college in Turin. As founder of the Congregation of St Joseph, his work lives on and may we recognise this today. Amen

31 March

John Donne, priest, poet (1631)

Born about 1571, a great-nephew of Thomas More, John Donne was brought up as a Roman Catholic, though in his youth religion did not attract him. Studying at Cambridge and then in continental Europe, he came to Christianity through the Church of England. Eventually he felt called to ordination and was appointed Dean of St Paul's Cathedral. His poetry changed from the satires, love-elegies and lyrics of his youth to the religious poetry of his troubled middle years, followed by the genius of his rhetorical preaching. His early cynicism gave way to his devotion to the vocation of a priest loving and loved by the crucified Christ.

Lord of life, on this day we rejoice at the ministry and inspiration of John Donne, a great-nephew of Thomas More, and a poet for all seasons. We thank you for his sermons, his verse, and his exploration of language and faith, which move and teach us in equal measure, even to this day. Amen

April

1 April

Frederick Denison Maurice, priest, teacher of the faith (1872)

Born in 1805, Frederick Maurice was one of the founders of the Christian Socialist Movement. Author of *The Kingdom of Christ* and known for his radical views on traditional concepts of hell, he ended his days as a professor at Cambridge University.

God of insight and teaching, we thank you for the life, learning and writing of Frederick Maurice, teacher of the faith. We especially remember his witness and his inspiration as founder of the Christian Socialist Movement. Amen

Hugh of Grenoble, bishop (1132)

Born in 1053 and educated in Valence, Hugh became Bishop of Grenoble when he was only 27. Always diffident and drawn to monastic life, he established through charter Bruno's order of Carthusian monks at the Grande Chartreuse in his diocese.

God of peace and contemplation, we remember with gratitude and fondness your servant Hugh, recognising his faithful duties as bishop. May his establishment of the Carthusian Order through the championing of Bruno be a lasting legacy of his faithfulness to you. Amen

2 April

Francis of Paola, founder of the order of Minims (1507)

Born in Calabria, Francis returned to his birthplace as a hermit after a period at a Franciscan friary. Famous for prophecy and miracles, and observing a perpetual Lent, Francis spent most of the rest of his life in France, advising Louis 11th and establishing his order, the Minims or 'Least Brethren'.

Lord of austerity and humility, we give thanks for the life, witness and obedience of Francis of Paola, founder of the Minims and spiritual adviser to Louis 11th. May his life of prophecy, integrity and order bring us hope and help in our daily lives, to your glory. Amen

Mary of Egypt, penitent (fifth century)

Moving to Alexandria in her teens, Mary led a life of prostitution until, at the age of 29, she went on a pilgrimage to Jerusalem, where she was converted. She then lived a solitary life of penitence in the desert, surviving on dates and berries, until her body was discovered by the monk Zosimus and buried by him, allegedly with the help of a lion.

Merciful God, on this day we look on your servant Mary of Egypt, transformed by your Spirit from prostitute to penitent. We remember her devotion and desire to know you through the simplicity of her life in the desert, an example to us of a straightforward but deep faith lived out in solitude. Amen

3 April

Richard of Chichester, bishop (1253) – *see under 16 June*

Pancras of Taormina, martyr (first century)

Pancras carried out most of his ministry in Sicily, where reputedly he was sent by Peter to evangelise. He was known as a preacher and miracle-worker and much loved in Sicily, but was stoned to death by brigands. He was venerated as far afield as Georgia and England, where a number of churches are dedicated to him.

Lord of miracle and marvel, we remember today the life and martyrdom of Pancras of Taormina, sent by Peter to evangelise Sicily. May we salute his mission and acknowledge his sacrifice as we seek to strengthen our own faith. Amen

4 April

Agape, Irene and Chione, martyrs (304)

Maidens from Salonika, born in the late third century, Agape, Irene and Chione left their homes to follow a life of prayer, but were brought to trial under the persecution of Diocletian for refusing to eat food offered in sacrifice to the gods. Two were condemned to be buried alive immediately, Irene suffering further questioning and an enforced confinement in a brothel, before herself being condemned to the flames.

> **God of sacrifice and sacrament, let us today admire, remember and revere the three martyrs Agape, Irene and Chione, victims of persecution and intolerance, but with a steadfast faith. May we learn from their witness and adherence to the Truth, whatever the consequences. Amen**

Isidore, scholar and Bishop of Seville (608)

Cartagena was the place of Isidore's birth, into a pious family, and he was educated mainly by his brother Leander, who became Archbishop of Seville and whom he succeeded. Known for converting the Visigoths from Arianism and presiding over the Councils of Seville (619) and Toledo (633), he was author of encyclopedic works of history, theology and etymology which were used throughout the Middle Ages.

> **Lord of all, we celebrate the life and works of Isidore, who brought scholarship and insight to the Christian story, in his ministry and writings. Let us admire and learn from his tireless search for the proper way to interpret, and live by, the faith your Son taught us. Amen**

5 April

Vincent Ferrer, missioner, Dominican friar (1419)

Born in Valencia in 1350, the son of an Englishman who had settled in Spain, Vincent joined the Dominican Friars in 1367 and was known as a philosopher and powerful preacher, who sought to bring an end to the papal schism. As a missioner, he converted many, including a rabbi, who went on to become Bishop of Cartagena, and many miracles have also been ascribed to him.

> Gracious God, we honour the memory today of Vincent Ferrer, for his zeal as preacher and missioner, for his faithful ministry as friar, and for his learning. May we be inspired by his service and his fervent efforts to end the papal schism. Amen

6 April

William of Aebelholt, abbot (1203)

Born in France in about 1127, William was a canon in Paris before being called to reform the abbey at Aebelholt in Denmark. Thereafter he became an influential figure in the development of the Danish Church, his letters providing an important history of events in the Church.

> God of vocations and ministry, we thank you for the fruitful following of your call by William of Aebelholt, who contributed to the advance of your Church in Denmark. Let us gratefully learn from his letters and his legacy, acknowledging the contributions of all those who record the pattern of ministry in the Church. Amen

Irenaeus of Sirmium, bishop and martyr (304)

Born in the latter part of the third century, Ireneaus was brought up at Sirmium in Serbia, which suffered persecution under Diocletian and Maximian. Refusing to offer sacrifices to the gods, he was imprisoned, tortured and beheaded, testifying to his faith to the last that 'my duty is to undergo torture rather than deny my God and sacrifice to demons'.

> Lord of lords, on this day we remember your servant Irenaeus, martyred for his steadfastness of faith, even under torture. May we be encouraged by his declaration of duty to follow you, whatever the pressures we face, knowing that you are with us always. Amen

7 April

John-Baptist de la Salle, educationalist and founder (1719)

Born in Rheims in 1651, John-Baptist, after being ordained priest, devoted most of his life to the setting up of schools and the training of teachers. He formed the 'Brothers of Christian Schools' and through his books *The Conduct of Christian Schools* and *Meditations for Sundays* was an influential figure in the development of education in both France and England.

Almighty God, we give thanks for the life and work of John-Baptist de la Salle, his pioneering work in education and his devotion to prayer. May his insights into the role of the teacher bring us new understanding of your Son, our teacher. Amen

Nilus of Sora, abbot (1508)

Born about 1433 of peasant origin, Nilus became a monk in Belozersk in Russia before going to Greece, where he studied monastic living on Mount Athos. Returning to his homeland in 1480, he founded a colony of semi-hermits by the River Sora, his beliefs combining serenity of discipline with an opposition to religious formalism and intolerance.

Generous Lord, you sent us Nilus to show us the importance of deep study, self-discipline and generosity of spirit. Help us to adopt his sense of freedom and moderation, in sound foundations of belief and religious life. Amen

8 April

Griffith Jones, priest, teacher of the faith (1761)

Griffith Jones was born in 1683, into a shepherding family, and after being educated at a grammar school in Camarthen, was ordained in 1708. A preacher of note, he was also dedicated to the setting up of circulating schools, improving literacy and contributing to the Welsh spiritual awakening.

Teacher, Lord, on this day we celebrate Griffith Jones, preacher, teacher and organiser of schools in Wales. We thank you that he inspired and instructed generations to know you better, helping to generate an awakening in faith. Amen

9 April

Dietrich Bonhoeffer, Lutheran pastor, martyr (1945)

Born in 1906, Dietrich Bonhoeffer was ordained in the Lutheran Church and gave lectures in a number of countries before returning to Berlin, where he was active in opposing Nazism. A leader in the Confessing Church, his stance resulted in his arrest by the Nazis in 1943 and he was murdered by the Nazi police in a concentration camp in 1945.

Loving Lord, we remember with thanks and admiration the witness of Dietrich Bonhoeffer, who taught us and showed the cost of discipleship, as your Son did. Let us rejoice at his legacy as we mourn a life cut short because of his stand against the evils of Nazism. Amen

Waudru, widow, Patroness of Mons (seventh century)

From a remarkable family of saints in seventh century Belgium, Waudru, after her husband became a monk, devoted herself to good works in caring for the poor and sick. Later, she was responsible for building a convent in what is now known as the town of Mons.

God of family love, today we celebrate the life, family and work of Waudru, Patroness of Mons. We give thanks especially for her good works and her establishment of a convent in this part of Belgium. Amen

10 April

William Law, priest, spiritual writer (1761)

William Law was born in 1686 in Kings Cliffe, Northamptonshire, educated at Emmanuel College, Cambridge, and after ordination as a deacon returned there as a Fellow. Becoming a priest, he published *A Serious Call to a Devout and Holy Life*, which influenced, among others, the Wesley brothers, retiring for his latter years to Kings Cliffe to a life of devotion and caring for the poor.

> **Lord of devotion and integrity, on this day we honour the life, writings and ministry of William Law, a man of learning and prayer, who led others into the path of faith and meditation. May we follow his path of truth and obedience, which takes us to you. Amen**

William of Ockham, friar, philosopher, teacher of the faith (1347)

From Ockham in Surrey, William was born about 1285 and joined the Franciscan Order, studying and teaching at Oxford. His writings on such matters as the principle of economy, papal primacy and the philosophy of religion were ground-breaking and controversial. He spent his later years in Paris and Bavaria.

> **We honour today the friar and writer William of Ockham, whose insights challenged and inspired his contemporaries in Britain and on the continent. Let us give thanks for his encouragement and his insights, which advanced the understanding of the philosophy of religion. Amen**

11 April

Stanislas, martyr, Bishop of Cracow (1079)

Born in 1010 at Szczepanow in Poland, Stanislas, after ordination as a priest, was given a canonry at Cracow, where he was consecrated bishop in

1072. Patron of Poland, Stanislas stood up to the blatantly adulterous behaviour of King Boleslav, who murdered him with his own hand after his soldiers refused to kill him.

Lord God, you gave Stanislas, Bishop of Cracow, the courage to challenge the scandalous behaviour of his king, for which he was martyred. May we, today, take heart that faith such as that of Stanislas can make us do courageous things in the face of temporal forces. Amen

George Augustus Selwyn, first Bishop of New Zealand (1878)

Born in 1809 and educated at Cambridge, George Augustus Selwyn was made curate of Windsor after ordination. In 1841 he became Bishop of New Zealand, where he stayed for twenty-seven years and was an advocate for Maori rights, before returning to England to become Bishop of Lichfield and a chief founder of the Lambeth Conference.

Lord of great protection, today we celebrate the life and witness of George Augustus Selwyn, defender of the rights of Maoris as Bishop of New Zealand and one of the architects of the Lambeth Conference. May we honour his sense of right and wrong, of rights as well as responsibilities as people of faith. Amen

12 April

Zeno, Bishop of Verona (c 371)

Born in Africa, Zeno became Bishop of Verona about 362, where he was known as a persuasive preacher and a good pastor, a defender of orthodoxy and founder of nunneries. Noted also for his charitable works and ministry of hospitality, he was an early advocate of human rights.

Creative God, Lord of all, we give thanks for the life and works of your servant Zeno, preacher, pastor, and friend of strangers. Let us learn from his openness of welcome and his firmness of purpose. Amen

William Forbes, bishop (1634)

Born in 1585 in Aberdeen, William Forbes became a professor there, ministering in various churches. He was a theologian of note who was appointed the first Bishop of Edinburgh, but died before he was due to be consecrated.

God of reconciliation and hope, we remember today the ministry of William Forbes, theologian and minister in Aberdeen. We especially remember his contribution towards understanding between Roman Catholics and Anglicans in the modern era. Amen

13 April

Martin 1st, pope and martyr (655)

Born at Todi in Umbria, Martin was a deacon in Rome and was sent to Constantinople, where in 649 he was elected pope. Presiding at a council which condemned the belief that denied Christ a human will, he was arrested by Emperor Constans and exiled to the Crimea, where he died, venerated as the last pope to be martyred.

God of vision and purpose, we rejoice at the strength of belief of Martin, pope and martyr, for his principles and faithfulness. May he be an inspiration to all those seeking the Way, the Truth and the Life, whatever the consequences. Amen

Carpus and Papylus, martyrs (c 170)

Brought before the Roman Governor at Pergamum, Carpus, Bishop of Gordus, and Papylus, deacon, were required to make sacrifices to the gods. They refused and, together with Agathonice, they were burned alive.

Merciful God, we remember on this day the faith and matyrdom of Carpus and Papylus who, alongside Agathonice, were burned at the stake for their beliefs. As we enjoy freedom of religion, let us remember those who died for professing the religion that your Son taught us and for which he died for us. Amen

14 April

Benezet of Avignon, bridge-builder (1184)

Born at Hermillon in Savoy, Benezet, a shepherd-boy, moved to Avignon in about 1178. There, following a vision, he devoted himself to a project to build a bridge over the Rhône, which was near completion by the time he died. His name was commemorated in the bridge and subsequently in Avignon Cathedral, where his body rests.

> **Almighty God, you sent your Son to rebuild a bridge between you and humanity. Today we remember the life and work of Benezet of Avignon, and may his dedication to the task of building a bridge over the Rhône, which was an inspiration to his fellow townspeople, encourage us also in our endeavours. Amen**

Caradoc, Welsh monk (1124)

Born in Brycheiniog, Caradoc entered the service of the Bishop at Llandaff before becoming a hermit in the Gower peninsula. From there he went to Menevia and was priested, but after retiring to an island off the Pembrokeshie coast as a hermit, he was forced by Viking raiders to move again, finally, to St Isell's, Haroldston.

> **God of peace and solitude, on this day we celebrate the life of Caradoc, a holy hermit and miracle-worker, who served you in isolated places and in difficult times. Let us admire his steadfastness and learn from his faithfulness. Amen**

15 (or 16) April

Paternus (or Padarn) of Wales, monk and bishop
(fifth or sixth century)

Born, brought up and educated in south-east Wales, Paternus was founder Abbot and Bishop of Llanbadarn Fawr (Dyfed) for twenty years. An evangelist of the neighbouring countryside, Paternus was closely associated with Roman civilisation, his ministry following a particular Roman road, and was said to have travelled to Jerusalem with David and Teilo.

Heavenly Father, we give thanks for the evangelical work in Wales of Paternus, known for his mission and ministry and much influenced by Roman civilisation. May we always be aware of building on the past in our own faith journey, following straight paths where these are available. Amen

16 April

Bernadette, visionary of Lourdes and nun (1879)

Born at Lourdes in 1844, Bernadette experienced a series of eighteen visions of the Virgin Mary in 1858, during which the Virgin described herself as 'The Immaculate Conception' and encouraged Bernadette to drink from a spring. These events led to Lourdes becoming one of the most important shrines in the history of Christendom. She died at the age of 35 at the convent at Nevers, where she was admitted as a nun in 1866.

Lord of life, we celebrate today the self-effacing life of your servant Bernadette, whose visions of the Virgin Mary echo in the lives and healing of so many, even today. May we be touched by her humble simplicity and trust exhibited in her short life. Amen

Magnus of Orkney, Earl of Orkney, martyr (1116)

Born about 1075, Magnus, son of Erling, one of two rulers of the Orkneys, became a pirate but was then converted to Christianity. He returned to the Orkneys to share government with his cousin, Haakon, who had him put to death on the island of Egilsay, demonstrating courage and faith to the last.

Lord of justice and mercy, help us to understand the courage and virtue of Magnus, cut down by his cousin in pursuit of supremacy over him. Let us admire his acceptance of sacrifice, as wronged ruler and martyr. Amen

Benedict Labre, confessor, mendicant, patron of tramps and the homeless (1783)

Benedict Labre was born near Boulogne in 1748, the eldest of fifteen children, who was too young and then too eccentric to join a religious order. Going on pilgrimage to Rome and then begging his way from shrine to shrine around Europe, sharing any food and money he was given with others who were more needy, he ended up in Rome from 1774, praying in churches and eventually seeking shelter in a hospice for poor men.

Generous God, we thank you on this day for sending Benedict Labre as a homeless mendicant and wandering holy man to minister to those less fortunate than himself. May his witness of care for the homeless show us the way to proper Christian care and concern for others. Amen

Isabella Gilmore, deaconess (1923)

The sister of William Morris, Isabella Gilmore was born in 1842 and became a nurse at Guy's Hospital in London, where she was asked to develop deaconess ministry in Rochester Diocese. This led to the establishment of a training house in Clapham, where she trained deaconesses from seventeen different dioceses.

God of the Spirit, we give thanks for the special ministry of training deaconesses pioneered by Isabella Gilmore, who followed the call of the Church to use and share her gifts. Let us listen out for your call to us and respond in a way that is true to the inspiration given to Isabella. Amen

17 April

Stephen Harding, Abbot of Citeaux (1134)

Born in Dorset, Stephen briefly joined the monastery at Sherborne before continuing his studies in Scotland and France, where he was converted and went to Rome, visiting monasteries along the way, then returned to

Burgundy and became a monk. He helped to found the austere monastery at Citeaux and went on to lay down the rules for the Cistercian order, which spread under his abbacy.

Founding Father, loving Lord, today we celebrate the life and works of Stephen Harding, who, with others, founded the Cistercian order of monasteries and wrote about its organisation and rule of life. We thank you for his example of clarity, austerity and scholarship, which has had a lasting legacy. Amen

Donnan, monk and martyr (618)

Donnan was an Irish monk who was with Columba in Iona and then founded a monastery on the island of Eigg in the Inner Hebrides. During Mass on Easter night in 618 an attack by robbers, probably Vikings, resulted in the killing of all fifty-three inhabitants and a number of churches in Scotland were dedicated to Donnan as a result of his martyrdom.

God of faith and fortune, we remember the dedicated life of Donnan, a monk of Iona, who founded a monastery on Eigg and who was put to death with his companions on Easter Day by bandits. May we mourn his passing but give thanks for his achievements. Amen

18 April

Laserian, Abbot of Leighton (639)

Born in Ireland, Laserian, who may have received his training in Iona, was Abbot of Old Leighton, set among the hills of County Carlow. An advocate of the Roman calculation of Easter, he also founded the community at Inishmurray in County Sligo.

God of peace and beauty, on this day we celebrate the life and works of Laserian, who did much to bring the monastic life to the west of Ireland. Let us reflect on his mission and your purpose in his example of righteous living. Amen

19 April

Alphege, Archbishop of Canterbury, martyr (1012)

Born in 954 of noble parents who gave him a good education, Alphege became a monk at Deerhurst in Gloucestershire, before becoming a hermit in Somerset for some years and then the Abbot of Bath. After a period as Bishop of Winchester he was translated to Canterbury as archbishop, where he was captured and held to ransom by the Danes. Refusing to pay and forbidding his people to do so, he was killed by the Danes at Greenwich.

Almighty God, we honour the wise ministry, humble service and great courage of your servant Alphege, Archbishop of Canterbury and martyr. May we learn from the way he treated others, his resistance of evil and his integrity, even unto death. Amen

Leo 9th, pope (1054)

Born in 1002 in Alsace, Leo was educated at Toul, where his teachers included Adalbert, later Bishop of Metz. Becoming Bishop of Toul in 1027, he was known as a reformer by Gregory 7th. Showing leadership in difficult times, Leo gave authority to Edward the Confessor's plan to re-found Westminster Abbey.

Lord of challenge and change, we remember on this day the inspiration for reform shown by Leo 9th in his life and leadership of your Church. Even in times of difficulty, let us always be alert to the need for change. Amen

20 April

Beuno, abbot (c 640)

Born at Llanymynech, Beuno was educated at the monastic school, Caerwent, returning home to establish a monastery before moving to Berriew. Following the English invasion of Wales he went on to found a number of monasteries and churches in his missionary work in North Wales.

God of mission, today we give thanks for the work, life and evangelism of Beuno, who tirelessly built and founded churches and monasteries in Wales. May his energy and zeal bring us hope and gratitude. Amen

Agnes of Montepulciano, virgin and abbess (1317)

Agnes was born in 1268 of a wealthy family, joining a convent in Montepulciano in Tuscany in her youth, a model of austerity. Eventually she established a convent of the Dominican order, in a home which had formerly been a brothel, and exhibited gifts of miracles and prophecy in her patient ministry.

God of patience and virtue, we celebrate the life and work of Agnes of Montepulciano, founder of a community and model of humility, charity and virtue. May her example be a guide to our Christian behaviour and faithful belief. Amen

21 April

Anselm, Abbot of Bec, Archbishop of Canterbury, teacher (1109)

Born at Aosta, in northern Italy, in 1033, Anselm left home as a young man and visited many monasteries in his travels, including Bec, where he became a monk under Lanfranc. He followed Lanfranc as Archbishop of Canterbury, wrote extensively on the incarnation and the atonement and reinforced the principle of celibacy amongst clergy. Despite exiles during periods of difficulty between Church and State, he strengthened the 'primacy' of Canterbury.

God of justice and mercy, on this day we remember the life, scholarship and leadership of Anselm, Archbishop of Canterbury after Lanfranc during turbulent times. May we admire his intellectual rigour, personal austerity and attractive character, as they were admired during his lifetime. Amen

22 April

Theodore of Sykeon, monk and bishop (613)

Born into a dysfunctional family of prostitutes and circus performers, Theodore fell under the influence of a devout cook, Stephen, and he was ordained priest at a very young age, visiting many holy places, including Jerusalem. A monk, a hermit, and a founder of a monastery, Theodore was appointed Bishop of Anastasiopolis, which proved a turbulent period in his life, stepping down after ten years to resume a contemplative life, healing and reconciling.

> **Lord of healing and reconciliation, we thank you for the healing powers and contemplative life of Theodore of Sykeon, who rose from a background of spiritual poverty to become a monk and a bishop of holiness and humility. Let us be glad at this transformation as we seek to transform our lives to your purpose. Amen**

23 April

George, martyr, Patron of England (c 304)

A soldier from Palestine, George was martyred in about 304, at the start of the Diocletian persecution. Known as 'the great martyr', churches were named after him in England and he was revered in other countries, including Germany, Russia and Ethiopia.

> **God of triumph and sacrifice, we give thanks today for the life and legacy of George, martyr and patron of the Byzantine armies, whose fame as a soldier and peaceful helper against evil forces became so potent in England and beyond. May we take heart from his bravery and rejoice at his deeds, legendary and factual, over dragons and evil. Amen**

Adalbert of Prague, bishop and missionary martyr (997)

Born in Bohemia of a princely family, Adalbert was educated by Adalbert of Magdeburg and at the age of 30 became Bishop of Prague but, exiled in Rome, he became a monk. He was subsequently recalled to Bohemia and founded the Benedictine Abbey of Brevnov. Following a further exile in Rome, he devoted his remaining years on a mission to convert Prussians, before being martyred near Königsberg.

God of surprises, on this day we celebrate the life and mission of Adalbert of Prague, who laboured as bishop and monk between exiles in Rome. May we recognise his perseverance as missioner and his sacrifice as martyr. Amen

24 April

Mellitus, bishop and archbishop (624)

A Roman abbot who was among the second band of monks sent by Pope Gregory to England, Mellitus became the first bishop of the East Saxons, with his see in London and his first church dedicated to St Paul. After a period of exile in France he returned and was appointed Archbishop of Canterbury in 619.

God of grace, we thank you for your servant Mellitus, who strengthened Christianity in England and followed the good work of Augustine. May we honour his name and seek to emulate his nobility in mind and spirit. Amen

Fidelis, Franciscan friar and martyr (1622)

Fidelis was born in 1577 in Sigmaringen, a town in Germany, educated at Freiburg in Switzerland and practised law at Colmar, where he was known as advocate for the poor. He was ordained priest and joined the Capuchin branch of the Franciscan Order in 1612. Sent to preach to Calvinists in the Grisons area to bring them back to Rome, he was killed by enraged Calvinist soldiers and a minister in the church at Seewis.

Almighty and ever-living God, we celebrate today the life and witness of Fidelis, who showed great virtues through his preaching and care of the sick. We remember his death at the hands of armed opponents of his faith and plead for restraint and generosity where there is religious difference. Amen

25 April

Mark, evangelist (first century)

The son of a woman householder in Jerusalem called Mary, Mark accompanied Barnabas and Paul on their first missionary journey. His gospel account is generally regarded as the earliest and was probably written during his time in Rome. Later he went to Alexandria and preached the gospel there, being martyred by pagans, but long after his death his body was brought to Venice and enshrined in the original church of San Marco.

God of the gospel, we give thanks for the life of Mark, evangelist and companion to Paul and Barnabas, the first to record the gospel account. May we learn from his directness, his energy, and his faithfulness to the events he witnessed and wrote about. Amen

26 April

Riquier, abbot (c 645)

Born near Amiens, Riquier, still a pagan, protected some Irish missionaries from the local population and, in return, they instructed him in the Christian faith. He was priested, went to England for some years before returning to France to found a monastery, and became a preacher, spending his last years as a hermit.

God of infinite fortitude, we celebrate today the life and ministry of Riquier, whose goodness towards others while still a pagan brought conversion by those he had helped. May we rejoice that he repaid that kindness in his ministry to others in England and France. Amen

Stephen of Perm, missionary bishop (1396)

Born in 1345, Stephen entered a monastery at Rostov in 1365 and stayed there for thirteen years, in preparation for a life of mission. As a priest he went to Komi, west of the Urals, where he invented an alphabet to enable the local population to use their own language in worship, translating sacred texts and training people to become priests. Fearless in defending the local population from oppression by the capital, he was made bishop at Perm in 1383.

God of justice, we give thanks for the fearless life and vigour of Stephen of Perm, who as a missionary defended the rights of the people he served and was made bishop as a result. Let us admire his faith and faithfulness and seek to bring both into the centre of our lives. Amen

27 April

Christina Rossetti, poet (1894)

Born in 1830, Christina Rossetti was associated with the Pre-Raphaelite group, but wrote poetry from a very early age. Known principally for her poetry dealing with religious subjects, she was also author of the carol 'In the bleak mid-winter'.

Lord of poetry and song, on this day we celebrate the work and vision of Christina Rossetti, poet and Pre-Raphaelite, who brought Christian insights and understanding into her verse. May we be grateful for her expressions of Christian faith in ways that are both accessible and meaningful. Amen

Zita, serving-maid, virgin (1272)

Born in 1218, Zita entered domestic service with the Fatinelli family in Lucca at the age of 12, where she stayed all her life. She was devout and austere in her living, but generous to the poor and eventually her patience and goodness became understood and at her death she was known as the patroness of maid-servants.

God of loving service, we thank you for the life and example of your servant Zita, in domestic service all her life, yet radiating devotion to you and generosity to others. Let us rejoice at her patient goodness in the face of misunderstanding, which is an example to us, even today. Amen

28 April

Peter Chanel, missionary in the South Pacific, martyr (1841)

Born at Cras in France in 1803, Peter Chanel went to the local seminary and after ordination was put in charge of a difficult parish, which he turned round, subsequently joining the newly-founded missionary society of Mary. Sent to the islands of the South Pacific in 1836, he and his companions were generally much loved and respected, but on the island of Futuna an enraged chief, whose son was seeking baptism, ordered him to be killed.

God of courage and mercy, on this day we recall the life of Peter Chanel, missionary and martyr, who served the people of the South Pacific islands with respect and care. We both mourn his violent death and wonder at his life of dedication to the faith. Amen

Louis Grignion de Montfort, priest and founder of the Company of Mary and the Daughters of Wisdom (1716)

Louis Grignion was born at Montfort in Brittany in 1673, educated by the Jesuits in Rennes and trained as a priest in Paris, where he introduced free schools and devoted himself to the poor and the sick. He became a 'missionary apostolic' and employed controversial revivalist techniques which nevertheless had an impact, founding the Company of Mary for priests who shared his ideals.

Lord of creativity and mission, today we celebrate all that Louis Grignion de Montfort achieved through both action and words. Let us take heart from his energy and willingness to use innovative ways to evangelise. Amen

29 April

Catherine of Siena, teacher of the faith, mystic (1380)

Born Catherine Benincasa in 1347, she was the second youngest of twenty-five children, and from an early age was devoted to a life of prayer and penance. Despite parental pressure to marry, she became a Dominican tertiary, nursed the sick, and entered into correspondence with many, including Pope Urban 6th, to encourage him to avoid the great schism in the Roman Catholic Church.

Lord of grace and love, on this day we give special thanks for the selfless life and work of Catherine of Siena, who cared for the sick and the pope equally. Her example of help for others and clear-sightedness in seeking to avert splits in the Church are beacons of hope to us all. Amen

Hugh of Cluny, abbot (1109)

Hugh was born at Semur in 1024, the eldest son of a Burgundian nobleman. Studious and clumsy in his youth, he was ordained priest in about 1044 and was elected abbot at Cluny when only 25. As a reformer and a man of great diplomatic ability, popes turned to him for advice and his integrity and generosity of spirit were widely known.

God of wisdom and patience, we offer our thanks and praise for the life and influence of Hugh of Cluny, abbot and reformer. May we rejoice at his wisdom and integrity and hope that we can find such people to turn to for our own spiritual guidance. Amen

30 April

'Pandita' Mary Ramabai, translator of the Scriptures (1922)

Born in 1858, the daughter of a Sanskrit scholar keen on the education of women, Mary Ramabai converted to Christianity yet, remaining loyal to her Hindu heritage, developed a pioneering Indian vision of the faith. She lived in great simplicity, founding schools and homes for women and orphans and opposing the caste system.

> **God of male and female, on this day we give thanks for the example of Mary Ramabai, who, remaining true to herself and her traditions, yet also took great steps in the Christian faith, showing courage and an inclusive heart in all that she did. May we learn from her witness and integrity. Amen**

Pius 5th, pope (1572)

Born in 1504 at Bosco in the diocese of Tortona, Liguria, Michael Ghislieri entered the Dominican Order at an early age, becoming well known as a preacher and teacher. After holding two bishoprics and the post of inquisitor general, he was elected pope in 1566 and became Pius 5th. He combined a devout, austere personal life with a generosity to the poor and a fierce approach to prostitution, bull-fighting and the Reformation in England.

> **Almighty God, we thank you for the life and work of Pius 5th, whose devotion and constancy to the principles of the faith shone out in his ministry, demonstrating integrity alongside intransigence on a number of issues. Let us, in turn, be aware of the need for core principles to determine our own way of life. Amen**

May

1 May

Philip and James 'the less', apostles (first century)
– commemorated in some traditions on 3 May

Philip and James were counted in the original twelve apostles, though Philip had a more prominent role, the third to be called by Jesus and himself bringing Nathaniel to the Lord. Philip, from Bethsaida, was actively involved in Jesus' ministry. James, the son of Alphaeus, was a witness at the crucifixion and was martyred in the year 62.

> **Today let us recall with thanksgiving the lives, mission and ministry of Philip and James, apostles beloved of Jesus and known for their servant hearts. May we remember their deeds and words as we celebrate their memory and legacy. Amen**

Joseph of Nazareth, foster-father of Christ and husband of the Blessed Virgin Mary (first century) – see under 19 March

Asaph, bishop in North Wales (early seventh century)

Asaph was a young disciple of Kentigern, working principally in Flintshire. Nominated Bishop of Llanelwy in the late sixth century, he remained there until his death, having endowed the cathedral which bears his name today.

> **God of truth, on this day we celebrate the life and work of Asaph, known for his charm of manners and holiness of heart, who graced the Church of North Wales, as bishop. May we remember his witness and rejoice at his effective ministry. Amen**

2 May

Athanasius, Bishop of Alexandria, teacher of the faith (373)

Born about the year 296, Athanasius was brought up in Alexandria and became a deacon under Bishop Alexander, attending and contributing to the Council of Nicaea in 325. Athanasius succeeded Alexander as Patriarch of Alexandria in 328 and spent much of the rest of his life defending the orthodoxy of the Church against Arianism, which led to a number of exiles before returning to Alexandria. One of the four great doctors of the Church, Athanasius wrote extensively on the Scriptures, notably the Psalms, and a 'Life of St Antony'.

Lord God, Father, Son, and Holy Spirit, on this day we recognise the major contribution of your servant Athanasius, tireless advocate for the faith, in the face of theological turmoil. We remember especially his championing of the Trinity, his scholarship and his commitment to the people of Alexandria. Amen

3 May

Philip and James 'the less', apostles – *see under 1 May*

Henry Vaughan, poet (1695)

Born in 1622 in Breconshire, Henry Vaughan qualified in medicine in London before returning home to practise. The Civil War saw him in action on the Royalist side, but he was captured, the Church he knew was suppressed and his wife died. His first volume of religious poetry was published in 1650 and his verse continued to explore his love of divine meanings in daily life, finding hope and peace through Jesus Christ.

Lord of hope and light, today we give you thanks and praise for your servant Henry Vaughan, religiously inspired poet in the tradition of John Donne and George Herbert. May we see, like him, the divine in the ordinary, peace and hope in the victory of your Son over death. Amen

Theodosius of the caves, abbot (1074)

Born in about 1002 near Kiev, Theodosius, despite the opposition of his mother, joined the monastic community of the caves of Kiev around

1032, taking over from the hermit St Antony as abbot. He brought direction to the austere life of the hermits, developing a more active tradition, under the influence of Theodore the Studite of Constantinople, and integrating his monastery with the society of the time.

Lord of integrity and inclusion, we rejoice today at the memory of Theodosius of the caves, who brought to the austerity of the hermit tradition the outgoing concern and care for society. Let us follow his tradition of holiness and outreach in our Christian lives. Amen

4 May

English saints and martyrs of the Reformation era

This day commemorates all holy Christian men and women who suffered for their own beliefs of interpretation of the truth of the gospel during the three centuries of conflicts of Church and State, but particularly during the sixteenth century, known as the Reformation era. Martyrs remembered in this way include Campion, Fisher, More, Cranmer, Latimer and Ridley.

Almighty God of power and forgiveness, may we remember with admiration and regret those English saints and martyrs who suffered for their strongly-held beliefs during the Reformation era. Let us honour their memory by seeking to bring Christian communities together rather than set them apart. Amen

5 May

Hilary, Bishop of Arles (449)

Born about the year 400, Hilary became a monk on the island of Lérins but was called to follow his former mentor, Honoratus, as Bishop of Arles at the age of 29. Energetic and impulsive, Hilary did not endear himself to Pope Leo 1st, who had to override him on occasions.

God of zeal, today we give thanks for the life and work of your servant Hilary, who became Bishop of Arles at a young age and showed his energy and devotion in all he did, establishing monasteries and showing great initiative. May we take risks for you, as your Son took risks for us. Amen

6 May

Edbert, Bishop of Lindisfarne (698)

Edbert, a priest of great biblical learning, was well known also for his generosity to the poor. As Bishop of Lindisfarne he improved the roof of the church built by Finan and, when he died, miracles were reported as taking place at his tomb.

Extravagant God, on this day we remember with grateful thanks the generosity in spirit and works of Edbert, who followed Cuthbert as Bishop of Lindisfarne. Let us also recognise his biblical learning and seek to emulate his eagerness to study the Scriptures. Amen

Marian and James, martyrs (259)

James, a deacon, and Marian, a lector, were tortured and condemned to death in the town that became known as Constantina, the chief city of Numidia. During torture they had visions, having openly affirmed their faith in front of their persecutors, and went to their death with others by the River Rummel.

Trusting and sympathetic Lord, today we mark the bravery and witness of your servants Marian and James, who went to their deaths unswerving in their faith. May their visions during torture have helped their sacrificial path to your heavenly kingdom. Amen

7 May

John of Beverley, Bishop of York (721)
– commemorated in some traditions on 25 October

John was born at Harpham in Humberside and went to Kent to study under Adrian, returning to the north to become a monk at Whitby. In 687 he became Bishop of Hexham and ordained Bede as both deacon and priest. Appointed Bishop of York in 705, John founded the monastery at Beverley, where he spent the last four years of his life, fulfilling all monastic duties.

> **Lord God, servant king, today let us celebrate the life and works of John of Beverley, devoted priest, pastor and bishop, who had a lasting impact on places and people in your Church. May we learn from his example of nurturing faith and building communities. Amen**

8 May

Julian of Norwich, spiritual writer (c 1417)

Born about 1343, Julian, at the age of 30, experienced a series of sixteen visions of the love of God during a grave illness from which she recovered. She recorded her reflections on these visions in what was the first book written by a woman in English, *Revelations of Divine Love*. She gained her name of Julian when she became an anchoress attached to the Church of St Julian in Norwich.

> **Loving Lord, on this day we offer our thanks and praise for the revelations of your love shown to Julian of Norwich. May we gain an insight through the writings she has left for our lasting benefit. Amen**

Peter of Tarentaise, Cistercian monk and archbishop (c 1174)

Born around 1102, near Vienne, Peter became a Cistercian monk at Bonnevaux. Joyful, modest, and humble throughout his life, Peter became Archbishop of Tarentaise in 1142 and was conspicuous all round his diocese, visiting, healing and taking an active interest in charitable works.

He courageously went against his emperor in continuing to support Pope Alexander in the great schism of the Church and used his diplomatic skills in seeking reconciliation between the Kings of France and England.

God of unity and purpose, we give thanks for the integrity, pastoral heart and diplomacy of Peter of Tarentaise, monk and archbishop, who showed courage and care in his ministry. Let us admire his example and learn from his faithfulness to your purpose. Amen

9 May

Pachomius, abbot (c 346)
– commemorated in some traditions on 15 May

Born about the year 290, near Esneh in Egypt, Pachomius spent some years in the army and became a Christian on returning home, living as a hermit before beginning to organise what became the first monasteries and nunneries. His skills of organisation and austere life were invaluable in this work and he greatly influenced Basil the Great and Benedict in their development of monastic life.

Lord of great discipline and order, today we acknowledge the devotion of Pachomius, who brought to communities of hermits a degree of order and austerity which laid the sure foundations for the development of monasteries. May we admire his insights and acknowledge his achievements. Amen

10 May

Antonino, Archbishop of Florence (1459)

Born Nicolo Pierozzi in Florence in 1389, Antonino took his name on becoming a Dominican friar at a young age under John Dominici, becoming prior at Cortona, Fiesole, Naples and Rome, displaying a reputation for wisdom and justice. In 1446 he was appointed Archbishop of Florence, where he wrote, visited extensively in the diocese and founded the College of St Martin to assist the unfortunate and needy.

God of great works, on this day we offer our grateful thanks for the life of your servant Antonino, called at an early age to the life of a friar, whose ministry flourished and developed as prior and bishop, as writer and pastor. May we learn from his devotion to the needs of the poor and his writings as a practical moralist. Amen

Comgall, Abbot of Bangor (602)
– commemorated in some traditions on 11 May

Born about the year 516, Comgall was trained under Fintan at Clonenagh and was the founder and first Abbot of Bangor Abbey, which became the largest monastery in Ireland. Comgall, who visited Columba in Iona and trained Columbanus, was an advocate of counselling alongside instruction, supporting the idea of the need for a 'soul-friend'.

Mighty Counsellor, we remember today the great contribution of Comgall, Abbot of Bangor, to the spread of your word and your Church in Ireland, Scotland and beyond. Let us recognise his insights into the importance of counselling alongside instruction. Amen

11 May

Comgall, Abbot of Bangor (602) – *see under 10 May*

Odo, Maieul, Odilo, Hugh the Great and Peter the Venerable, Abbots of Cluny, 927-1157

Founded in Burgundy in 909, the Abbey of Cluny played an important role during a period of decline and difficulty for the papacy, enabling it to contribute to, and benefit from, the reformed papacy. Led by a succession of able and holy abbots, including Odo, Maieul, Odilo, Hugh the Great and Peter the Venerable, the Abbey of Cluny played an important role in helping to shape the development of the Church in Europe.

God of sure foundations, we celebrate the lives and leadership of successive Abbots of Cluny, notably Odo, Maieul, Odilo, Hugh the Great and Peter the Venerable, during difficult times for the Church. Let us give thanks for their vision, ability and holiness in shining your light during dark times. Amen

12 May

Thomas Rattray, bishop (1743)

From a Perthshire family, Thomas was already a distinguished theological author as a layman and exercised considerable influence on the eucharistic worship of the Episcopal Church in Scotland. He was an advocate of bishops being appointed by the clergy of the diocese and with the approval of the laity and himself became Bishop of Brechin, then of Dunkeld.

Lord of learning and service, we mark today the scholarship and insights of Thomas Rattray, who had a great influence on the development of the Episcopal Church in Scotland, both as layman and later as bishop. May his example of learning and contribution to liturgy and order in the Church be acknowledged with grateful thanks. Amen

Nereus and Achilleus, Roman martyrs (second century)

Nereus and Achilleus were Roman soldiers who became Christians and refused to continue in the army carrying out the orders of cruel tyrants. Professing their faith, they were martyred.

Almighty God, on this day we remember the martyred Roman soldiers, Nereus and Achilleus, who bravely refused to continue to carry out the cruel orders of tyrants and went to their death professing the faith. We give thanks that the strength of their new-found faith sustained them and brought them to you. Amen

Pancras of Rome, martyr (c 304)

Pancras, a Roman martyr who is usually remembered on the same day as two other Roman martyrs, Nereus and Achilleus, was probably born at Phrygia and brought to Rome by his uncle. There they were converted and Pancras was only a teenager when he was martyred. St Augustine dedicated a church to him in Canterbury and the cemetery and railway station in North London take their name from one of the other churches dedicated to him.

> **Lord of hope and salvation, we give thanks for the witness of Pancras, whose life was cut short in Rome in the days of the persecution. Let us remember the sacrifices made by the early Christians and be glad of the freedom we enjoy to worship you today. Amen**

13 May

John the Silent, bishop and hermit (559)

Born at Nicopolis in Armenia in 454, John built a monastery in which he and ten companions lived from the age of 18. Made a bishop at the age of 28, but resigning his position, he became a solitary and a hermit and lived for forty years in the desert.

> **God of stillness and holiness, on this day may we remember the devotion, humility and conscience of John the Silent, who forsook his episcopal position to live in the desert. Help us to understand the wilderness experience, as your Son did. Amen**

Andrew Fournet, priest (1834)

Born near Poitiers in 1752, Andrew Fournet, influenced by an uncle who was a priest, himself became a priest, but at the French Revolution refused to take the oath of the civil constitution of the clergy, carrying out his duties in secret. He assisted Elizabeth Bichier in the establishment of the Daughters of the Cross and drew up their rule of life. He is said to have performed miracles in the provision of food for the sisters.

God of mystery and resolve, we celebrate all that Andrew Fournet brought to his Christian life, including the courage to resist the State and the wisdom to help found the Order of the Cross. May we remember the difficulties under which he ministered when we recall his achievements. Amen

14 May

Carthage, abbot-bishop (637) – *see under 15 May*

Matthias, apostle and evangelist (first century)

Matthias was a constant attendant on our Lord from the period of baptism to ascension and was then chosen by lot to fill the place among the twelve apostles left vacant by Judas Iscariot. The exact dates of his subsequent ministry are not known, but it is said that he preached in Judaea and perhaps later in Cappadocia.

Heavenly Father, on this day may we remember the life and devotion of Matthias, recognised by his fellow disciples when he was chosen by lot to replace Judas Iscariot as the twelfth apostle. May we always be as faithful, ready to fulfil any role you may ask of us. Amen

15 May

Carthage, abbot-bishop (637)
– commemorated in some traditions on 14 May

Born in Kerry, Carthage became a hermit and then lived in various monasteries, settling eventually in Rathan, where he formed his own community, writing their rule in verse. Forced to move out, he re-established the community at Lismore, which became one of the foremost Irish monastic schools.

God of great gifts, we remember all that Carthage was able to achieve for communities in Ireland, especially at Lismore, through his ability and perseverance. May we recognise the firm foundations he laid for monastic life. Amen

Hallvard, martyr (1043)

Born in Husaby, Norway, Hallvard is known principally for his defence of an innocent woman accused of theft, to whom he gave refuge in his boat. Her pursuer caught up with her and killed them both. Regarded as a Patron Saint of Oslo, his body was enshrined at Christ Church in that city.

Just God, defender of innocence, on this day we recall the bravery of Hallvard, defender of an innocent woman, for which out of his bravery both were martyred. May we have the courage to resist evil, however it confronts us. Amen

Pachomius, abbot (c 346) – see under 9 May

16 May

Caroline Chisholm, social reformer (1877)

Born Caroline Jones in 1808, on marrying she took the Roman Catholic faith of her husband, Archibald Chisholm, setting up, with him, a school for soldiers' daughters in Madras. Moving to Sydney in 1838, Caroline worked on behalf of vulnerable immigrants, especially women, and campaigned for improved conditions, continuing the fight for emigration reform on return to Britain in 1846.

God of the oppressed, we give thanks for the campaigning work of social reformer Caroline Chisholm, who tirelessly strove for improved conditions for women emigrants abused on arrival as immigrants. May we follow her example in seeking to end human trafficking in our own times. Amen

Brendan the voyager (navigator), abbot (c 577)

Brendan was born in Kerry, brought up under the care of Ita and educated by Erc, Bishop of Kerry, becoming a monk and later abbot. He founded the monastery of Clonfert in Galway as well as other monastic communities, but is remembered especially for his voyages, certainly to Iona and western Scotland and, it is said, much further afield in the Atlantic.

God of great journeys, today we celebrate the life, work and voyages of Brendan, founder of monasteries in western Ireland and navigator across the seas. May we always set out on journeys in faith, as Brendan did. Amen

Simon Stock, Carmelite friar (1265)

Probably born at Aylesford in Kent, Simon went on a pilgrimage to the Holy Land as a young man, joining the Carmelites there. When he came back to Britain he returned to Aylesford and was elected supervisor-general of his order in London, helping to oversee the development of the order from hermits to mendicant friars and founding homes in university towns, attracting young graduates to join.

Holy and life-giving Lord, we rejoice at the devoted and long-lasting work of Simon Stock, whose experiences in the Holy Land brought new meaning into his life. We especially remember his development of the Carmelite Order in England to reflect new needs and opportunities. Amen

John of Nepomuk, priest and martyr (1393)

Born at Nepomuk in Bohemia in about 1345, John was educated in Prague, where he became a priest and a canon and a confidant of the Empress Jane who grew more devout under his counsel. A victim of the struggles between King Wenceslas and the Archbishop of Prague, John was murdered on the orders of Wenceslas after refusing to divulge secrets of the confessional, his body being thrown into the River Vlatava.

God of secrets and service, on this day we remember the learning and integrity of your servant John of Nepomuk, unjustly murdered by King Wenceslas and thrown into the river at Prague. Let us pay tribute to his keeping of confidentiality, even at the expense of his life. Amen

17 May

Pascal Baylon, Franciscan lay brother (1592)

Pascal was born in 1540 at Torre Hermosa in Aragon, Spain, into a poor shepherding family, then becoming a shepherd and receiving an elementary education but gaining increased religious awareness, becoming a lay brother in a series of convents. Known for his devotion to the Mass and his love of mystical prayer, he also cared for the sick and the poor, remaining in perpetual good humour.

God of great expectations, we thank you on this day for Pascal Baylon, who showed devotion, humility and austerity, alongside unfailing good humour, in his worship and his ministry to the poor and the sick. Let us, like him, fulfil our duties and devotions in a spirit of joy and dedication. Amen

18 May

Eric, King of Sweden (c 1160)

Eric came from a family of landed gentry and married Christina from the royal family, subsequently becoming King of Sweden. Along with the English Bishop Henry he set out to convert the neighbouring Finns to Christianity. Eventually dissident Swedes teamed up with Prince Magnus of Denmark and killed Eric on Ascension Day, just after he had heard Mass, and he was buried in Uppsala.

Lord of life and legend, today we remember your servant Eric, King of Sweden, who resisted the attacks of pagan Finns, whom he then sought to convert to Christianity, helped by Bishop Henry. We remember his life and mourn his martyrdom after attending Ascension Day Mass. Amen

John 1st, pope (526)

Born in Tuscany, John became a priest and held the position of archdeacon in Rome, being chosen Bishop of Rome towards the end of his life. Much of his time was taken up in seeking accommodation with the Arians, which led to imprisonment by the Arian emperor Theodoric, but he did introduce to the West the Alexandrian calculation of Easter.

God of East and West, we honour the contribution of Pope John 1st, who struggled to reconcile differences within the Church in East and West, while bringing unity to the calculation of the date of Easter. May his efforts in times of difficulty in the Church bring us hope of seeking greater church unity today. Amen

19 May

Dunstan, Archbishop of Canterbury (988)

Born into a noble family in Glastonbury about the year 910, Dunstan received a good education and, encouraged by his uncle Anthelm, he became a monk. In 943 King Edmund made him abbot and asked him to restore monastic life, starting in Glastonbury, and extended to other monasteries through a national code of monastic observance. Becoming Archbishop of Canterbury enabled him to extend his reforms throughout the Church in England, as well as allowing him to pursue his interests in metal-working, singing and teaching.

Lord of change and continuity, on this day we remember the life and work of your servant Dunstan, called to restore and develop your Church and monasteries in England. May his example as a great Archbishop of Canterbury encourage present Archbishops in their task of restoration and renewal. Amen

20 May

Bernardine of Siena, Franciscan friar (1444)

Born in 1380 at Massa, Bernardine was left an orphan in 1386 and brought up lovingly by an aunt. As a young man he took charge of a hospital in Siena where other staff had succumbed to an epidemic and in 1402 he became a Franciscan friar, proving to be a fiery and controversial preacher all over Italy, setting up schools of theology at Perugia and Monteripido.

Lord of joy and inspiration, we celebrate the life, preaching and creative ministry of Bernardine of Siena, brought up an orphan and great carer for others. Let us admire and seek to emulate his tireless efforts to spread your word and bring people to Jesus. Amen

Alcuin, deacon, Abbot of Tours (804)

Born into a noble Northumbrian family around 735 in York, Alcuin spent much of his education and working life in the cathedral school of York, rising to become Master. He then went to advise Charlemagne on religious and educational matters at Aachen, where he set up an important library at the Palace School before continuing his ministry as Abbot of Tours, completing considerable liturgical work and revising the lectionary.

Loving Lord, we thank you for the life and work of Alcuin, deacon, who devoted his life to religious and educational matters, as writer, adviser, and master and Abbot of Tours. May we value and mark his contributions, which advanced our understanding of your kingdom. Amen

21 May

Godric, hermit (1170)

Born about the year 1069, Godric took to the sea after a period as a pedlar and became a prosperous trader, travelling widely and also making pilgrimages. Returning to England, he went first to a hermitage near Whitby, then to Finchale on the Bishop of Durham's land. He led a life of austerity in a hut he built himself, was fond of all creatures, became known for his wise counsel and gifts of prophecy, wrote lyrical verse and composed melodies.

Holy Lord, we rejoice today at the long life and immense variety of skills and qualities of your servant Godric, pedlar, trader, prophet, hermit. May his life inspire us to take stock of our lives and change direction where necessary, in order to use the gifts you have provided. Amen

Helena, empress, protector of the Holy Places (330)
– commemorated in some traditions on 18 August

Helena, mother of the Emperor Constantine, was a Christian given a position of great honour by her son. In 326 she made a pilgrimage to the Holy Land, where she funded the building of basilicas on the Mount of Olives and at Bethlehem. It is said that she also discovered the cross used to crucify Christ.

God of loyalty and honour, on this day we remember with gratitude the dedicated life and work of Helena, mother of Constantine, who protected the holy places in Bethlehem and on the Mount of Olives. Just as she sought to preserve the memory and sacredness of those places, may we recall her part in that process today. Amen

22 May

Rita of Cascia, widow, nun, patron of desperate cases (1447)

Born about the year 1377, Rita wanted to become a nun but deferred to her parents' wishes and entered into a marriage which proved disastrous, owing to her husband's violence and infidelities, though they had two sons. On his death she sought entry to a convent of Augustinian nuns in Cascia, Umbria, where she was known for her holiness and the performing of miracles.

> **God of first and last, we give thanks for the long-suffering life of Rita, who put up with a violent domestic life for nearly twenty years, before being released to do your will as a nun. We ask for your comfort and blessings on all those trapped in unsatisfactory relationships, as we remember her perseverance in times of trouble. Amen**

23 May

William of Rochester (or Perth) (1201)

Born in Perth and either a fisherman or a baker, William was converted as a young man and dedicated himself to working with the poor and orphans, beginning a pilgrimage to the Holy Land in 1201. He was, however, killed by a companion en route, near Rochester, where he was buried and where miracles were claimed.

> **God of miracles, we celebrate today the dedication of William, who cared for the poor in his native Perth, but was murdered on his way to the Holy Land, in Rochester, where his body rests. Let us recall the caring concern he had shown in his Christian life and marvel at the miracles which followed his death. Amen**

Alexander Nevsky, Prince of Novgorod, defender and protector of Russia (1263) – *see under 23 November*

John Baptist Rossi (1764)

Born in 1698 near Genoa, John was sent to the Roman College, where his epilepsy caused a breakdown. On his recovery he was priested and worked tirelessly among the sick, the deprived and the destitute, including beggars and prostitutes. He was known as an outstanding preacher and teacher amongst people right across the social spectrum.

God of humanity, we remember the life and service of John Baptist Rossi who, despite his epilepsy, became a respected teacher and preacher, alongside his work for the poor and needy. Let us admire and emulate his example and witness. Amen

24 May

John and Charles Wesley, evangelists, hymn writers (1791 and 1788)

John and Charles Wesley were brought up at Epworth Rectory in Lincolnshire, the sons of an Anglican priest and a Puritan mother. John was ordained and, on 24 May 1738, had a religious experience when he felt his heart 'strangely warmed' and began to travel throughout the country, often with Charles, as an itinerant minister, preaching and building up early Methodist societies. Although both remained Anglican throughout their lives, the Methodist Church developed and grew worldwide after their death, with Charles' thousands of hymns as a wonderful resource for worship.

Wonderful Counsellor, Almighty God, we give thanks on this day for the creative, tireless mission and ministry of John and Charles Wesley, whose hearts were moved by your Holy Spirit to a life of evangelism through prayer, preaching and praise. May we feel our hearts warmed by your presence and our lives be inspired by their service to you and your Church. Amen

David of Scotland, king (c 1153)

David was born about the year 1085, the youngest son of Malcolm 3rd and his wife Margaret. Although reluctant to become king, David proved to be one of the best Scottish kings, introducing improved systems of justice and land tenure, and reorganised the Church, founding the bishoprics of Brechin, Dunblane, Caithness, Ross and Aberdeen as well as numerous churches and monasteries.

God of grand designs, today we honour the memory of David, King of Scotland in the twelfth century, who showed gifts of organisation in Church and State and lived a devout life. Let us recall his legacy and give thanks for his Christian action as an individual and as king, showing an integrity which serves as a model for us. Amen

25 May

The Venerable Bede, monk of Jarrow, scholar, historian (735)

Born near Sunderland in 673, Bede was educated from the age of 7 by monks, first at Wearmouth and then at Jarrow, where he was a monk for the rest of his life, never travelling further than York. He wrote twenty-five works of scripture commentary and his great Ecclesiastical History of the English People was completed in 731. He is said to have dictated the last lines of his translation of John's Gospel when he was almost at the point of death.

Loving Lord, we thank you that you sent your servant Bede to work tirelessly as monk, scholar, writer and teacher, recording so much about the Church and Christian life in England up to the early eighth century. May we rejoice at his love of accuracy and truth and marvel at his ability to communicate it to others. Amen

Mary-Magdalen dei Pazzi, mystic (1607)

Born at Florence in 1566, Mary-Magdalen became a Carmelite nun at the age of 17. After some initial inner turmoils she found her vocation in prayer and penance, dictating work which reflected her love of the natural beauty around her.

God of truth and beauty, on this day we recall the devout prayer and writing of Mary-Magdalen dei Pazzi, Carmelite nun and mystic. May we be set free in our contemplation by her example and expression of the glories of our surroundings. Amen

Gregory 7th (Hildebrand), pope (1085)

Born of humble origins in Tuscany about the year 1020, Hildebrand, as he was first known, went to Rome as a young man, became a monk, and then was made the chaplain of Pope Gregory 6th, with whom he was exiled in 1046. Elected as Pope Gregory 7th in 1073, he wielded great power in a long dispute with Emperor Henry 4th in seeking to develop the authority of the papacy and safeguard it from secular powers, establishing more freedom of practice for the Church through what has become known as Gregorian reform.

Almighty God, today we commemorate the life and impact of your servant Gregory, known also as Hildebrand, whose integrity and force of argument were unflinching in reforming and strengthening the Church. Let us renew our Christian life with equal vigour, but always listening to your will for this world. Amen

26 May

Augustine, first Archbishop of Canterbury (605)
– commemorated in some traditions on 27 May

Born in Italy, Augustine became a monk and later prior of the monastery of St Andrew in Rome. Sent by Pope Gregory the Great on a mission to England, he nearly turned back, but was given encouragement by Gregory to continue, landing on the Isle of Thanet in 597 and establishing the cathedral, Christ Church, in Canterbury and founding the Abbey of St Peter and St Paul, which became known as St Augustine's.

God of purpose and vision, on this day we celebrate the life and mission of Augustine, first Archbishop of Canterbury, sent by Pope Gregory to re-evangelise the English Church. May we rejoice at his successful establishment of the Church in Canterbury, Rochester, and then in London, and give thanks. Amen

Philip Neri, founder of the Oratorians, spiritual guide (1595)

Born in Florence in 1515, Philip Neri was a devout student who, after ordination in 1551, joined a company of priests meeting in Girolamo Church, where an oratory was built to enable them to carry on their work of teaching, discussion and organisation of relief for the poor and the sick. A kind and gentle man, he preached about love and spiritual integrity and was known for his laughter and love of practical jokes.

Lord of love and laughter, today we remember with thanks and joy the life and work of Philip Neri, whose gentle love and humour were underpinned by deep spiritual insight. May our faith benefit from his example of cheerfulness and humility. Amen

John Calvin, reformer (1564)

Born in Picardy in 1509, John Calvin was initially prepared for holy orders but after switching from theology to law at university he came under Protestant influence at Orleans and following a religious experience saw his destiny as reforming and restoring the Church of Christ, so broke from the Roman Catholic Church, accepting a position in Geneva to introduce Reformation principles, his ideas shaping the development of the reformed churches in many countries.

God of grace, we give thanks for the great reformer John Calvin, whose writings so influenced the development of your Church in many countries and heightened our understanding and awareness of the origins of our salvation. Let us learn from his insights on grace and be influenced by his understanding of faith. Amen

27 May

Augustine, first Archbishop of Canterbury (605) –
see under 26 May

Melangell, religious (seventh century)
– commemorated in some traditions on 28 May

Fleeing from an unwanted marriage in Ireland, Melangell spent fifteen years in isolation in the countryside of Pennant, in the principality of Powys, before being discovered by Prince Brockwell sheltering hares from his hunting dogs. Thereafter, for a further thirty-seven years, she had his protection in a sanctuary which became a community of nuns and a safe haven for her beloved hares.

God of peace and love, we rejoice at the steadfast faith and prayerful protection of animals shown by your servant Melangell. May those who seek solitude and careful stewardship of your creation take heart and hope from her ministry of service. Amen

28 May

Melagell, religious (seventh century) – *see under 27 May*

Lanfranc, Prior of Le Bec, Archbishop of Canterbury, scholar (1089)

Lanfranc was born and educated in Pavia, Italy, in 1005, moving to Burgundy and Normandy, before joining the community of Le Bec in his late 30s, rising to become prior in 1045. A writer and a scholar, he became Archbishop of Canterbury in 1070, rebuilding the cathedral damaged by fire and bringing order to the Church in England by a combination of energy, rigour and a love of regular, liturgical life.

We give thanks on this day for the life and ministry of Lanfranc, Prior of Le Bec and Archbishop of Canterbury, who brought order to your Church in England. Grant that his legacy of scholarship, love of liturgy and energetic extension of cathedral monasteries be remembered as an example of your Holy Spirit at work. Amen

Germanus, Bishop of Paris (576)

Germanus was born near Autun in Burgundy around 496, educated at Avallon, becoming a monk and a priest, and then Bishop of Paris, earning a reputation for his healing powers. He founded a monastery in Paris and his daughter, Bertha, married the King of Kent, Ethelbert.

God of great expectations, we recall the life and work of Germanus, Bishop of Paris. By his concern for the sick, the disabled and the possessed and his efforts to counter warring factions among the Frankish kings, may he continue to show us the way to true ministry in difficult times. Amen

29 May

Bona of Pisa, pilgrim (1207)

Born about 1156, in Pisa, Bona experienced childhood visions involving St James the Greater and in her teens travelled to Jerusalem to see her father, who was engaged in the crusades. Captured and rescued from pirates, she undertook numerous pilgrimages to Santiago de Compostella and has become the patron saint of travellers and those who guide and assist travellers.

Today we recognise and honour the memory of Bona of Pisa, inveterate traveller from an early age and pilgrimage guide. May our travels and pilgrimages be blessed with the care and attention of those infused with the same qualities of care shown by Bona. Amen

30 May

Ferdinand 3rd, King of Castile and Léon (1252)

Born near Salamanca in 1199, Ferdinand became King of Castile in 1217 and of Léon in 1230. His achievement included founding several bishoprics and building or repairing many cathedrals, churches, monasteries and hospitals. He undertook the campaigns which recovered much of Spain from the Moors, including Seville.

On this day we celebrate the deeds of Ferdinand, great king, leader and founder of many Christian institutions. May his energy and success in reversing the tide of Moorish domination in Spain be recognised and honoured and his faithful service to Christendom celebrated. Amen

Joan of Arc, visionary (1431)

Joan was born in 1412 at Domrémy, a peasant girl who began to hear voices from the age of 14, telling her to save France. Following some accurate predictions of French defeats, she was brought to the attention of the Dauphin who became Charles 7th and led French troops to victory in the relief of Orléans from the English. Later she was handed over to the English by the Burgundians, tried and burnt at the stake in 1431, becoming second Patron of France in 1920, on her canonisation.

God of grace and purpose, we remember with admiration the single-mindedness of Joan of Arc, resolute in her convictions, brave in leading French troops, and fearless in her defence at her trial. May we honour and learn from her faith and actions at such a tender age. Amen

Josephine Butler, social reformer (1906)

Born in 1828, Josephine grew up in Northumberland, was married to an Anglican priest and became active in seeking reform for the treatment of prostitutes. Her campaign, underpinned by prayer, led to the repeal, in 1883, of the Contagious Diseases Act, which had stigmatised the women affected.

We give thanks for the reforming zeal of Josephine Butler, who fought injustice for marginalised women, as your Son did. May the power of her prayer and social action inspire us and future generations to justice, love, mercy and walking with you, our God. Amen

Apolo Kivebulaya, priest, evangelist in Central Africa (1933)

Apolo was born and grew up close to the capital of Uganda and after seeing the ravages of disease, which killed his sister, and the atrocities carried out in the name of Islam, he became a Christian in 1885 and then a teacher in the Ugandan Church. He went to Boga in the Congo as an evangelist, where he was priested and where he developed a special ministry towards the pygmy people of the forest, for whom he translated Mark's Gospel, his lasting legacy.

Lord of mission and ministry, we thank you for the life and work of Apolo Kivebulaya, who brought hope and love to the people of the forest in Central Africa. May his perseverance and his skills of translation be a beacon of light and a source of encouragement for all engaged in mission. Amen

31 May

Petronilla, early Roman martyr (first century?)

Petronilla was born into the family of Domitilla in early Roman times. In sixth century accounts she was reputedly a daughter of Peter and died following a fast after refusing to marry a suitor. She is remembered especially in France and is often depicted in English churches in stained glass or on a painted screen of the Middle Ages.

We thank you on this day for Petronilla, who lives on in pictures and stained glass, as a link with Peter. Only you know her full life history, but may we always be curious about those we only know about in glimpses of their lives and your glory. Amen

June

1 June

Justin, martyr at Rome (c 165)

Born in Samaria around 100, Justin spent his youth reading the works of poets, orators and historians and then studied philosophy, becoming a Christian in about 130 and making his way to Rome halfway through the century. There he wrote two Apologies, seeking to reconcile the claims of faith and reason. In 165 he and five others were denounced as Christians and beheaded.

> **Today we give thanks for your faithful servant Justin, whose insight and erudition in proclaiming the gospel won hearts and minds as well as enemies. May his fearless exploration of faith encourage us to go the extra mile to know your ways, faithful God. Amen**

Pamphilus, martyr (309)

Pamphilus was born in Beirut around 240, studied at Alexandria and went to live at Caesaria in Palestine, where he was priested. A teacher who worked on the text of the Bible, he was a supporter and advocate of the teaching of Origen, but was put to death for his beliefs along with Elias and six companions in 309.

> **God of learning and hope, we thank you for the studies and writing of Pamphilus, spreading the teaching of the early fathers and suffering death for his beliefs. As we learn about and share the faith, may we be mindful of the sacrifices made by Pamphilus and others who stood up for their faith and were cut down. Amen**

2 June

Marcellinus and Peter, Roman martyrs (c 304)

Marcellinus, a priest, and Peter, an exorcist, were imprisoned and martyred under the persecution of Diocletian. Before their death they were said to have converted their gaoler and when their bodies were moved to the monastery of Selingenstadt miracles were recorded as happening.

We remember today the ministry of Marcellinus and Peter, Roman martyrs, who sought conversions, even of their gaoler, up until their death and whose witness led to miracles when they were put to death. May we admire their fortitude and learn from their faithful devotion to your Truth. Amen

Oda, Archbishop of Canterbury (958)

From East Anglia, Oda became a priest as a young man and was appointed as Bishop of Ramsbury around 925. A counsellor of King Athelstan, Oda was a negotiator with the French and was with Athelstan at the Battle of Brunangburgh which established the supremacy of Wessex over northern England. As Archbishop of Canterbury he was known as 'Oda the Good', restoring churches, engaging in pastoral activities and influencing the ministry of Dunstan, among others who followed him.

Lord of inspiration and purpose, we remember on this day the devoted archbishop Oda, whose pastoral ministry and concern for good order of churches and clergy set standards for his successors. As we thank him, may we set our standards high by example and service. Amen

Martyrs of Lyons (177)

During the persecution of Marcus Aurelius some fifty Christians from Lyons and Vienne, including bishops, priests and deacons, lay men and women and slaves, suffered abuse, violence and death at the instigation of both the heathen mob and official sanction. Among those martyred were the woman Blandina and the young Ponticus, both of whom showed great courage in the face of appalling treatment and agonising death.

God of mercy, we pray that the martyrs of Lyons, received into your kingdom after barbaric deaths, and resolute in their witness to the end, may live on in the collective Christian memory. We give thanks that they died that the Christian faith might survive in the hearts and minds of those who remained. Amen

3 June

Kevin of Glendalough, hermit (c 618)

Born in Leinster, Kevin came from a noble family which fell out of favour with the kingship. Educated by monks, he was priested and became a hermit at Glendalough in the Wicklow hills, where a community gathered around him which became a monastery. A man of prayer and with a love of nature, including wild animals, Kevin was also a poet and a musician.

God of peace and love, may the example of Kevin, bringer of music and poetry, at one with nature, and attracting others to his community, be a beacon of hope to Christians everywhere. Let us remember today this man of God and rejoice in his ministry. Amen

Clotilde, Queen of France (545)

Born about the year 475, survivor, with her sister, of the murder of the rest of her family by her uncle, the tyrannical King of Burgundy, and brought up in his court, she was married to the pagan King of the Franks, Clovis. Clovis was converted after his victory at the Battle of Alemanni, having prayed to 'the God of Clotilde'. After his death she devoted herself to prayer and building churches and monasteries.

On this day we give thanks for the life of Clotilde, begun in troubled times and ending in prayer and devotion. We remember her prayers for, and example to, her husband, Clovis, resulting in his conversion, and take inspiration from her faith and constancy to you, Lord. Amen

Charles Lwanga and companions, martyrs of Uganda (1885-7 and 1978) – *commemorated in some traditions on 4 June. Janani Luwum also commemorated on 17 February*

The first group of Ugandan martyrs, Yusufu Lugalama, Mako Kalumba and Nuwa Sewanga, shortly followed by Joseph Mkasa Balikuddembe, met their death in 1885 on the orders of Mwanga, kabaka of Buganda.

Further persecution followed after Mwanga received criticism from Christians about his behaviour and at least forty-six were martyred, mostly on Ascension Day, 3 June 1886, including one of the leaders, Charles Lwanga, and ending with the death of Jean-Marie Muzeyi the following year. Much later, in the 1970s and 1980s, renewed pressures on the Churches in Uganda surfaced and among those to be put to death was Archbishop Janani Luwum, in 1978.

> **God of justice and mercy, today we recall the bravery and suffering of the Ugandan martyrs, under different rulers, in two centuries. May their faith and resistance in the face of tyranny be recognised as laying the foundations of a rebirth of Christian and civil life in a free and independent Africa. Amen**

4 June

Charles Lwanga and companions, martyrs of Uganda
(1885-7 and 1978) – *see under 3 June*

Petroc, Abbot of Padstow (sixth century)

One of the foremost British Celtic saints, Petroc was the son of a Welsh chieftain who came to be known as the 'captain of Cornish saints'. He founded a monastery at modern-day Padstow, which was his base for the monastic and missionary activities with which he was engaged as a hermit for the rest of his life.

> **God of greatness and humility, we recognise and honour the pioneering ministry of Petroc, helping to build your Church rather than taking on a kingly role. As we honour his humility and charity, may we commit ourselves to a life of service and righteousness. Amen**

John 13th, Bishop of Rome, reformer (1963)

Pope John was born Angelo Roncalli near Bergamo in Italy in 1881, became a priest and then a bishop and succeeded Pope Pius 12th in 1958. Expected to be a 'caretaker' appointment, John proved to be a reforming pope, beginning the process of far-reaching change with the second Vatican Council, before his death in 1963, when he was greatly mourned.

> **On this day, let us honour the memory of John, a reforming pope with a vision for the Church and a personal piety which proved a powerful combination. May we be surprised by you, O Lord, in our own ministry, as we seek to follow your way and learn daily from your truth. Amen**

5 June

Boniface (Wynfrith) of Crediton, bishop, apostle of Germany, martyr (754)

Born Wynfrith about 675, he took the name Boniface on entering the monastery in Exeter as a young man, being priested in 716 and becoming a Latin scholar and poet. Called to be a missionary in Frisia, in the footsteps of Willibrord, he became Bishop of Mainz, founding monasteries and famously felling a tall oak consecrated to Jupiter and using the timber to build a chapel. Resuming his mission to Friesland, he was martyred there in 754.

> **Almighty God, you conferred great courage and learning on your servant Boniface, whom we remember and celebrate today. As we recall his ministry as missionary, bishop and reformer, may we gain insight and encouragement in our understanding of your purpose for us today. Amen**

6 June

Norbert, Archbishop of Magdeburg, founder of the Premonstratensian Order (1134)

Born around 1080 into a noble family, Norbert initially led a worldly life, even as a deacon and a canon, but a riding accident caused him to have a sudden conversion and he renounced his old ways. Taking priest's orders, he put himself at the disposal of Pope Gelasius 2nd and became an itinerant preacher in northern France, founded a community of canons at Prémontré and was then appointed Archbishop of Magdeburg, later on supporting the cause of Pope Innocent 2nd.

> **God of faithfulness and forgiveness, let us give thanks for the conversion of Norbert and his subsequent ministry as archbishop and founder, in difficult times for the Church. May we learn from his story of the transformative power of your love in our lives. Amen**

Ini Kopuria, founder of the Melanesian Brotherhood (1945)

Born and brought up in the Solomon Islands, Ini Kopuria's job as a policeman was transformed by a vision of Jesus. This led him to a life of evangelism throughout Melanesia, founding a brotherhood for Melanesians in 1925, which had striking success in bringing people to Jesus.

> **God of great expectations, we rejoice today at the life and work of Ini Kopuria, extraordinary evangelist and founder of the Melanesian Brotherhood. Let us honour his memory as we recall his deep spirituality, his joy of living and his wise common sense; and learn from his example. Amen**

7 June

Colman of Dromore, monk and bishop (sixth century)
– commemorated in some traditions on 20 November

Born in Ulster, Colman was founder of the monastery at Dromore in County Down, where he was also bishop. A teacher of Finnian, Colman continued the tradition of Patrick in his zeal for truth and faith.

May we reflect on the life and influence of Colman of Dromore, teacher of Finnian and follower of the pastoral tradition of Patrick. Let us be fierce in our search for truth and passionate about our faith. Amen

Robert of Newminster, Cistercian abbot (1159)

Born at Gargrave in Yorkshire around 1100, Robert became a parish priest in his own town and later joined the Benedictines at Whitby. One of the founders of Fountains Abbey in 1132 and known as a man of prayer, Robert was appointed as Abbot of Newminster in 1139.

Lord of the Spirit, we remember on this day the life and work of Robert Newminster, model monk and abbot. Let us, in our turn, share his appreciation of prayer and meditation as the sure foundation of the Christian life. Amen

8 June

Thomas Ken, Bishop of Bath and Wells, non juror, hymn writer (1711)

Born at Berkhampstead in 1637, Thomas Ken was educated at New College, Oxford, was priested in 1662, and served in Winchester Diocese, before becoming chaplain to King Charles 2nd and then Bishop of Bath and Wells. A man of conscience and integrity, as well as a writer of hymns, he refused to comply with James 2nd's reforms, yet when the king was succeeded by William and Mary he felt unable to forswear the anointed monarch.

Lord God, may the words of Thomas Ken's most famous hymn remind us of this man of God, whose praise joins with ours:
'Praise God, from whom all blessings flow,
praise him, all creatures here below,
praise him above ye heav'nly host,
praise Father, Son and Holy Ghost.'
Amen

William of York, archbishop (1154)

From a noble background, William became treasurer of York as a chaplain to the king, before being appointed Archbishop of York in 1140. Bitter dispute arose about his appointment, which was rescinded by the Cistercian Pope Eugenius on the intervention of Bernard of Clairvaux. He bore this with fortitude and later, under Pope Anastasius 4th, he was reinstated, but died a year later, allegedly poisoned.

God of reconciliation, help us to understand the injustice done to William of York, who remained conscientious and without rancour during difficult times. We ask that in the face of such setbacks as he experienced, we may gain strength through prayer and patience, even in adversity. Amen

9 June

Columba, Abbot of Iona, missionary (597)

Born in 521 at Gurton in Donegal, Columba trained under Finnian, founding a number of monasteries, including Durrow, Derry and probably Kells. He and twenty companions left Ireland to settle at Iona, off the Scottish coast, where they built up the monastery and engaged in missionary work and advised kings. An austere and striking man, he brought Christianity to many parts of Scotland and the north of England, including Lindisfarne.

On this day we give thanks for the ministry and mission of Columba, austere yet loving, energetic yet prayerful, who brought Christianity from Ireland to Scotland and the north of England. May we wonder at his impact and be inspired by his legacy. Amen

Ephrem of Syria, hymn writer and teacher of the faith (373)

Born around 306 at Nisibis in Mesopotamia, Ephrem became a deacon and a teacher there until the Persian invasion and occupation in 363. He then settled in Edessa in Turkey, where he wrote hymns and homilies, which were translated into a number of different languages. He was also known for his charitable works to feed victims of famine and plague.

God of wisdom and melody, today we remember the gifts of words and music of Ephrem of Syria and give thanks for all his works. May we be inspired by his charity as well as his writing ability as we seek to use our gifts in the way you would want. Amen

10 June

Ithamar, Bishop of Rochester (c 660)

Born in Kent, Ithamar was a man of learning who became the first Anglo-Saxon bishop when he was appointed by Honorius to the see of Rochester. He also consecrated the first Anglo-Saxon Archbishop of Canterbury, Deusdedit.

O God who raises up leaders in your Church, we give thanks today for Ithamar, Bishop of Rochester, who served the early Church in Britain well. We pray that in every age leaders come forward to bring your kingdom closer. Amen

11 June

Barnabas, apostle (first century)

A Levite from Cyprus, Barnabas had a close association with Paul, whom he introduced to the leaders of the Church in Jerusalem. After a period in Antioch he undertook, with Paul, the first 'missionary journey', beginning in Cyprus. He later returned to Cyprus alone, founding the Church there, and was martyred at Salamis.

Lord of all, on this day let us recall the pioneering missionary work of Barnabas, especially in Cyprus as founder of the Church there. May we take heart and inspiration from the zeal of his ministry and the energy of his mission. Amen

12 June

John Skinner the elder (1807) and John Skinner the younger (1816)

John Skinner the elder, born in Birse, Aberdeenshire, in 1721, was ordained in 1742 and was also known as a poet and historian, with liberal sympathies, who was imprisoned with his son for conducting worship in 1753. John Skinner the younger, his son, became Bishop of Aberdeen in 1786 and elected Primus in 1788, in which capacity he successfully campaigned for the repeal of the Penal Laws under which he and his father had been imprisoned. He was a leading figure in the development of the Episcopalian Church.

> **Today we celebrate the ministry and persistent discipleship of John Skinner the elder and John Skinner the younger, whose service to the Episcopalian Church in Scotland and beyond was special. Grant to us the same commitment to our Church, whatever the difficulties and pressures. Amen**

13 June

Antony of Padua, Franciscan friar and priest (1231)

A native of Lisbon, Antony was a biblical scholar of note who joined the Franciscan friars and used his gift of preaching to great effect in both France and Italy. Known as the 'hammer of heretics', he left a legacy of masterly sermons and is also venerated as the saint of lost articles, because of an incident involving a lost psalter, returned to him by a novice who had an apparition.

> **Lord of the lost, we give thanks that you found your servant Antony and gave him the gifts of preaching and confronting heresies. May we learn from his life and scholarship as we seek the best ways to serve you. Amen**

14 June

Richard Baxter, Puritan divine (1691)

Born in 1615 at Rowton, Shropshire, Richard Baxter studied divinity before being ordained. Disillusioned with the episcopacy, he became a curate in a deprived area of the West Midlands, opposing the Civil War and being a powerful advocate for the recall of Charles 2nd. An authority on pastoral organisation, he declined preferment as a bishop and devoted himself to writing many hymns.

We celebrate today the words and wisdom of Richard Baxter, who lived a life of piety and moderation, contributing much to the hymn-singing tradition in your Church. May his humility and pastoral sensitivity serve to remind us today of your holy angels bright. Amen

Methodius of Constantinople, bishop (847)

Born at Syracuse, Methodius was a great lover of icons and sacred images, for which he was punished and imprisoned under Emperor Michael 2nd. Restored under Theodora's regency, he was appointed Patriarch of Constantinople and reaffirmed the place of the right to venerate religious images, as well as writing many hymns.

God of majesty and might, may we wonder at the art, icons and images created in the Orthodox tradition, thanks to Methodius' stand. Let his faith shine through these works, just as his hymns must have been wonderful accompaniment to his prayers and praise. Amen

15 June

Vitus and companions, martyrs (c 303)

Vitus grew up in a noble family in southern Italy, or possibly Sicily, and suffered under the persecution of Diocletian, remaining steadfast in the faith. Together with his Christian nurse, Crescentia, and her husband Modestus, he was martyred and has best been remembered for the ailment known as 'St Vitus' dance' and has become the patron saint of epilepsy and nervous diseases.

> **On this day we give thanks for Vitus and his companions, dying for their faith under Roman persecution. Let us remember their suffering each time we hear about those with epilepsy and nervous diseases and read about St Vitus' dance. Amen**

Evelyn Underhill, spiritual writer, exponent of the spiritual life (1941)

Born in 1875, the daughter of a distinguished barrister, she studied at King's College, London, and wrote on the mystics, publishing *Mysticism* in 1911. Becoming a communicant member of the Church of England, she was in demand as a retreat conductor and spiritual director and published her most important work, *Worship*, in 1936. In her later years she became a pacifist.

> **Lord of mystery and imagination, today we mark the insights and learning of Evelyn Underhill, who sought to understand and interpret the mystics and to aid our appreciation of worship. In our own prayers, meditations and contemplation, may we be equally careful to be true to these gifts and the revelations they inspire. Amen**

16 June

Richard of Chichester, bishop (1253)
– commemorated in some traditions on 3 April

Richard was born in 1197 at Droitwich, the son of a yeoman farmer. Studying at Oxford, Paris and Bologna, he returned to Oxford and became chancellor there, before being called by Edmund of Abingdon, the Archbishop of Canterbury, to become his chancellor. After a spell in France, where he was priested, he was elected Bishop of Chichester in 1244, where he was a model diocesan bishop, strict, accessible and generous.

As we remember the life, ministry and writings of your servant, Richard of Chichester, may we seek always to know you more clearly, love you more dearly and follow you more nearly, day by day. Let his work inspire us in our daily lives. Amen

Joseph Butler, Bishop of Durham, philosopher (1752)

Born into a Presbyterian family at Wantage in 1692, Joseph studied in Tewksbury but abandoned Presbyterianism in 1714 to join the Church of England. Ordained in 1718, he was known as a fine preacher, becoming Bishop of Durham and well known as the foremost exponent of ethics and natural theology of his generation.

God of hope, we rejoice at the life and works of Joseph Butler, who inspired a generation by his preaching and writing. Let us be glad that his scholarship and his exploration of ethical issues and theology were both recognised and available to Christians in his age and ours. Amen

17 June

Botolph, abbot (c 680)

Born in Britain, Botolph, together with his brother Adulf, spent time abroad, where he became a monk. In 654 he established a monastery called Icanhoe, originally thought to have been in Lincolnshire at Boston (a contraction of 'Botolph's town' or 'Botolph's stone') but now believed to have been at Iken in Suffolk. He was long known as the patron saint of travellers and was renowned as a man 'of remarkable life and learning'. Today there are nearly seventy churches which bear his name, many of them close to ancient city gates.

God of great enterprise, on this day we remember Botolph, who journeyed far and wide before founding a monastery at Icanhoe. May the many churches that bear his name be blessed with the same love of life and learning that he showed. Amen

Samuel and Henrietta Barrett, social reformers
(1913 and 1936)

Born in Bristol in 1844, Samuel Barrett was educated at Wadham College, Oxford, priested and became vicar of St Jude's, Whitechapel, where he stayed from 1873 till 1894. He and his wife, Henrietta, born in Clapham in 1851, became a formidable partnership in ministry to a very deprived area, and were instrumental in setting up Toynbee Hall in 1884. Later, Henrietta founded Hampstead Garden Suburb. Both showed exceptional spiritual gifts, energy and Christian commitment to mission.

Lord of life, today we remember Samuel and Henrietta Barrett, pioneers in Christian ministry and community living in East London. May their legacy continue to shape Christian witness in places of need in this country as well as abroad. Amen

18 June

Gregorio Barbango, Bishop of Padua (1697)

Born into a noble family in 1625, Gregorio Barbango was educated at Venice and after ordination showed his pastoral skills during the plague of 1657, became a cardinal in 1660 and was appointed Bishop of Padua in 1664. He was a polymath who demonstrated great ability in reconciliation between Eastern and Western Churches, in learning and as a founder of a college, a library and a seminary, as well as in dispensing charity.

We remember on this day the public service and Christian commitment of Gregorio Barbango, Bishop of Padua, a man of great learning and diplomacy. As we contemplate his works, let us appreciate and emulate his commitment to faith and to its dissemination through learning and training. Amen

Bernard Mizeki, apostle of the Mashona, martyr (1896)

Bernard Mizeki was born in Portuguese East Africa, worked in Cape Town and became a Christian through the Cowley Fathers. As a translator and evangelist he served the Mashona, but in 1896 was murdered because of his association with Europeans in a tribal uprising, the site of his martyrdom becoming a place of pilgrimage for Christians throughout Central Africa.

God of service and sacrifice, let us today mark and recall the witness of Bernard Mizeki, tireless in evangelism and steadfast in faith. May we acknowledge his commitment in bringing faith to the Mashona and pray that his martyrdom is remembered as a turning point in the development of Christianity in Central Africa. Amen

19 June

Romuald of Ravenna, Benedictine abbot (c 1027)
– commemorated in some traditions on 7 February

Born into a noble family in Ravenna, Romuald entered the Cluniac monastery of S. Apollinaire-in-Classe in reaction to his father's killing of a relative in a duel. His study of the desert fathers and his advocacy of penance and solitude in monastic life led to the incorporation of the hermit life within the Benedictine Rule. His foundations included Fonte Avellana in the Apennines and Camaldoli, near Arezzo.

We thank you, Lord, for the example of Romuald, who turned his back on the life of the nobility to enhance the contemplative solitude of the life of the hermit within the Benedictine Rule. Grant us the same ability to adapt our spiritual life in order to respond to your call. Amen

Sundar Singh of India, evangelist, teacher of the faith (1929)

Sundar Singh was born into a wealthy Sikh family, but following a vision he became a Christian. Convinced that faith and experience come first and understanding will follow, he travelled extensively around the Indian sub-continent dressed in the robes of a holy man or 'sadhu', sharing his gospel experience and interpreting it for the lives of those he met.

God of experience and miracles, we remember today the ministry and mission of Sundar Singh of India, tireless evangelist. Let us give thanks for his willingness to witness to you in sometimes hostile communities and may our knowledge of his life and work encourage us in our mission today. Amen

20 June

Alban *(also commemorated alone on 22 June)*, Julius and Aaron, martyrs (c 250)

Julius and Aaron were among the first Welsh citizens to have their names recorded and known to this day. They died during the Emperor Diocletian's persecutions at the beginning of the fourth century. Alban, who took the place of the priest who had converted him, was the victim of the same persecution and died after being tortured without renouncing his faith.

We give thanks for the early Romano-British martyrs, Alban, Julius and Aaron, who professed their faith and died for their faith. May we remember their steadfast courage in the face of persecution and not be afraid of any attempts to belittle our own faith. Amen

Adalbert of Magdeburg, archbishop (981)

A monk from Trier, Adalbert was sent by Emperor Otto the Great into Russia at the instigation of his wife, Olga of Kiev. Ejected by her son, who was a heathen, he returned to Germany, where he became Abbot of Weissenburg. Known for his encouragement of learning, in 968 he was made the first Archbishop of Magdeburg, engaging in missionary work and founding three dioceses.

God of great encouragement, we celebrate today Adalbert, who brought hope and learning to many as abbot and archbishop, missionary and scholar. Let his example of faith and works be a sign to us of the importance of both in our lives in your service. Amen

21 June

Aloysius Gonzaga, Jesuit (1591)

Born in 1568, in the castle of Castiglione, Aloysius seemed destined for a military career. However, at the age of 16 he decided to become a Jesuit and entered training as a novitiate in 1585, against his father's wishes. Ministering to those suffering from the plague, he was himself infected and recovered, but was much weakened, dying shortly afterwards. He was known for his single-minded devotion to God and was heavily influenced by the spiritual direction of Robert Bellarmine.

> **Lord of all, we recall and commemorate the life of Aloysius, called at an early age to become a Jesuit and to engage in ministry to the sick. May his courage and devotion be constant reminders of the gifts we need to show in witnessing to our faith. Amen**

22 June

Alban, first martyr of Britain (c 250) – *also commemorated with Julius and Aaron on 20 June*

Alban was a citizen of Verulamium, a Roman city now known as St Albans. In a period of persecution he gave shelter to a priest, known subsequently as Amphilbalus, who converted him. When soldiers came looking, Alban put on the priest's clothes, allowing the priest to escape. Refusing to renounce his new-found faith under torture, Alban was beheaded around the year 250.

> **God of steadfastness, we give thanks for your servant Alban, whose conversion was quickly followed by sacrificial courage as he took the place of a priest pursued by Roman persecutors. Let his heroic example remain in our hearts and inspire our faith. Amen**

John Fisher and Thomas More, Reformation martyrs (1535) *– also commemorated in some traditions on 6 July*

John Fisher was born at Beverley in 1469 and became a distinguished scholar and a faithful bishop, who was opposed to Lutheran reforms despite being a reformer himself. Refusing to take the oath which would have repudiated the pope, Henry 8th brought him to trial and he was executed on Tower Hill.

Thomas More had a legal training and entered Parliament in 1504. A writer, reformer and scholar, he was given a series of posts by Henry 8th, including Speaker of the House of Commons, and pursued William Tyndale relentlessly. Refusing to sanction Henry's demand for his marriage to Catherine of Aragon to be declare invalid, he was tried and executed a few days after John Fisher at Tower Hill.

> **On this day we cherish the memory of John Fisher and Thomas More, distinguished men of scholarship and faith, who refused to bow to demands from the king which would have compromised their beliefs. May their courage and service make them beacons of hope in a period of change. Amen**

23 June

Etheldreda, queen, foundress and Abbess of Ely (c 679)

Born around 630, Etheldreda was the daughter of King Anna of the East Angles, married twice, without consummation of the marriages, and became a nun at Coldingham. She founded a religious house at Ely for both men and women, where she became abbess until her death. Wearing only wool, eating only one meal a day and remaining at prayer half the night, she was known as a woman of prayer, austerity and prophecy and is one of the most revered of Anglo-Saxon saints.

> **Lord of dedication and holiness, we honour the life and memory of your servant Etheldreda, who served both Crown and Church with distinction and patience. May we show her dedication and desire to spread your word in our own intercessions and spiritual life. Amen**

Joseph Cafasso, diocesan priest (1860)

Joseph Cafasso, born in Piedmont, educated at Chieri and after priesting was appointed to the Turin dioceses, where he was known for his preaching and spiritual direction. He became Don Bosco's teacher, adviser and spiritual director, helping him to found the Salesian congregation.

We remember the spiritual life and influence of Joseph Cafasso, mentor of John Bosco, founder of the Salesians. Never let us take lightly the power of the Holy Spirit encountered through teachers, friends and spiritual directors. Amen

24 June

The birth of John the Baptist

Endowed with grace before his birth, John was the son of Zechariah, a Temple priest and the elderly Elizabeth, a cousin of the Virgin Mary. Struck dumb on hearing the news about the impending birth and chosen name of the baby, Zechariah only regained his voice when John was born. Known as the forerunner of Christ, John marks the boundary between the Old and New Testaments.

God of beginnings and endings, we celebrate today the birth of John, the forerunner of Christ, who gave encouragement to the people of God and prepared them for the arrival of the Messiah, our Redeemer. May we gain confidence from John's life and works as we mark the beginning of his pivotal role in the Christian story. Amen

25 June

Prosper of Aquitaine, theologian (c 460)

Sometimes confused with Prosper of Reggio, Prosper of Aquitaine was born about the year 390 and spent most of his adult life in Provence. A follower of Augustine and a lay theologian of note, he was said to have become the secretary of Leo the Great. His writing, in both prose and verse, concentrated on the theological controversies of the time, in which he upheld Augustine's teaching on grace and attacked Pelagian heresies.

On this day let us remember the writings of Prosper, who sought to explore and maintain Augustinian teaching in the face of controversy. May we be as passionate and focused in our understanding and teaching of all that your Son taught us. Amen

Moluag of Lismore, bishop (592)

Arriving in Scotland around the same time as Columba, Moluag founded a community on the island of Lismore, which later became the Church of St Moluag and the seat of the bishopric of the Isles. From here, as bishop, he established other centres of mission in the isles.

God of infinite reach, we thank you that you touched Moluag with your Holy Spirit and sustained him in his work of mission in the Scottish Isles. May we always seek to extend our reach, but always with you as our guardian and our guide. Amen

26 June

Robert Leighton, Archbishop of Glasgow (1684)

Born in 1611, Robert, the son of a puritanical doctor, studied first in Edinburgh, then on the continent, where he came under the influence of the Jansenists, who taught tolerance and piety. Principal of Edinburgh University under Cromwell, under the Restoration he became Bishop of Dunblane and tried to heal the rifts in the Scottish Church, a task he continued as Archbishop of Glasgow. Despite his best efforts, reconciliation with the Presbyterian Church was not achieved and he returned to England.

We recall with gratitude today the efforts of Robert Leighton, Archbishop of Glasgow, to heal schisms in the Scottish Church. May we take risks in our Christian lives to uphold or seek the things which are righteous in your sight. Amen

27 June

Cyril of Alexandria, Bishop of Alexandria, teacher of the faith (444)

Born in Alexandria, the nephew of Theophilus, Cyril succeeded his uncle as Bishop of Alexandria, but stirred up trouble between religious factions and drove out the Jews. Later he became a stout defender of the Trinity against Nestorius' heresy and presided over a special Council at Ephesus to decide the issue. An outstanding theologian and disciple of the Early Fathers, he wrote extensively and left a formidable legacy.

God who is Father, Son, and Holy Spirit, we celebrate today the life and work of Cyril of Alexandria, champion of the Trinity, theologian of note and advocate for the Early Fathers. We give thanks that difficult issues of faith were explored and clarified under his leadership. Amen

Richard FitzRalph, Archbishop of Armagh, reformer (1360)

Born about the year 1295, Richard FitzRalph was a learned scholar and celebrated preacher who was Chancellor of Oxford University, then Dean of Lichfield, becoming Archbishop of Armagh in 1347. A great supporter of, and advocate for, the people of Dundalk and Drogheda, especially during the Black Death, he nevertheless criticised the mendicants of the day, maintaining that voluntary begging was against the teaching of Christ. His thinking and writing greatly influenced John Wyclif.

On this day we recall with gratitude the ministry of Richard FitzRalph, preacher and scholar, whose insights and sermons about a Christian stewardship of possessions influenced many. May we give thoughtful consideration to the issues he raised, as the poor are always with us, as your Son reminded us. Amen

28 June

Irenaeus, Bishop of Lyons, teacher of the faith (c 200)

Thought to have been born at Smyrna about the year 130, Irenaeus was strongly influenced by Polycarp, studied at Rome and became Bishop of Lyons in 177. Irenaeus showed great powers of reconciliation as a very conscientious bishop, while writing powerfully against Gnostic heresies and about the theology of the incarnation.

God of tough love, today we celebrate the life and work of Irenaeus, bishop, theologian and reconciler, whose rigours of scholarship safeguarded the foundation of the faith. Let us be thankful for the benefits of his understanding and learning in our own journey of faith. Amen

Austell, monk (sixth century)

A disciple of Mewan, whom he accompanied from South Wales to Cornwall, Austell founded the Church in Cornwall at the town which now bears his name. He then followed Mewan to Brittany, where he died.

Lord of west and east, we give thanks on this day for your servant Austell and especially for his ministry in Cornwall. Let his legacy be known by the town which bears his name and in the lives of the generations of Christians brought up in Cornwall. Amen

29 June

Peter and Paul, apostles (c 65)

Born Simon, a native of Bethsaida, Peter was a fisherman when, along with his brother Andrew, he was called to follow Christ as a 'fisher of men'. Jesus gave him the name Peter, as the 'rock' on which he would build his Church, as the foremost of the apostles. His warm impetuosity and very human feelings made many identify with him, while his key role was in witnessing to the Lordship of Christ.

Paul, born at Tarsus, is often known as 'apostle to the Gentiles'. A Roman citizen known as Saul before his conversion on the road to Damascus, he had been a strict Pharisee searching out and persecuting Christians. Some time after his conversion he embarked on his great mission to the Gentiles, spreading understanding of the meaning of the Lordship of Christ.

Both Peter and Paul met their death in Rome, by crucifixion upside down and by beheading respectively, about the year 65.

> **Lord of great gifting, we give thanks on this special day for the two towers of strength to your Son's ministry and mission, Peter the 'rock' and Paul, the 'apostle to the Gentiles'. May we acknowledge our debt of gratitude to their humanity and their dedication and commitment to spread the good news, even to death. Amen**

30 June

The martyrdom of Paul and the first martyrs of the Church of Rome (first century)

During the time of persecution under Nero in the latter part of the first century, many died in addition to Paul. Known collectively as the 'martyrs of Rome', they are remembered alongside Paul, and their death is commemorated separately from Paul in some traditions.

> **God of first and last, we recall today all those Christians who died in the persecution of Nero, including Paul, whose martyrdom we also mark on this day. May their sacrifice serve to remind us of the cost of discipleship at that time and of the freedom we have today to worship the one true God. Amen**

July

1 July

Henry, John, and Henry Venn the Younger, priests, evangelical divines (1797, 1813, 1873)

Born in 1725 in Barnes, Henry studied in Cambridge and developed his evangelical principles as a curate in Surrey and Clapham. Working with great dedication as a vicar in Huddersfield and then Huntingdonshire, Henry was a cheerful man of piety.

John Venn also studied at Cambridge, becoming rector of Little Dunelm in Norfolk and then of Clapham in 1792, where he was at the heart of the philanthropic group known as the Clapham Sect, and was a prime mover in the establishment of the Church Missionary Society.

John's son Henry was born at Clapham in 1796, also studied at Cambridge and served as secretary of the Church Missionary Society for thirty-two years. He was regarded as one of the leading evangelical figures in the Church of England.

> **God of movement and might, today we celebrate the dedication and influence of Henry, John and Henry Venn the Younger, whom we remember for their philanthropic principles leading to the establishment of the Church Missionary Society. May their work be our inspiration and may the Church Missionary Society continue to flourish in our day and age. Amen**

Oliver Plunkett, Archbishop of Armagh, martyr (1681)

Born in County Meath in Ireland, Oliver studied in Rome and was priested in 1654, becoming Archbishop of Armagh in 1669, where he revived the Catholic Church despite continuing disputes over whether Dublin or Armagh had primacy. Promulgating the Treaty of Trent and recognising papal authority, he was the object of spurious charges of treason, removed to London and being condemned of 'setting up a false religion', was condemned to death, suffering horribly at Tyburn, where he was hanged, drawn and quartered.

> **Lord of judgement and justice, we remember on this day the gifts and influence of your servant Oliver Plunkett, who led the Catholic Church with distinction at Armagh before being the victim of an**

unjust plot to disgrace him and his ministry. May his dedication and service shine through his suffering and prompt us to renewed efforts in your service. Amen

2 July

John Francis Regis, Jesuit priest (1640)

Born and brought up in south-eastern France, John Francis Regis became a Jesuit in Toulouse, to where he returned to be priested after serving in different houses. Surviving the plague and the effects of the Wars of Religion, he devoted his life to missionary work among those who had lost their religion and cared for the poor and the marginalised. His final illness was the result of continuing his mission work in extremely cold conditions.

God of mission and mercy, we hold up to you the work of John Francis Regis amongst the least, the lost and the lonely. Let his zeal and pastoral sensitivity be a guide and a spur to our own work in the field of mission, at home and abroad. Amen

3 July

Thomas, apostle (first century)
– commemorated in some traditions on 21 December

Known as Didymus ('The Twin'), Thomas was a Galilean Jew who became one of the apostles. Sceptical about Christ's resurrection until his wounds were shown to him, his response was the wholehearted belief expressed in his exclamation 'My Lord and my God!' Later he is thought to have taken the gospel to the Indian sub-continent, where he was martyred, killed by a spear or a lance.

Our Lord and our God, we honour today the life and work of mission of Thomas, apostle, who wanted confirmation of the resurrection, but in receiving the evidence from Jesus became a fearless advocate for the Way, the Truth and the Life. May we who have not seen but believe thank you for the openness and honesty of Thomas, whose doubt enabled Jesus to banish all doubt. Amen

4 July

Elizabeth of Portugal, queen (1336)

Born in 1271, the daughter of Peter 3rd, King of Aragon, Elizabeth married King Denis of Portugal, and bore two children. Known for her good works, prayer and piety, she sought to bring reconciliation to her family and nation in their disputes and cared for her husband in his last illness, despite his wayward behaviour. She then went on a pilgrimage and became a Poor Clare nun, dying after an attempt to reconcile conflict between her son and grandson.

> **God of trust and fidelity, let us rejoice in the prayerful piety and reconciling love of Elizabeth of Portugal, who always looked for ways to build bridges in family and national relationships. May her faith and diplomacy inspire us to follow her example in our own family life and faith journeys. Amen**

5 July

Antony Zaccaria, founder of the Barnabite Order (1539)

A doctor at Cremona, Antony became a priest in 1528, drawn to practise spiritual as well as physical healing. He founded the Barnabite Order, based on the love of divine worship, frequent preaching and the Eucharist, part of the revival of Christian life in Italy. He died peacefully at the age of 37.

> **Lord of healing and wholeness, we give thanks for Antony Zaccaria, doctor and priest, whose passion for worship, the sacraments and preaching led him to found an order of priests. May his contribution to the revival of Christian life remind us of our need continually to review our own Christian life and witness. Amen**

6 July

John Fisher and Thomas More, Reformation martyrs –
see under 22 June

Maria Goretti, virgin and martyr (1902)

Born into a peasant family near Ancona in 1890, Maria lost her father in 1900 and while her mother was working she was attacked by a local man, who tried to rape her and when she resisted stabbed her to death. Eventually her assailant, after a lengthy time in prison, was released, a changed man.

God of purity and forgiveness, we remember on this day the fortitude and suffering of Maria, who became a martyr for the Christian life when she was attacked, preferring death to dishonour. Let us be thankful that her assailant repented and took communion before you and side by side with Maria's mother, forgiving Lord. Amen

Palladius, bishop (fifth century) –
commemorated in some traditions on 7 July

Born in Gaul and probably a deacon in Auxerre before going to Rome, Palladius was sent by Pope Celestine to continue the anti-Pelagian work being carried out in the British Isles by Germanus. Firstly in Ireland and then in Scotland Palladius preached with great zeal and built up a strong Church, for which he became known as the apostle of Scotland.

God of destiny, on this day help us to understand the pioneering work in Ireland and Scotland of your servant Palladius, who countered the Pelagian heresy and built up the Church in Scotland. May we acknowledge and learn from the formative work and formidable preaching of this Christian leader. Amen

7 July

Thomas Becket, Archbishop of Canterbury and martyr (1170)
– *see under 29 December*

Palladius, bishop (fifth century) – *see under 6 July*

Willibald, Bishop of Eichstadt (786)

Born in Wessex about 700, Willebald became a monk at Bishops Waltham and travelled widely in Europe and the near East before living as a monk in Monte Cassino. Sent by Pope Gregory to assist Boniface in Bavaria, he was priested and became Bishop of Eichstadt, founding monasteries in Heidenheim and displaying great qualities as a pastor, educator and missioner.

We honour and commemorate the ministry of Willibald, from Wessex, whose work and witness took him to many lands, in support of Boniface and as a founder of monasteries. May we be inspired and encouraged by the dedication of his pastoral work and personal example of devotion and good works. Amen

Hedda, Bishop of Winchester (705)

Educated at Whitby, Hedda became the first bishop to be based at Winchester and was known as a good and just man, naturally virtuous, sought out for his wisdom and prudence by the great and the good to help in framing laws.

God of justice and peace, on this day we give thanks for your servant Hedda, adviser to kings and first episcopal leader of the West Saxons in Winchester. Let us rejoice that his example and the esteem in which he was held have been recorded and remembered. Amen

8 July

Kilian, bishop and martyr (689)

Born in County Cavan in Ireland, Kilian became a missionary in Germany, converting the local ruler to Christianity and rebuilding the Church in

Baden and Bavaria. Returning from Rome, where he visited the pope, he was killed at Würzburg after he had tried to intervene to separate the king from his brother's widow.

> God of sure foundations, we celebrate the efforts of Kilian to bring Christianity and a godly way of living to parts of Germany lacking in both. We recall his stand against a wrong relationship and mourn his untimely death. Amen

9 July

Veronica Giulani, mystic (1727)

Born at Mercatello in 1660, Veronica's early devotion led to her becoming a novitiate nun, against her father's wishes, experiencing mystical union with Christ and visions of Christ being on the cross, manifested on her person with stigmata and a crown of thorns appearing on her forehead. She became mistress of novices at Città di Castello in Umbria and, later, abbess. She was known for her integrity and efficiency and left a spiritual diary in ten volumes.

> Lord of the extraordinary, we commemorate today the devotion of Veronica Giulani, mystic and abbess, whose experience and visions of Christ attested to her faith and calling. May those who follow their vocation learn from her dedication and openness to the immediacy of Christ in her spiritual life. Amen

10 July

Antony of the Caves, abbot and hermit (1073)

Antony was born near Chernigov in 983 and in 1028 went to live as a hermit, possibly on Mount Athos. Later he returned to Russia and lived in a cave by the River Dnieper near Kiev. This became the first Russian monastery, which was developed further by Theodosius of the Caves when Antony left in search of greater solitude, only returning to Kiev at the end of his life.

God of solitude, we thank you for the example of simple austerity and devotion of Antony of the Caves, who drew others to his life as a hermit and founded the first Russian monastery. Let us savour and appreciate his dedication to you in the silence and stillness of the caves. Amen

11 July

Benedict, abbot, patriarch of the Western monks (c 547)

Born at Nursa in Central Italy in about 480, Benedict studied briefly in Rome, leaving to become a hermit at Subiaco, where others joined him and he formed a community of monks, becoming their abbot, though he was never priested. He established twelve communities, including, in 529, the monastery of Monte Cassino. Here he developed his monastic Rule, which served as a model for monasteries and communities throughout the Western Church.

Lord of community, on this day we remember Benedict, author of the 'Rule for Monks', which has guided the conduct of monasteries over the centuries. May his prudence, moderation and obedience be a model for our relationship with each other today, as we seek your kingdom, by your grace. Amen

12 July

John Gualberto, abbot (1073)

Born at Florence into a rich family, John underwent a conversion experience after an encounter with the murderer of his brother, Hugo, on Good Friday, sparing him and immediately committing his own life to Christ. Although never priested, he became the founder and abbot of the Vallambrosian monks, basing their order on Benedict's Rule, but also developing this in new ways. John was known for his gifts of prophecy and healing and a commitment to the poor and hungry.

We give thanks for John Gualberto, a man who foreswore revenge and followed Christ in word and deed, establishing the Vallambrosian monks and demonstrating miraculous powers. Let his life be an example and his rule of life be emulated. Amen

Veronica, a woman of Jerusalem (first century)

Veronica, a woman of Jerusalem, is said to have wiped the face of Christ with a cloth as he carried the cross to Golgotha, leaving an image of Jesus' features on the cloth.

God of compassion, on this day we remember the act of love of Veronica for Jesus on his way to Golgotha, wiping his face with a cloth. May such tenderness and kindness be recalled with gratitude and as a demonstration of how we can respond to your love for us, gracious Lord. Amen

13 July

Henry, Holy Roman Emperor (1024)

Henry was born in Bavaria, the son of Henry, Duke of Bavaria, and educated at Hildersheim, succeeding his father in 995 and becoming emperor in 1002. He waged wars in defence of Christendom and was engaged in the reform and reorganisation of the Church, including the foundation of the see of Bamberg, where he was buried.

Lord of Church and State, we thank you for the vision and leadership of Henry, Holy Roman Emperor, stout defender and unifier of the German empire and advocate of reform and order in the Church. We honour his achievements and recognise his protective powers. Amen

Mildred, abbess (c 700)

The daughter of Merewald, King of Mercia, Mildred studied at a convent in Chelles, near Paris. Refusing an offer of marriage, she returned to

England and joined the convent founded by her mother, Ermenburga, at Minster-in-Thanet in Kent, becoming abbess by 694. There she was noted for her kindly and generous disposition, especially in her dealings with children and widows.

On this day we honour the memory of Mildred, abbess at Minster-in-Thanet, and give thanks for her overflowing kindness, 'a comforter to all in affliction'. May her generosity of spirit be our guide as we seek to do your will in our own communities. Amen

Silas (Silvanus), companion of Paul (first century) – *commemorated in some traditions on 30 July*

Silas, a companion and co-worker of Paul, was entrusted by Paul to deliver a letter to the Christians of Antioch, where he stayed before accompanying Paul to Syria and eventually to Macedonia, where he died.

God of faith and fellowship, we recall with gratitude the important work of Silas in supporting and working with Paul on his journeys and in ensuring the safe arrival of his letters. May we be blessed with trusty and faithful companions on our faith journeys and in our ministry. Amen

14 July

John Keble, priest, tractarian poet (1866)

The son of a priest, John was born in 1792 at Fairford and showed brilliance as a poet at Oxford University, becoming a fellow of Oriel College before being ordained deacon in 1816. After a spell in parish ministry he was elected Professor of Poetry at Oxford in 1831 and became increasingly involved as a leading light in the Oxford movement, co-operating with Newman in writing a number of 'Tracts for the Times'. He later became a parish priest near Winchester.

We remember today the gifts and talents of John Keble, poet and tractarian, a prime mover of the Oxford movement, who remained faithful to the high church principles of the Church of England. We give thanks for his poetry, his spiritual guidance and his ministry, which have inspired the Church even to this day. Amen

Camillus de Lellis, founder of the Servants of the Sick (1614)

Born in Abruzzi in 1550, and losing his parents when he was young, Camillus joined the army. A big man with a big appetite for gambling, his life was changed around when he lost everything and he sought to join the Franciscan order, but was denied because of a chronic leg ailment, which led him to offer his services to the hospital of San Giacomo in Rome, becoming its bursar. Later he was priested and, in association with Philip Neri, founded a congregation of priests and lay brothers known as the Servants of the Sick, setting up hospitals in Naples and elsewhere. Ahead of his time in insisting on fresh air, correct diets and isolation of contagious cases, he has become the patron saint of nurses and the sick.

God of healing and pastoral care, we give thanks for the ministry to the sick of Camillus de Lellis, his dedication, his ability to organise others and his identification of correct conditions for convalescence and recovery. May we extend his principles of care in our ministry and care of others. Amen

15 July

Swithun, Bishop of Winchester (c 862)

Born in Wessex and educated in Winchester, Swithun was chosen by King Egbert to be his chaplain and tutor of his son, Ethelwulf, who later made him Bishop of Winchester. Although famous for his charity and building of churches, he is principally remembered for what happened after his death. Despite dire warnings, when his remains were removed and put into a shrine in the new cathedral by Ethelwold, forty days of rain followed, as predicted, giving rise to the belief that if it rains on this day, forty days of rain will follow.

We recall on this day the ministry and charitable works of Swithun, Bishop of Winchester, builder of churches and exemplar of Christian simplicity and holiness. Help us to remember his life in your service when we look out for rain on this date. Amen

Bonaventure, friar, bishop, teacher of the faith (1274)

Bonaventure was born at Bagnoreggio in Italy about 1218 and was sent to Paris to study under Alexander of Hales, becoming Master of the Franciscan school there in 1253, and was elected Minister-General of the Franciscan Order in 1257. A theologian of note, he was regarded as the second founder of the Franciscan Order, adding study to the tenets of Francis' teaching and putting learning on a par with poverty and spirituality. He was also known for his courtesy, compassion and accessibility.

God of reconciliation and reform, we honour the life and work of your servant Bonaventure, who remained true to Francis' rule of life, supplementing it with the benefits of study and teaching. Let us in our own spiritual lives seek to develop our gifts in the way Bonaventure showed us and demonstrated himself. Amen

16 July

Osmond, Bishop of Salisbury (1099)

Following William the Conqueror to England, Osmond became Chancellor in 1072 and, later, Bishop of Salisbury, supervising the completion of the cathedral at Old Sarum. He was known for his administrative skills and lack of ambition and was involved in the completion of the Domesday Book and its presentation to the king in 1086.

God of great works, we give thanks for the life and work of Osmond, who oversaw the completion of the cathedral at Old Sarum and of the Domesday Book. May we learn from his commitment to projects others had started and follow his careful example. Amen

Helier, martyr, first saint of Jersey (sixth century)

A hermit from Tongres in Belgium, Helier lived in a cave above the town named after him in Jersey, having been converted by Cunibert in his native country before fleeing because of the murder of Cumbert. Helier was himself killed by pagan searovers to whom he tried to preach the gospel.

On this day we remember the martyrdom of Helier, who fled Belgium fearing persecution and lived as a hermit in Jersey, before being murdered by those with whom he was trying to share the good news. Let us rejoice at his courageous work of mission in the face of hostility and ignorance. Amen

17 July

Alexis of Rome, 'Man of God' (fifth century)

Based on the life of Mar Riscia of Edessa, the legend of Alexis is that he embarked on a pilgrimage, leaving his wife on their wedding night to live in Syria. Returning to Rome, he lived incognito as a beggar for seventeen years, unrecognised in his father's house. His legend gave rise to his choice as patron saint of the Alexian Brothers, a nursing society, in about 1350.

God of mystery, we recall the legend of Alexis of Rome, who assumed the role of a beggar on his return from pilgrimage and remained unrecognised for many years in his own community. May we retain an element of mystery in our lives, but only if it brings us closer to you, loving Lord. Amen

Kenelm, prince of the Mercian royal family (c 812)

The son of Coenwulf, King of Mercia, he was assigned the ownership of Glastonbury by Leo 3rd in 798. Although a legend grew up around his death on the instruction of his jealous sister, Kenelm probably died in battle at a young age and his body taken to Winchcombe in Gloucestershire.

Today we remember the short life of Kenelm from the royal family of Mercia, heralded as a martyr and known throughout the South West. Let his name invoke interest and enquiry and a strong faith in the churches bearing his name. Amen

18 July

Elizabeth Ferard, first deaconess of the Church of England, founder of the Community of St Andrew (1883)

After she had been encouraged by her bishop to visit various institutions of deaconesses in Germany, Elizabeth returned and in 1861 set up a group of women dedicated 'to minister to the necessities of the Church, as servants in the Church'. Receiving the first licence as deaconess from Bishop Tait, she established a community of religious sisters and deaconesses working in different parts of London.

God of small beginnings, on this day we mark the life and ministry of Elizabeth Ferard, a pioneer deaconess in the Church of England. May we honour her faithfulness, her servanthood and her ability to organise, qualities we seek to emulate in our own ministry and faith journeys. Amen

Elizabeth of Russia, religious and martyr (1918)

Born in 1867, Elizabeth was married to Sergei, a son of the Tsar of Russia, who was assassinated in 1905. She used the wealth of her possessions to set up the Martha and Mary home in Moscow, bringing together seventeen women as Sisters of Love and Mercy, ministering to the sick and needy. Although immediately after the 1917 Revolution their work was encouraged, in July 1918 she and others were taken by the authorities and murdered, along with members of the Royal Family.

We remember with thanks the groundbreaking active Christian service of Elizabeth of Russia at the Martha and Mary home in Moscow, cut short by her martyrdom. Let us take heart from her unstinting service to needy neighbours in the name of Christ and be inspired. Amen

Pambo of Nitria, abbot (385)

A disciple of Antony in the desert, Pambo was admired by Antony for his purity of faith, touched by the Holy Spirit. Settling in the desert of Nitria, he was known for his crafting of mats and baskets, always austere in his way of life, secure in the Lord and uncomplaining in his faith.

May we learn from the humility and austerity of your servant Pambo, disciple of Antony, who lived in a cell in the desert, but who earned his keep by weaving mats and baskets. Let his purity of faith and the self-sufficiency of his way of life show us a simple alternative to being busy and acquisitive. Amen

19 July

Gregory of Nyssa, bishop, and his sister Macrina, deaconess, teachers of the faith (394 and 379) – *for Gregory alone see under 9 March*

The younger brother of Basil the Great, Gregory was born at Caesarea in Cappadocia and was introduced to the spiritual life by his elder sister, Macrina, who is also remembered today. Educated at Athens and married to Theosiba, who was highly respected in her own right, he was priested about the year 362 and made Bishop of Nyssa in 371. There he used his considerable rhetorical skills in defence of orthodoxy against Arianism and is considered to be a spiritual writer of substance in the tradition of Origen.

God of authority and insights, today we celebrate the life and wisdom of Gregory of Nyssa, one of the Cappadocian fathers responsible for building up the foundation beliefs of the Church, and his sister Macrina, whose spiritual depth influenced him. May we wonder at their powers of theological understanding and ability to transmit this to others. Amen

Arsenius, monk (c 412)

Thought to have been born in Rome, where he became a deacon, Arsenius may have been tutor to the sons of Theodosius 1st, Emperor of

Constantinople. Later he joined the desert fathers, showing great self-discipline and self-sufficiency. Known for the saying 'I have often been sorry for having spoken, but never for having held my tongue', Arsenius was also the author of many other maxims and moral anecdotes.

> **Gracious Lord, we remember on this day the wisdom and words of Arsenius, desert father, monk and noted solitary, who nevertheless left us important sayings to make our life more spiritual. May we learn from his austerity of life and be inspired by his way with words. Amen**

20 July

Margaret of Antioch, martyr (fourth century)

According to legend, Margaret was the daughter of a pagan priest who became a Christian and a shepherdess. She resisted a powerful suitor, the governor of Antioch, who kidnapped her, and lived to become an inspiring preacher, converting many to Christianity. She was beheaded in the Diocletian persecutions and her cult had a powerful influence in medieval times, resulting in two hundred English churches being dedicated to her.

> **God of mystery and imagination, we recall at this time the power of the legend of Margaret of Antioch, shepherdess and preacher, whose sufferings only inspired those who heard her preaching and converted to Christianity. We thank you, Lord, that people such as Margaret resisted evil and demonstrated their fearless faith in the face of death. Amen**

Bartolomé de Las Casas, apostle to the Indies (1566)

Bartolomé was born at Las Casas in Seville and was converted after seeing the injustices faced by the Indians when he went to Haiti in 1502. He became a Dominican priest and the Bishop of Chiapa in Mexico in 1543. Outspoken in his prophetic role and deep in his theological thinking, he became known as 'the defender of the Indians'.

God of justice and judgement, we thank you for the clear-speaking and prophetic life and work of Bartolomé de Las Casas, champion of the rights of Indians in the Americas, who saw that the injustice he observed was an affront to Christ. May we, in our age, be reminded of his saying that 'Christ did not come into the world to die for gold'. Amen

21 July

Lawrence of Brindisi, theologian and missioner (1619)

Born at Brindisi of a wealthy Venetian family, Lawrence became a Capuchin Franciscan at 16 and then studied at Padua University, studying languages and the Bible with some distinction. He preached widely amongst Lutherans and Jews and was sent to establish the Capuchin reforms in Germany, also founding houses and advising generals, even leading troops into battle bearing a crucifix. He was a prolific writer of, among other works, sermons and commentaries and a polemic against Lutherans.

Lord of all, we wonder at the industry, energy and scholastic ability of Lawrence of Brindisi, theologian and missioner, who attempted and achieved much for you. Let his all-round abilities encourage us in our many tasks for you, our God of gifts and grace. Amen

Victor of Marseilles, martyr (c 290)

Victor was a soldier who was killed in Marseilles in the persecution of Maximian, along with three guards whom he had converted, having prepared and encouraged the local Christians in the face of death.

Transforming God, today we remember the courage and encouragement of Victor of Marseilles, faced with the death of fellow Christians along with his own execution. Let his example of steadfastness during such persecution be an example for us when our faith is challenged. Amen

Howell Harris, preacher (1773)

Born at Talgarth in Wales in 1714, Howell became a school teacher until a profound religious experience on Whit Sunday 1735 transformed his life. He became an 'exhorter', leading informal services in his community. Turned down for ordination, he helped develop a Welsh Methodist movement before setting up a Christian Moravian community. He was a powerful preacher who had a considerable impact on Christianity in Wales.

We give thanks on this day for your enthusiastic servant Howell Harris, moved to preach and lead services in unorthodox but effective ways. May his energy and innovation be the qualities we remember and seek to incorporate in our own ministry and worship. Amen

22 July

Mary Magdalene (first century)

Mary was a follower of Christ who had been a sinner and possessed of seven demons until cleansed and healed by Jesus. She then accompanied Jesus, stood by the cross, anointed the body and was the first to see the risen Christ in the garden, taking the good news to the disciples. Known as 'the apostle to the apostles', she is also regarded as patron to repentant sinners and of the contemplative life.

God of forgiveness and revelation, we remember with grateful thanks the faithfulness of Mary Magdalene, repentant sinner, who stood by your Son at his death and was there to witness to his resurrection and give the good news to his disciples. May we have the faith, the loyalty and the perseverance of Mary in our faith journey – and rejoice in hers. Amen

23 July

Declan, bishop (early fifth century) – *see under 24 July*

Bridget of Sweden, foundress and visionary (1373)

Born in 1303, the daughter of Berger, the governor of Upland, she was married at the age of 14 to Ulf Gudmarrson and had eight children, one of whom, Catherine, became an abbess. She experienced mystical visions, which intensified after her husband's death in 1344 and led her to take pilgrimages and then to found a monastery at Vadstena on Lake Vattern, where sixty nuns and twenty-five monks lived in separate institutions but shared the same church. Her advice was much sought after by rulers and church leaders.

God of divine revelation, we remember the devotion of Bridget of Sweden, the visions which inspired her actions and the skills she showed as foundress and adviser. Let us rejoice at her inspiration to others both in her lifetime and through the centuries. Amen

Philip Evans, Jesuit priest and martyr (1679) – commemorated with the Welsh martyrs on 25 October in some traditions

Born at Monmouth and educated at St Omer, Philip became a Jesuit in 1665 and was priested in 1675. His ministry in South Wales was cut short when he was accused of involvement in a supposed 'Popish plot' and after a period of imprisonment he was executed declaring he was dying 'for God and religion's sake'.

God of mercy and grace, on this day we recall the faithfulness, even to death, of your servant Philip Evans, whose work and witness in South Wales exemplified a deep faith and a true heart. May his example be a beacon of hope in the face of opposition and hate. Amen

John Lloyd, priest and martyr (1679)

John Lloyd was born at Brecon, entered the English seminary of Valladolid in 1649 and was priested in 1653. Returning to Wales, he pursued his ministry for the next twenty years before being arrested and imprisoned in connection with the so-called 'Popish plot'. He was executed with Philip Evans on 22 July 1679.

> **Remembering the ministry and martyrdom of John Lloyd today, we give thanks for his faithful service in Wales, in the face of religious scares and bigotry. Let us share in his work and his vision of the Christian life. Amen**

John Cassian, abbot (c 433) –
commemorated in some traditions on 29 February

A Romanian by birth, John Cassian became a monk in Bethlehem, went to Egypt with Germanus and later was made a deacon in Constantinople. A disciple of John Chrysostom, he pleaded John's cause with the pope before becoming a priest in Marseilles, establishing two monasteries, one for men and one for women. His writings, including *The Institutes and the Conferences*, were influential in the West, particularly in Benedictine monastic life, his views on Augustine's teachings more controversial.

> **We rejoice in recalling John Cassian's life and works, his defence of John Chrysostom, his influence on monastic life and his ministry as founder and abbot. May his challenging writings inform us today in our understanding of the faith. Amen**

24 July

Declan, bishop (early fifth century) –
commemorated in some traditions on 23 July

Born of noble blood into a Christian family of the tribe of Decies, Declan was brought up near Lismore in Ireland, then studied abroad and founded the church at Ardmore, where he became bishop. His ministry predated that of Patrick, who went on to give order and organisation to the Irish Church.

Loving God, we remember on this day the life of Declan, a bishop in Ireland before Patrick's mission and founder of the church at Ardmore. May his pioneering work inspire us in our own faltering steps in mission and ministry to others. Amen

25 July

James, apostle and martyr (44)

James 'the Great' was the son of Zebedee and brother of John, all fishermen from Bethsaida. James and John were called to follow Jesus and were known as the 'sons of thunder'. They were with Jesus as witnesses to Jesus' transfiguration and also in the Garden of Gethsemane. He was the first apostle to be martyred, put to the sword by Herod Agrippa. Said to have travelled to Spain to preach and promote the gospel, James became associated with Santiago di Compostella, where his relics were interred.

We celebrate the apostle James, present with Jesus at the transfiguration and at Gethsemane and martyred on the orders of Herod Agrippa. May his zeal and impetuosity be both a spur and a lesson to us in our demonstration of faith. Amen

Christopher, martyr (third century)

Christopher, so named as 'one who carries Christ', was, according to legend, a Canaanite of great status who became a Christian on discovering that even the Devil was afraid of Christ. Carrying a child over a river, Christopher could hardly get across and the child is said to have told him that he had carried 'him that created and made the whole world on his shoulders'. Because in legend it was thought that no one who looked on him would die that day, he became known as the patron saint of travellers and, later, of motorists.

God of great journeys, we recall Christopher, Christ-bearer, whose story has given comfort to wayfarers and travellers over the centuries. Let his choice of Christ over the Devil be an inspiration for our own lives. Amen

26 July

Anne and Joachim, parents of the Blessed Virgin Mary

According to John of Damascus, Anne and Joachim were a 'blessed and spotless' couple who led a devout and holy life and to whom, as parents of the Virgin Mary, much is owed.

God of great faithfulness, we thank you on this day for Anne and Joachim, parents of the mother of your Son. May their lives be an example of the importance of a holy education for our children. Amen

27 July

Brooke Foss Westcott, bishop, teacher of the faith (1901)

Born in 1825 and educated at Birmingham and Trinity College, Cambridge, Brooke Foss Westcott became a master at Harrow School and then Regius Professor of Divinity at Cambridge, where he wrote three celebrated biblical commentaries and shared in the preparation of a critical edition of the Greek New Testament, leading a revival in British biblical studies and theology. He also devoted energy to the training of students and encouragement of missions, founding the Clergy Training School in Cambridge, later renamed Westcott House. In 1890 he was consecrated Bishop of Durham.

Today we mark the life and achievements of Brooke Foss Westcott, theologian and biblical expert, who strove to develop and enhance the training of clergy for the good of the Church. Let us be thankful for his insights and for his tireless work to improve understanding among ministers. Amen

Pantaleon, doctor and martyr (c 304)

The son of a pagan father and Christian mother, Pantaleon became court physician to Emperor Galerius Maximanus, leading to pagan ways before being brought back to the faith by a Christian by the name of Hermolaus.

Thereafter Pantaleon sought to make amends, was denounced as a Christian by his colleagues, and in the Diocletian persecutions he was arrested, tortured and beheaded, having distributed all his possessions to the poor. He is honoured as the chief patron of physicians after Luke.

> God of healing and wholeness, we give you thanks for the life and service of Pantaleon, who not only practised the medical skills of the physician, but also returned to the true path of faith, for which he was martyred. May we honour his sacrifice and follow his example of care for others. Amen

28 July

Samson, bishop (565)

Born in Wales about the year 485, Samson was educated and ordained deacon at Illitud's school at Llantwit, where he was also priested. He left for the monastery on Caldey Island, becoming abbot. Missionary journeys followed, to Ireland and Cornwall, where he spent twenty-five years, founding monasteries there and in Brittany, where he established the monastery at Dol, which became a great centre of evangelism and where he took on an episcopal role.

> God of mission and movement, today we recall the ministry and mission of Samson, the wandering Celtic monk-bishop, who brought the good news in word and deed to many parts of the West of the British Isles and France. Let us rejoice at his energy and be glad of his success in planting the seed of faith in so many places. Amen

29 July

Mary, Martha and Lazarus, companions of our Lord (first century) – *in some traditions only Martha is commemorated*

These siblings lived at Bethany, close to Jerusalem, where they gave Jesus hospitality. Martha, the eldest, was particularly solicitous in ministering to

Jesus, was present for the raising of her brother, Lazarus, and recognised Jesus as the Messiah while her sister Mary washed his feet. She was also one of the women at the foot of the cross.

God of great generosity, on this day we commemorate Martha, Mary and Lazarus, who among them looked after Jesus in different ways, showing both affection and loyalty when others deserted him. May we show in our lives the same sense of service to you, Lord. Amen

Lupus of Troyes, bishop (478)

Born at Toul in the late fourth century, Lupus became a monk at Lérins and Bishop of Troyes in 426. He joined forces with Germanus of Auxerre in coming to Britain in 429 to preach against the Pelagian heresy. After engagement with Attila the Hun and following a period as a hermit, he resumed his diocesan role until his death.

God of great associations, we thank you for the active life and ministry of Lupus of Troyes, bishop and preacher, diplomat and hermit, who showed determination and faith in all he did. May we admire and acknowledge the work he did in Britain with Germanus and be glad. Amen

30 July

Silas (Silvanus), companion of Paul (first century) – *see under 13 July*

Peter Chrysologus, Archbishop of Ravenna (c 450)

Born at Imola in about 400, Peter was a deacon there, before becoming Bishop of Ravenna. Noted for his preaching on the gospels in clear and practical terms, he also enjoyed the patronage of Valentinian 3rd and his mother Galla Placidia in his church reforms and building projects, including those at the port of Classis.

We recall the sermons, reforms and building projects of Peter Chrysologus, Bishop of Ravenna, who left his mark both spiritually and architecturally. In rejoicing at his legacy, may we seek the clarity and practicality of his teaching style in our own learning. Amen

William Wilberforce, social reformer (1833)

Born in 1759 in Hull, William Wilberforce was educated at St John's College, Cambridge, and then became an MP, initially for Hull and then for Yorkshire. Converted to Evangelicalism and committed to lead a disciplined Christian life, he became a member of the 'Clapham sect' and supported missionary societies, helping to found the Bible Society. He is particularly known for his campaign for the abolition of the slave trade, for which he spoke eloquently and passionately in Parliament and which he lived to see implemented.

God of great objectives, we commemorate the oratorical skills and the campaigning, evangelical determination of William Wilberforce, who led the movement to abolish slavery. May we be inspired by his single-mindedness and his perseverance in pursuing this endeavour successfully. Amen

31 July

Joseph of Arimathea, disciple (first century)
– see under 17 March

Germanus of Auxerre, bishop (c 448) –
commemorated in some traditions on 3 August

Born at Ravenna about the year 378, Germanus trained and practised as an advocate in Roman law. Elected Bishop of Auxerre in 418, against his will, he showed himself to be a bishop of exceptional ability. He twice went to Britain to counter the Pelagian heresy, the second time also directing the British forces sucessfully against the Picts and the Scots. He later presented the case of the people of Brittany to the emperor at Ravenna, where he was known for his sanctity and miracles.

On this day we remember with grateful thanks the ministry and mission of Germanus of Auxerre, whose skills of advocacy, diplomacy and leadership won hearts and minds in Gaul and Britain, as well as Ravenna. May his example encourage us always to set our sights high for you. Amen

Ignatius of Loyola, founder of the Jesuits (1556)

Ignatius was the youngest of eleven children from a noble Basque family. He served as a soldier and was wounded fighting the French at the Battle of Pamplona in 1521. In a long convalescence he was converted after reading a Life of Christ and dedicated himself to prayer and penance and writing his Spiritual Exercises. Along with six disciples he sought the approval of the pope for an order dedicated to poverty and chastity, ready to go wherever the pope decreed. In 1540 approval was given and Ignatius became the first General of the Society of Jesus, directing the work of the order for sixteen years as it spread around the world.

Almighty God, today we recall and rejoice at the vision, insight and inspiration of Ignatius of Loyola, who changed his life from battlefield exploits to a life of dedication to spiritual work as founder of the Society of Jesus. Let his influence continue to work wonders in your world and may his spiritual exercises underpin our Christian life. Amen

August

1 August

Alphonsus Liguori, bishop, founder and theologian (1787)

Alphonsus was the son of a Neopolitan nobleman, studied law and practised as a barrister until losing a high profile case, whereupon he studied theology and was called to the ministry. Priested in 1726, he became famous as a preacher, re-founded a community of nuns and founded a congregation of priests known as Redemptorists in 1732, writing his most important work on moral theology, published in 1745, and becoming Bishop of Sant' Agata dei Goti in 1762. He was known for his gentleness, simplicity and clarity.

> **God of gentleness and patience, we give thanks for the great clarity of expression and simplicity of living of your servant Alphonsus Liguori, bishop and founder of the Redemptorists. May his moderation be an example and an inspiration for the way we lead our lives and develop our faith. Amen**

Ethelwold, Bishop of Winchester (984)

Born at Winchester, Ethelwold became a monk after serving at the court of King Athelstan. He was priested on the same day as Dunstan, serving under him at Glastonbury before re-establishing Abingdon Abbey and becoming Bishop of Winchester in 963. He went on to reform, found or re-found a number of monasteries, including Peterborough, Ely and Thorney. He was a champion of music and of vernacular writing, a translator of the Rule of St Benedict and possessed many practical and artistic gifts. He was also austere, demanding and known for his intransigence.

> **God of great gifts, on this day we mark the energy and achievements of Ethelwold, Bishop of Winchester, who galvanised the English Church in so many ways, reforming, founding and modernising monasteries and worship. Let us celebrate his ability to present and explain the wonder of your love for humankind in word, illumination and buildings. Amen**

2 August

Eusebius, Bishop of Vercelli (371)

Born in Sardinia, into a family persecuted for their faith, Eusebius was brought to Rome, where he was educated and became a priest. He served in the Church of Vercelli in Piedmont, where he later became its first bishop, living with his clergy in an organised community, founding, with Augustine, the Austin Canons. He suffered for his defence of orthodoxy against Arianism and is thought to have been involved in the composition of the Athanasian Creed. He worked with Hilary of Poitiers in the fight against Arianism.

Lord of reconciling love, we remember today the perseverance and suffering of Eusebius in his efforts on behalf of Athanasius against the Arians and to end the schism in the Church on this issue. May his resolute defence of orthodoxy be a beacon of hope and light for the true faith. Amen

Thomas of Hales (of Dover), Benedictine monk (1295)

Reported to have been the victim of a French raid on Dover, Thomas was said to have been a devoted and holy Benedictine monk who was killed in his bed by French soldiers.

Lord of life and death, we recall the untimely death of Thomas of Hales, a monk who had the misfortune to be murdered in Dover by a French raiding party. Let us mourn those who are the victims of random attacks and ask that they be welcomed into your kingdom, by your grace. Amen

Peter Eynard, priest and founder (1868)
– commemorated in some traditions on 3 August

Peter Eynard, a contemporary of John-Baptiste Vianney, was a parish priest and a member of the Marist congregation who founded the Priests of the Blessed Sacrament, among other communities of sisters and lay brethren.

God of mercy and sacrament, we celebrate today the life and works of Peter Eynard, his pastoral ministry as well as his founding of the Priests of the Blessed Sacrament. May his love for you inspire and enhance our service too. Amen

3 August

Germanus of Auxerre – *see under 31 July*

Peter Eynard – *see under 2 August*

Waldef, Cistercian Abbot of Melrose (c 1160)

The son of Simon, Earl of Huntingdon, Waldef (also the name of his grandfather) was brought up at the Scottish court and then became an Austin canon at Nostell in Yorkshire, becoming prior at Kirkham in 1134. Prevented by King Stephen from taking up his appointment as Archbishop of York, Waldef became a Cistercian and in 1140 was appointed abbot at Melrose, where he was known for his mercy, simplicity and kindness.

Lord of all, we thank you for the service and humility of Waldef, Cistercian abbot and founder of monasteries. Let us rejoice at his kindness and mercy and hope to emulate these qualities in our own lives. Amen

4 August

Jean-Baptiste Vianney, spiritual guide (1859)

Born near Lyons in 1786, the son of a peasant farmer, Jean-Baptiste became a shepherd on his father's farm and had little formal education before he began studying for the priesthood. What he lacked in academic performance he made up for in devotion and holiness. He served as a priest for most of his life in the village of Ars-en-Dombes, where he was known and loved as a preacher and confessor and which became a place of pilgrimage. He showed gifts of counselling inside and outside the confessional, underpinned by an abiding love of God.

Listening Lord, we celebrate the gifts of Jean-Baptiste Vianney, which brought thousands of pilgrims to his confessional. May we rejoice at his powers of insight into personal lives and his demonstration of the love of God at work. Amen

5 August

Sixtus 2nd, pope and martyr and companions (258)
– *see under 6 August*

Oswald, King of Northumbria, martyr (642) – *commemorated in some traditions on 8 or 9 August*

Born about the year 605, Oswald was the son of Ethelfrith, King of Northumbria, but was forced to flee to Scotland after Ethelfrith's death and became a Christian at Iona. Oswald eventually returned and defeated the tyrant Cadwalla, assembling his men round a wooden cross on the eve of the decisive battle. Oswald worked closely with Aidan, bringing unity and Christianity to Northumbria, but was killed by the pagan King Penda of Mercia in 642.

God of great endeavour, we recall on this day the feats of fortitude of Oswald, King of Northumbria, in defence of Christendom, working in partnership with Aidan. Let us give thanks for his skill and bravery in battle and his wisdom in faith and leadership. Amen

6 August

Sixtus 2nd, pope and martyr and companions (258) – commemorated in some traditions on 5 or 7 August

Sixtus became pope in 258 and only served for twelve months before the Emperor Valerian ordered the death of bishops, priests and deacons. He and some deacons were seized in a cemetery on the Appian Way while he was addressing a congregation of Christians and he died by the sword there and then, along with four of the deacons, and was buried in the cemetery of Callistus nearby.

God of service and sacrifice, we remember the short papacy of Sixtus, killed for his beliefs by a pagan emperor, along with four companions. Let us not forget the cost of discipleship in early Roman times, give thanks for the freedom to worship today and pray for those parts of the world where it is still dangerous for people to declare themselves Christians. Amen

7 August

Sixtus 2nd, pope and martyr and companions (258) – see under 6 August

Cajetan, founder of the Theatine Order (1547) – commemorated in some traditions on 8 August

Born at Vicenza in 1480 into a noble family and educated at Padua University, Cajetan only became a priest in 1516. Active in charitable works, serving the sick and the poor in confraternities of clergy and laity, he went on to found, with Pietro Caraffa, an order of clergy modelled on the lives of the apostles, which sought to restore the dignity and spirituality of worship, spearheading reform in the Church, notably in Verona, Venice and Naples, where he governed the house until his death.

Today we honour and celebrate the life and witness of Cajetan, bringing much needed order to the Church on apostolic principles. May we learn from his emphasis on worship, spirituality and care for the sick and the poor as core ingredients of our Christian life. Amen

John Mason Neale, priest, hymn writer (1866) – *commemorated in some traditions on 9 August*

Born in 1818, John Mason Neale was educated at Sherborne and Trinity College, Cambridge, where he was influenced by the Tractarians. A co-founder of the Cambridge Society and ordained in 1842, he played an important part in the revival of Catholic ritual in the Church of England. But it is as a hymn writer and translator of hymns from the Latin and Greek that he remains principally known, especially for Hymns, Ancient and Modern and the English Hymnal.

God of harmony and hymnody, on this day may we recall with grateful thanks the life and writing of John Mason Neale. Let the choirs of new Jerusalem rejoice with happy bands of pilgrims to laud and honour his name, to your praise and glory. Amen

8 August

Oswald, King of Northumbria, martyr (642)
– see under 5 August

Cajetan, founder of The Theatine Order (1547)
– see under 7 August

Dominic, founder of the Order of the Franciscan Preachers (1221)

Born in 1170 at Calaruega in Castile, Dominic was the youngest of four children, studied at Palencia, and became an Austin canon of Osma Cathedral, leading a disciplined life of prayer and penance, becoming a prior in 1201. Accompanying his bishop through France he came across the Albigenses, or Cathars, who held heretical beliefs, which he sought to change by preaching and, forming an Order of Preachers, approved by the pope in 1216, to combat such beliefs. Establishing friaries at Bologna and other places in Europe, Dominic's communities of sacred learning and sound teaching had a huge impact in securing the Orthodox faith in the medieval Church in Europe.

God of truth and light, we give thanks that you sent your servant Dominic to spread your word and practise your Son's teaching to such great effect. May his impact and the order he founded continue to influence our daily lives and learning in modern times. Amen

9 August

Oswald, King of Northumbria, martyr (642)
– *see under 5 August*

John Mason Neale, priest, hymn writer (1866)
– *see under 7 August*

Mary Elizabeth Sumner, founder of the Mothers' Union (1921)

Born in 1828 at Swinton, Mary Heywood married George Henry Sumner, then a young curate, in 1848. As a mother of three children, she called a meeting in 1876 which launched the Mothers' Union, based on the importance of baptism and parental example as the foundation stones of family life. The first Diocesan Conference of the Mothers' Union was held in 1887, later becoming an international organisation which encouraged the ideal of a Christian home.

God our Father, you gave to Mary the sacred job of becoming the mother of your Son. On this day we remember with gratitude the vision and perseverance of Mary Sumner in explaining and encouraging the principles of Christian family life, both nationally and internationally. May we seek to support and sustain that vision as the bedrock of our society today and tomorrow. Amen

Edith Stein (Teresa Benedicta of the Cross), religious and martyr (1942)

Born into a devout Jewish family at Breslau (near Wroclaw) in 1891, Edith was converted to Christianity on reading the autobiography of Teresa of Avila, becoming a leading light in the German Catholic Women's Movement. She became a Carmelite and took the name of Teresa Benedicta of the Cross, escaping the terror of Kristallnacht in November 1938 by being sent to the Netherlands, where later she and all Roman Catholic Jews were taken by the Nazis, and she was sent to Auschwitz and executed within a week of arrival.

God of mercy and transformation, we recall and acknowledge the witness of Edith Stein, convert and faithful religious, who endured exile and death for her origins and background. Let us never forget the terrors of that time in our own times, just as we never forget the sacrifice of your Son for us. Amen

10 August

Laurence (Lawrence), deacon at Rome, martyr (258)

Martyred a few days after Pope Sixtus 2nd as part of the persecution of Emperor Valerian, Laurence, a deacon, was given a few days to bring together the riches of the Church. Assembling the poor supported by the Church, he declared: 'Here is the treasure of the Church'. It is said that this caused him to be toasted on a gridiron, limb by limb, praying all the while, though some scholars suggest that he was beheaded.

Lord of great inspiration, today we remember Laurence, brave deacon of Rome, who defied attempts by Emperor Valerian's prefect to extract the Church's money by assembling the real treasures of the Church, the faithful poor. May this gesture and his subsequent painful death be an indication of faith and true worth in the Christian tradition. Amen

11 August

Attracta (Araght), nun (fifth or sixth century)
– see under 12 August

Clare of Assisi, founder of the Minoresses or Poor Clares (1253)

Born at Assisi in 1194, of a noble family, Clare, withstanding pressure to marry, was inspired by Francis, whom she joined and, renouncing her possessions and taking the habit of a nun, she was formed in the religious life. In 1216 she became abbess of a community of women seeking to follow a life of poverty and austerity, in the spirit of Francis. Though the movement spread across Europe, she never left her convent at Assisi, remaining devoted to a life of contemplation, serving her community with great joy.

On this day we recall and honour the contemplative life and devotion of Clare of Assisi, inspired by Francis and having an influence spreading across Europe through the founding of convents. Let her example show how the light of Christ can shine brightly through faith and such holiness. Amen

John Henry Newman, priest, tractarian and cardinal (1890)

Born in 1801, John Henry Newman first came under evangelical influence, entering Trinity College in 1817, becoming a fellow of Oriel in 1822 and ordained deacon in 1824. Gradually he developed a more

Catholic view of the Church, especially in the light of liberal trends in both politics and theology reducing the authority of the Church of England. As one of the leading tractarians, he was keen to see the Church follow a middle way between Roman Catholicism and Protestantism. However, he joined the Roman Catholic Church in 1845, continuing to influence Christian thinking in his writings, becoming a cardinal in 1879.

God of transformation. may we celebrate the intellectual power and personal rigour of John Henry Newman, influential churchman and writer. Let his faith journey show that the Christian path is not easy, but that staying true to belief is a foundation stone of faith. Amen

12 August

Attracta (Araght), nun (fifth or sixth century) – *commemorated in some traditions on 11 August*

Attracta, an Irishwoman, is said to have run away from home and given the veil as a nun by Patrick, then founded a shelter for travellers by Lough Gara, called Killaraght today. Surprising miracles were attributed to her.

God of vocations, we give thanks that you called Attracta to the devotional life as a nun and her foundation of a shelter for travellers. In our own travels may we experience the kind of hospitality she offered when we find ourselves without a refuge as we journey. Amen

Murtagh (Muredach), bishop (c 480)

A convert of Patrick, or possibly a contemporary of Columba, Murtagh is said to have become a presbyter towards the end of Patrick's mission to the West, staying in west Sligo and Mayo. It is also suggested that he became the first Bishop of Killala and the founder of Innismurray, a monastic island, where he lived as a hermit.

Today we honour the life and ministry of Murtagh, a protegé and companion of Patrick, who brought monasticism to the west of Ireland, becoming a hermit later in his life. Let us follow his example of simplicity in our way of life, alongside a quiet commitment to mission. Amen

13 August

Jeremy Taylor, Bishop of Down and Connor, teacher of the faith (1667)

Born in Cambridge in 1613, Jeremy Taylor was educated at Gonville and Caius College, becoming a fellow there and being priested in the same year, 1633. A chaplain to the Royalist forces in the Civil War, he was captured and imprisoned briefly and then went to Wales, becoming chaplain to Lord Carberry, where he wrote prolifically. His works on *Holy Living* and *Holy Dying* were two of his most influential treatises. He went to Ireland in 1658 and became the Bishop of Down and Connor in 1660, but came under attack from both Catholics and Protestants, which affected his health.

Lord of inclusion and diversity, on this day we acknowledge the lucidity of thought and active engagement of Jeremy Taylor in his life and writing. May we learn from the way he took things on – and took opponents on – but also be aware of the costs. Amen

Hippolytus, martyr (252)

A Roman priest, Hippolytus was also a controversial theologian who disagreed publicly with successive bishops of Rome, Zephrynius and Callistus 1st, and was banished to Sardinia, in the persecution of Maximinus, where he became reconciled with the Church and where he died, probably a martyr. However, other legends link him, erroneously, with a fictional figure who was put to death by being tied to wild horses and torn to pieces. His writings were rediscovered relatively recently and have been widely admired, especially his *Apostolic Tradition*.

God of mystery and tradition, today we mark the controversial contributions of Hippolytus, in his writings and pronouncements. Let us admire his outspokenness, which led to exile and death. Amen

Florence Nightingale, nurse, social reformer (1910)

Born in 1820, into a well-to-do family, Florence Nightingale was determined to train as a nurse, against her parents' wishes. This she achieved and in 1833 headed a private nursing institution in London. After many efforts to improve the conditions for treatment of the wounded during the Crimean War, she devoted the rest of her life to the reform of nursing care, especially at her school at St Thomas' Hospital, which was at the forefront of raising the status of nursing into a profession. She was an Anglican who held a personal mystical faith which meant a great deal to her, especially in her later years of poor health.

Lord of caring and healing, we remember the major contribution of Florence Nightingale to the health of the nation, her devotion to nursing matched by her personal faith. May we be inspired to integrate our work and personal faith by her example. Amen

14 August

Maximilian Kolbe, Franciscan priest, martyr (1941)

Born at Zdunska Wola near Lodz in Poland in 1894, of parents who were Franciscan tertiaries, Maximilian Kolbe entered the Franciscan Order in 1910. He studied in Rome and after contracting tuberculosis retired to Poland, teaching church history in a seminary and then publishing a Christian magazine, which gained a huge circulation. Imprisoned by the Nazis in Auschwitz, he volunteered to be a substitute for a man chosen to die because of an escape and after two weeks of starvation he received a lethal injection.

Generous and self-giving Lord, we commemorate on this day the life, example and self-sacrifice of Maximilian Kolbe, who took the place of a condemned man in Auschwitz. Let his courage and selfless faith remind us of our own saving grace through your Son's sacrifice and resurrection. Amen

15 August

The Blessed Virgin Mary –
commemorated in some traditions on 8 September

Pre-eminent among all the saints, Mary, the mother of Jesus, was a Jewish maiden, called Miriam in Hebrew, by tradition of the family of David and often described as 'the second Eve', who unlocks Eve's disobedience. According to John's Gospel, at the time of his death Jesus commended the care of his mother to 'the beloved disciple', which may explain why her final years are associated with both Jerusalem and Ephesus.

Father God, today we honour and venerate the life of Mary, the mother of your Son, whose humility and obedience brought about the revelation of your relationship with humankind through your Son. May we wonder at her faithfulness and rejoice at her response to your calling. Amen

Tarsicius, Roman martyr (third or fourth century)

Tarsicius was probably a young deacon in Rome who was carrying the consecrated sacraments when he was waylaid by a pagan mob who asked him what he was carrying. In trying to protect the host he was killed by his assailants.

Sacred Lord, we remember the steadfast defence of the holy sacrament by Tarsicius, set upon in Rome by a mob who searched him and beat him to death. Let his example of courage and witness be a beacon of hope and faith. Amen

16 August

Stephen, King of Hungary (1038)

Born at Esztergom in about 975, Stephen was the son of Geza, Duke of the Magyars. In 995 he married Gisela, the sister of Henry 2nd and in 1001 was crowned the first King of Hungary, bringing order and Christianity to the country and establishing a number of monasteries including the most famous at Esztergom. Severe with pagans and wrongdoers, Stephen also endeared himself to people through his accessibility and holds a special place in Hungarian history.

God of majesty and might, we commemorate the immense contribution to Hungary and to Christendom of Stephen, King of Hungary, known for his organisation of Church and State. May his accessibility and firmness of purpose be recalled with gratitude today. Amen

Rock (or Roch), healer (c 1380)

Born around the year 1350 at Montpellier, into a rich merchant family, Rock nursed the sick during an epidemic in northern Italy. He spent much of his life as a hermit or on pilgrimages, on one of which, to Rome, he is said to have caught the plague and was fed, and saved, by a dog. He was also said to have been taken for a spy and died in prison in Lombardy.

On this day we recall the short life of Rock, who went out of his way to cure and care for the sick, leading to his own illness. May we honour his dedication to healing and his appreciation of the place of animals in the healing process. Amen

17 August

Hyacinth of Cracow, Dominican friar and confessor (1257)

Known as the 'apostle of the north', Hyacinth was born of a noble family at Kammien and educated at Prague and Bologna. After being priested he joined the Order of Preachers and was sent to Cracow, establishing

Dominican houses here and elsewhere in Poland. Known as a wonderworker, he is said to have evangelised many parts of northern Europe during extensive missionary journeys.

God of north and south, east and west, we give thanks for the ministry and mission of Hyacinth, noted Dominican, who evangelised large areas of northern Europe. Let his missionary zeal inspire us today in rolling back secularism. Amen

Clare of Montefalco, Augustinian nun (1308)

At a young age Clare became a member of a community of Franciscan hermits, refounded as Augustinians, becoming abbess in 1291. Through her exposure to the Passion of Christ in austerities, ecstasies and miracles, she became famous as her cult began very soon after she died.

Today we honour and recall the devotion to the Passion of Christ of Clare of Montefalco, hermit and Augustinian nun. As we celebrate her spiritual heart, may we also seek to follow Christ through our own devotion and observance. Amen

18 August

Helena, empress, protector of the Holy Places (330)
– see under 21 May

Alipius, Bishop of Tagaste (c 430)

Born at Tagaste in Numidia in c 360, Alipius studied in Carthage under Augustine and then went to Rome, where he made a name for himself in the Law, but was converted to Christianity, with Augustine, in Milan before they returned to Tagaste. They moved on to Hippo to live in community and ordination as priests followed. Alipius was consecrated Bishop of Tagaste, keeping in close touch with Augustine, who had become Bishop of Hippo.

God of friendship and hope, we give thanks today for Alipius, close colleague of Augustine of Hippo, studying together and near neighbours as bishops. May their willingness to open up to each other help us to open up to you, Lord. Amen

19 August

John Eudes, founder of the Congregation of Jesus and Mary (1680)

Born into a farming family in Normandy and educated by the Jesuits at Caen, John Eudes was a priest of the French Oratory for twenty years, where he was noted for his preaching in missions and his care for the sick during epidemics. In 1643 he founded a new congregation for the education of priests in seminaries, which later founded refuges for fallen women. He was also responsible for providing a doctrinal basis to the devotion to the Sacred Heart, thus encouraging its spread.

Loving Lord, we give thanks today for the ministry and doctrines of John Eudes, faithful priest and founder. Let his love of preaching and devotion be an example and a model for our ministry to each other. Amen

20 August

Bernard, Abbot of Clairvaux, teacher of the faith (1153)

Born into a Burgundian noble family, Bernard, one of six brilliant brothers, entered the Benedictine abbey at Cîteaux in 1112, along with some of his companions and brothers. He was behind some of the reforms in Benedictine thinking at the time and established a new monastery at Clairvaux (literally 'Valley of Light'), where he built up the community, preached widely and gained fame for his theological thinking and both the vigour and rigour of his arguments, as a result of which hundreds of Cistercian houses were set up and his influence spread far and wide.

God of order and worth, we remember and celebrate the work and influence of Bernard of Clairvaux, who gave the Cistercian Order a new impetus across Europe. We thank you that, through his insights and efforts, he has influenced so many lives today. Amen

William and Catherine Booth, founders of the Salvation Army (1912 and 1890)

Born respectively in Nottingham and Ashbourne in 1829, William and Catherine (née Mumford) were married in 1855. William left the Methodist Church in 1861 as a result of criticism of his aggressive style of preaching and founded a revivalist mission in Whitechapel, London, known as the Christian Mission, shortly afterwards. This evolved into the Salvation Army, undertaking evangelistic, social and rescue work which developed into a worldwide denomination. Both William and Catherine were noted for their preaching, based on a strong moral fervour and commitment to the poor.

Saviour God, we give you great thanks for the ministries of William and Catherine Booth, drawn together in common aspirations for mission amongst the poor. May the worldwide impact of the Salvation Army they founded continue to bring hope and help to millions today and tomorrow. Amen

Oswin, King of Deira in Northumbria (651), martyr

Oswin was the cousin of Oswald, King of Northumbria. When his father Osric was killed by the pagan King Cadwalla in 634 he went south to Wessex for safety, but returned to Northumbria to become King of Deira. A devoted friend of Aidan, Oswin's virtue, moderation and humble manner were valued by his people and he ruled successfully and courteously, unlike his cousin Oswiu, who ruled neighbouring Bernicia and who had him put to death at Gilling after a betrayal.

God of trust, we recall on this day Oswin, King of Deira, who was genuinely loved for his kingly qualities of mind and courtesy before his untimely death. Let his legacy be that a monastery was founded in his memory and his virtues long remembered. Amen

21 August

Pius 10th, pope (1914)

Born at Riese in Venetia in 1835, into poor circumstances, Giuseppe Sarto was ordained priest in 1858, served as curate and rector and was made a canon of Treviso in 1875, Bishop of Mantua in 1884, and became patriarch of Venice and cardinal in 1893, succeeding Leo 8th as Pope Pius 10th in 1903. Aspiring to 'renew all things in Christ', his changes and reforms were far-reaching, especially those relating to Church-State relations, public worship, including frequent communion, and the revision of the Latin translation of the Bible. He was known for his simplicity of life, healing powers and obvious goodness.

God of healing and wholeness, we rejoice at the many and long-lasting contributions of Pope Pius 10th to your Church and to the life of Christians. May we look back and give thanks for his wisdom, energy and humility. Amen

Abraham of Smolensk, abbot (1221)

Born at Smolensk, Abraham became a monk there and immersed himself in biblical study and preaching. He had a large following among the laity, particularly the sick and disturbed, despite his stern character. Changes from the clergy led initially to his being disciplined by the bishop, who later reviewed his case, acquitted him and made him abbot of a monastery, where he saw out his ministry without any further trouble.

Lord of second chances, just as you gave humankind another chance through your Son, we remember today Abraham of Smolensk, whose ministry was restored by his bishop and who was regarded as a notable figure in Russia. May we be reminded by Abraham of your willingness to give us all a second chance. Amen

22 August

Symphorian, martyr (second or third century)

Hauled before the Roman governor at Autun in Gaul, apparently for showing contempt for a local goddess, Symphorian resisted all attempts to convert him from his beliefs, despite being flogged. Sentenced to death, his mother showed support and encouragement for him as he was led out to be beheaded.

We remember the suffering and steadfastness of faith of Symphorian in Roman Gaul, whose refusal to deny his faith led to his beheading. Let us learn from the example of his mother, who fearlessly continued to encourage her son, even to the point of his death. Amen

23 August

Rose of Lima, virgin (1617)

Born into a Spanish family in Lima, Peru, Isabel de Flores y del Oliva, known in infancy as Rose because of her beauty, supported her impoverished parents by growing flowers and taking on embroidery work. Taking a vow of virginity and influenced by Catherine of Siena, she became a Dominican tertiary and lived as a recluse in a hut in the garden. Through penances, mystical experiences and her sympathy for the sufferings of others, especially the poor and the sick among the Indian population, she was shunned by friends and family but heralded as the originator of social services in Peru.

God of grace, we thank you today for the life, witness and penance of Rose of Lima, who rejected the worldly, widespread corruption of the day to be true to you and to herself. May there always be those, like Rose, who stand out from the crowd to be faithful to you. Amen

Philip Benizi, Servite friar (1285)

Born at Florence in 1233, Philip Benizi was educated at the universities of Paris and Padua, studying medicine and philosophy, but soon after became a lay brother with the Servites at Monte Senario and then was priested, becoming the head of the order in 1267. Proposed as pope in succession to Clement 4th, he apparently hid himself away to avoid becoming a serious candidate. A talented and effective preacher, Philip was also a skilful peacemaker and a founder of the Servite nuns.

Lord of love and example, we give thanks today for the erudition and practical work of reconciliation of Philip of Benizi, Servite friar and founder of the Servite nuns. Give us a glimpse of his insights and motivation as we undertake our journey of faith. Amen

24 August

Bartholomew, apostle (first century)

Also known as Nathaniel, Bartholomew was one of the twelve apostles who was also present beside the sea of Galilee at the resurrection. He is usually associated with evangelistic work in Lycaonia, India and Armenia, where he is said to have met his death, a martyr. In the eleventh century an arm reported to have been Bartholomew's was given to Canterbury by Cnut's wife, Queen Emma.

God of great reach, we honour the apostle Bartholomew, who witnessed the miracle of the resurrection and who spread the gospel far and wide. Let us, like Bartholomew, see and believe through the witness of the disciples. Amen

Ouen, Bishop of Rouen (c 684)

Born around 600 at Sancy, near Soissons, Ouen became an important official at the court of the Frankish Kings, Clotaire 2nd and Dagobert 1st, receiving Holy Orders rather late in life, and became Bishop of Rouen in 641. He was a tireless evangelist in his diocese and founded monasteries as centres of learning and piety. Relics of Ouen were said to have been brought to Canterbury and placed with those of Wilfrid and Blaise in a chapel in the crypt of the cathedral.

Today we remember Ouen, high official and then priest and Bishop of Rouen, where he served with zeal and distinction. Create in us, Lord, that same desire and ability to spread the good news of your Way. Amen

25 August

Louis 9th, King of France (1270)

Born at Poissy in 1214, Louis became King of France at the age of 12 with his mother as regent. Marrying Margaret, elder sister of Eleanor, wife of Henry 3rd of England, in 1234, he showed himself to be a model Christian king, impartial and merciful, just and trustworthy, a man of integrity. He was sincerely religious and twice led crusades, both ending unfavourably, the second leading to his death, of dysentery.

King of kings and Lord of lords, we salute the Christian life and example of King Louis 9th of France, a ruler of integrity who sought to do the right thing for his people and his neighbours. May that integrity be a benchmark and a beacon to all those who hear his story. Amen

Joseph Calasanz, educationist and founder (1648)

Born at Peralta de la Sal in Aragon in about 1557, Joseph was educated at Estadilla, Lerida and Valencia and priested in 1583. Already committed to educating the urban poor, when he went to Rome in 1592 he was shocked by the squalor there among the ordinary people and in 1597 he established a free school in a slum area across the Tiber. This grew and became an institute with numerous priests and 1,200 students and was recognised as a religious congregation. These Piarist schools grew into an international movement.

Lord of learning, on this day we commemorate the calling of Joseph Calasanz to educate the urban poor in the worst districts of Rome and founding an institute and international order. May his vision inform and inspire the educational efforts in our most deprived areas today. Amen

26 August

Ninian, bishop and missionary (fifth century) – *commemorated in some traditions on 16 September*

After formation in Rome, Ninian is reputed to have come to Whithorn in Galway and built a stone church there inspired by and dedicated to Martin of Tours. He is also said to have been the apostle to the southern and possibly the northern Picts. His cult later spread to Kent and Denmark.

God of far and wide, we recall with gratitude the influence of Ninian on the Picts and on Whithorn, where he built a church. In honouring his memory may we commit ourselves to leaving a mark in your world to advance your kingdom and to your praise and glory. Amen

Elizabeth Bichier des Âges, foundress (1838)

Born at Château des Âges, near Poitiers, Elizabeth Bichier later lived with her widowed mother at La Guimitière in Poitou where, during the French Revolution, she organised secret worship meetings. An encounter with Andrew Fournet led to the establishment of a community of sisters, teaching girls and caring for the sick, known as Daughters of the Cross, leading to the opening of sixty small convents spread across southern France.

God of hope and help, we recall today the fruitful life and service of Elizabeth Bichier, who kept the flame of faith alive in difficult times during the French Revolution. Let her example and witness, in setting up the community of the Daughters of the Cross, show that even in the darkest hour, the light, your light of the world, will show itself. Amen

27 August

Monica, mother of Augustine of Hippo (387)

Born in North Africa into a pious family in 332, Monica married Patricius, a pagan who later converted to Christianity. They had three children, the eldest of whom was Augustine (also known as Austin), but she was left a widow when he was 18. Patient and persistent, Monica sought to restrain Augustine from his early excesses and dabbling in heresies. When, in 1883, Augustine went to Rome, Monica pursued him and, with the help of Ambrose, her prayers were rewarded when he committed himself to the Christian faith in 386 and was baptised in 387. On returning to North Africa that same year, she was taken ill and died at Ostia.

Lord of love and influence, let us rejoice at the patient care and persistent prayers of Monica, who never gave up on her wayward son, Augustine, and whose love was rewarded by his conversion and subsequent ministry. Bless all parents who seek the right balance between letting go and showing tough love. Amen

Caesarius, Bishop of Arles (543)

Born into a noble Gallo-Roman family at Chalons-sur-Saône in Burgundy, Caesarius served as a monk at Sérins, was priested and appointed abbot of a monastery which he successfully reformed, introducing a proper Rule. Becoming Bishop of Arles three years later, he showed remarkable skills as a preacher and in matters of liturgy, seeking to bring together worship and daily living in order to 'match your behaviour to the words you say'. He also set up an enclosed nunnery at Arles, to which he left most of his possessions.

Today we commemorate Caesarius of Arles, a great teacher, scholar and pastor, who brought order and integrity to monastic life and use of liturgy. May his holistic approach speak to us today in our efforts to bring relevance and order to our society. Amen

28 August

Augustine of Hippo, bishop, teacher of the faith (430)

Born in North Africa in 354, of a Christian mother and pagan father, Augustine initially had a Christian upbringing, but as a young man he neglected Christianity, preferring the study of philosophy and Manichaeism, taught rhetoric at Rome and Milan, and had a son by a long-term mistress. Coming under the influence of Ambrose in Rome and his mother's efforts, he was baptised, with his son, in 387 and in 391 was ordained priest, becoming Bishop of Hippo in 396. During his long episcopacy Augustine was a prolific writer on major theological themes, from the Trinity to original sin, from charity to the grace of God.

Great God, we offer you our thanks and praise for the life, works and ministry of Augustine of Hippo, who revealed your grace through his humanity and his writings. May we be informed and inspired by his special insights into your reconciling love for the world in and through Christ. Amen

29 August

The beheading of John the Baptist –
see under June 24 for the birth of John the Baptist

The forerunner and herald of Jesus Christ, in his death, John, son of Zachary and Elizabeth, was an itinerant preacher who gained many followers in his ministry of repentance and baptism. Soon after baptising Jesus, John was arrested and thrown into prison for condemnation of Herod's incestuous marriage to Herodias, who was his half-brother's wife. Taking revenge by tricking Herod into a rash promise, John was beheaded and, by his own suffering, showed that Christ also would suffer.

God of true promise, on this day we remember the sacrifice of John the Baptist, who always heralded and acknowledged Jesus as Lord, even unto death. Never let us underestimate the importance of his ministry and his message of the freedom of heavenly peace. Amen

30 August

John Bunyan, spiritual writer (1688)

Born at Elstow in Bedfordshire into a poor family, he probably acquired his knowledge and mastery of language from the Bible and was introduced to some Protestant texts by his wife, a woman of piety. He suffered much from repressive measures of the Royalists after the Restoration and wrote extensively while he was in prison. Best known for what is widely held to be a work of spiritual genius, *Pilgrim's Progress*, John Bunyan showed in his writings that salvation of the soul was what mattered most to him.

Master, friend, Saviour, may we rejoice at the inspiring life and work of John Bunyan, writer of *Pilgrim's Progress*, who saw that the world was full of spiritual warfare. May we never flinch from his message and from your grace abounding in bringing us salvation. Amen

Margaret Clitherow, one of the forty martyrs of England and Wales – *commemorated in some traditions on 25 October (1586)*

Born in York, Margaret was brought up as a Protestant, marrying John Clitherow, a butcher, in 1571. Becoming a Roman Catholic a few years later, Margaret actively professed her Catholicism, even though her husband, who became a chamberlain of York, remained a Protestant. Later imprisoned and charged with harbouring priests and attending Mass, she did not enter a plea, to avoid implicating others, and was sentenced to being crushed to death.

God of mercy and justice, we recall on this day the fortitude and single-mindedness of Margaret Clitherow, Roman Catholic activist and martyr. Let her faith and witness show through the religious divisions of her time, so that her character and faith shine through. Amen

31 August

Aidan, abbot, Bishop of Lindisfarne, missionary (651)

Born in Ireland, Aidan became one of Columba's monks in the monastery at Iona. He was chosen as a missionary to Northumbria, to replace a colleague who had failed in his efforts there. Aidan, however, succeeded in his more gentle and discreet approach and worked closely with King Oswald, who became a friend. From his base at Lindisfarne, through his evangelistic efforts of preaching, teaching and example of self-discipline and walking everywhere, he inspired widespread support and strengthened the Church beyond the boundaries of Northumbria.

God of great journeys, today we give thanks for all that Aidan brought to his ministry in Iona and Northumbria: his obvious pastoral heart, his gentleness and his holiness. Let his quiet persistence in mission be a strength of our ministry in your Church today, Lord. Amen

Eanswyth, virgin (c 640) – *commemorated in some traditions on 12 September*

Eanswyth was the daughter of Edbald, King of Kent, and the granddaughter of Ethelbert. Refusing to marry a prince from Northumbria, Eanswyth was trained as a nun in France and founded a nunnery in Folkestone, thought to be the first in England. Her remains were moved into the current church building there in 1138.

Transforming God, on this day we remember the selfless devotion of Eanswyth, who followed her faith in becoming a nun, forgoing the opportunity to marry a prince, and founding the first nunnery in England at Folkestone. May her memory encourage others making difficult decisions about walking in the way of the cross. Amen

September

1 September

Giles of Provence, hermit, abbot (c 710)

Thought to be Athenian by birth, Giles travelled to Provence, settling at the mouth of the Rhône as a hermit on land owned by Visigoth King Wamba, who reputedly wounded and crippled him with an arrow while hunting a hind which Giles was protecting. His fame spread and eventually his monastery was recognised by the pope. Giles has become known as the patron of the crippled and wounded.

God of the differently able, we celebrate today the devotion of Giles to your creation, living as a hermit in prayer and solitude, but as a witness to your love. May his example of drawing others in to this contemplative life demonstrate the power of the gift of your Son to change lives. Amen

Fiacre, hermit (seventh century)

Originally from Ireland, Fiacre (or Fiacra) travelled to France and was given a piece of land by Faro at Meaux, on which he built a hospice for travellers. Care and intercession were offered to the sick and his hermitage was known for the excellence of its vegetables, leading to his becoming the patron of gardeners. His name is also given to the French four-wheeler, the fiacre, because the cab-stand in Paris was near the Hotel Saint-Fiacre.

Lord of coming and going, on this day we celebrate the journey of Fiacre from Ireland to France, his establishment of a hermitage, hospice and garden and his care and intercession for the sick. Let his name be long remembered through his association with gardens, travel and the patients he looked after and prayed for. Amen

Drithelm, monk of Melrose (c 700)

Drithelm lived at Cunningham in greater Northumbria and experienced a momentous revival after apparently dying a few hours previously. As a result he spent the night in prayer and then gave away his possessions to his family and the poor after seeing a vision of the next life, including hell, purgatory and heaven. He spent the rest of his life as a monk at Melrose.

> **God of revelation and resurrection, we marvel at the experiences and vision of your servant Drithelm, who was given a glimpse of eternity which changed his life. May our recollection of this story heighten our awareness of our purpose in life and the destination you have prepared for us. Amen**

2 September

William of Roskilde, bishop (1070)

William was an English priest who accompanied King Canute to Scandinavia as his chaplain. There he stayed to preach the gospel, becoming Bishop of Roskilde and proving to be an excellent pastor, even standing up to the King, Sweyn Estridsen, in condemning his behaviour. After confessing his misdeeds, the king worked closely with William to bring Christianity to more people across the land.

> **Thank you, Lord, for the calling and bravery of William of Roskilde, who left his native land to work to your praise and glory in Scandinavia, showing himself a wise pastor and a strong diplomat. May we be inspired by his willingness to take risks for you, empowering God. Amen**

Lucian Tapiedi and the Martyrs of Papua New Guinea (1901 and 1942)

Two waves of martyrdoms were experienced in Papua New Guinea. First, in 1901, James Chalmers, Oliver Tomkins and companions, sent by the London Missionary Society, met their death. Later, in the Second World War, during Japanese occupation, a total of 333 Christians died for their faith, including Lucian Tapiedi and many priests, evangelists, teachers and nurses. Bernard Moore was shot while presiding at the Eucharist. Later, after the war, a revival took place.

Lord of all, on this day we remember the martyrs of Papua New Guinea, struck down in peace and war because of their faith and witness. Let their memorial be the strength of the Christian faith in that country today. Amen

3 September

Gregory the Great, pope, teacher of the faith (604)

Born in 540, Gregory was the son of a Roman senator and started his career working for the government, becoming a prefect of the city of Rome in 573. He founded six monasteries in Sicily and one in Rome, St Andrew, before becoming a monk there himself. Called out of the monastery by Pope Benedict 1st, he went initially to Constantinople, returned to Rome and was elected pope in 590. He proved to be a skilful diplomat, bringing about peace with the Lombards, initiated the conversion of the Anglo-Saxons through the mission of Augustine, was a prolific writer and a great pastor who came to be known as 'the servant of the servants of God'.

God of great enterprise, today we mark the life, ministry and inspiration of Gregory the Great, pope, pastor and principal architect of the re-evangelisation of England. As we rejoice in the Church today and face the challenges ahead, may we take heart from his achievements and his devotion to your will. Amen

4 September

Cuthbert, Bishop of Lindisfarne, missionary (687) – *see under 20 March*

Oengus Mac Nisse (or Macanisius) of Dalriada, Bishop of Connor (514)

Reputed to have been a hermit at Kells and a disciple of Patrick, Macanisius became Bishop of Connor. As an indication of his dedicated service, it is said that he carried his book of the Gospels on his shoulders, remaining hunched as he walked.

> **Holy God, we give thanks on this day for the witness and reverence shown by your servant Macanisius in his duties and his position when bearing the Gospels. Let us accept, with grace, his veneration of Scripture and his dedication to his ministry. Amen**

Birinius, Bishop of Dorchester (on Thames) (c 650) – *commemorated in some traditions on 3 or 5 December*

Born in northern Europe in the second half of the sixth century, Birinius became a priest in Rome and was sent by Pope Honorarius to continue the re-evangelisation of Britain, concentrating his efforts on King Cynigils and the West Saxons. Dorchester on Thames became his see and he built churches elsewhere in the area, extending also to Winchester. He became known as 'Apostle of the West Saxons'.

> **Father of all, today we celebrate the missionary life and work of Birinius, sent to Britain to extend the bounds of Christendom and establish the faith firmly among the West Saxons. May we note and learn from his persistent pastoral work and desire to establish churches wherever he went. Amen**

5 September

Laurence Justinian, Archbishop of Venice (1455)

Born of a noble Venetian family in 1380, Laurence lived devoutly at home before being drawn to the Augustinian monastery of San Giorgio, becoming a priest in 1406 and prior a year later and then general of the congregation in 1424. Although made Bishop of Castello in 1433, he preferred to delegate his administrative duties and be a preacher to his flock, but his appointment as first Bishop of Venice led him to embark on a period of reform, accompanied by practical writings and a book of prayers, all aimed at raising the standard of the clergy.

On this day may we honour the determination of Laurence Justinian to follow your Way and clear the path for Christians to follow by equipping clergy to do your will. Let the heavens rejoice at Laurence's response to your call as we seek out our own vacation. Amen

6 September

Cagnoald, Bishop of Laon (c 635)

The brother of Faro, Cagnoald was at Luxeuil under Columba and became Bishop of Laon. His sister, Fare, founded a nunnery, which became known as Faremoutiers, over which she presided for many years.

God of friendship and family, today we commemorate the life and ministry of Cagnoald, brother of Faro and Bishop of Laon. Let him be a beacon of your love, just as Laon stands out above the countryside as a sign of hope. Amen

Allen Gardiner, founder of the South American Mission Society (1851)

Born in 1794, Allen Gardiner joined the Royal Navy as a young man, resigning in 1826. After the death of his wife in 1834 he devoted himself to missionary work, first amongst the Zulus for the Church Missionary Society, founding the city of Durban. Less successfully, he became absorbed in the desire to evangelise the tribes of South America and died on the shores of Tierra del Fuego after being shipwrecked. The work of the South American Mission Society, which he founded, is a legacy of his efforts and vision.

God of great strength, we thank you for the selfless missionary work of Allen Gardiner in South Africa and South America, bringing little immediate reward but a lasting legacy. Let us acknowledge and learn from his thwarted efforts and his passionate zeal. Amen

7 September

Cloud, prince (560)

Born in 522, Cloud was the son of Clodomir, King of Orleans, who was killed when he was only three and so Cloud was brought up by his grandmother, Clotilde. Narrowly missing being murdered by his uncle, he renounced all claims to the Frankish throne, became a monk and was known for his good works, founding a monastery near Paris, in an area known as St Cloud.

God of peace, we thank you today that Cloud found a way of life away from power and violence, offering hope and help to the poor and the pious. Let his wisdom touch our hearts and heal our souls. Amen

8 September

The birth of the Blessed Virgin Mary, the mother of Jesus Christ

Chosen by God to be the mother of his Son Jesus Christ, Mary is accorded pre-eminence among all saints by many churches. This festival in honour of her birth is celebrated on this day in both Eastern and Western Churches, falling, as it does, nine months after the Feast of the Conception of Mary and representing the boundary between the old and the new covenants and the start of the dispensation of grace.

Father God, on this day we rejoice at the birth of the Blessed Virgin Mary, the mother of your Son, Jesus Christ, and wonder at her faith and fortitude. Endow us with the patience and the care she showed in all that she did and all that she was and remains for us now. Amen

9 September

Ciaran of Clonmacnoise, abbot (c 545)

Born in Connaught, the son of a carpenter, Ciaran left home, driving a cow to sustain him, in order to be trained by Finnian at Clonard. Moving to Enda on Aran Island in c 534, he was ordained priest there, before going eastwards to Senan and then to Clonmacnoise on the Shannon, where he founded a monastery but died shortly afterwards. The monastery became an outstanding centre of prayer and study.

Today we remember the life and inspiration of Ciaran, who followed your guiding hand in his formation and in his founding of the monastery at Clonmacnoise, which became greatly influential in Ireland. Let his initiative and encouragement to others be a source of motivation to our own faith journey. Amen

Peter Claver, Spanish Jesuit priest, missionary to black slaves (1654)

Born in Catalonia in 1580, Peter Claver was educated at Barcelona University, becoming a Jesuit at Tarragona in 1600. He came under the influence of Alphonsius Rodriguez at college in Palma, Majorca, and was sent to Cartegena in what is now Colombia, where he was priested in 1616. Thereafter his work was principally with the black slaves who arrived in Cartegena, caring for them, baptising them and doing his best to follow up his contacts in the mines and on the plantations where they went to work. He also ministered to others in need, both white and black, and stood up for them against the rich and powerful.

God of high and low, your servant whom we remember today, Peter Claver, showed us how to care for those without wealth and position and to fight their cause. May his example inform our own lives, with the help of your Holy Spirit. Amen

Charles Fuge Lowder, priest (1880)

Born in 1820, Charles Lowder studied at Exeter College, Oxford, where he became influenced by the Oxford Movement and, after ordination, was a supporter of the Tractarians. Moving to London in 1851, first as a curate in Pimlico and Stepney and then as a vicar in the London Docks, he was not only dedicated and tireless in his ministry to the poor and destitute, but he was fiercely supportive of faith, even in the face of complaints to his bishop about his practices.

Lord of order and integrity, on this day we recall the pastoral ministry and attention to liturgical practice and ritual of your servant Charles Lowder, in particular his service in London's docklands. Let his combination of servanthood and ordered worship be prized and acknowledged in our own day and age. Amen

10 September

Finnian of Moville, abbot (579)

Reputedly of royal birth, Finnian was educated partly at the monastery founded by Ninian at Whithorn. Returning to Ireland after some twenty years in Scotland, he founded a monastery at Moville around 550 and one later on at Dromin. It is said that one of his pupils was Columba and that he was responsible for bringing to Ireland its first copy of the Vulgate version of the Bible. Finnian became known as 'the master and teacher of the saints'.

God of greatness and majesty, today we commemorate the pioneering work of Finnian of Moville, missionary in Scotland and 'teacher of the saints' in Ireland. Let his mastery of ministry and the Scriptures be a model for holistic priesthood and discipleship and shape our own faith in present times. Amen

Nicholas of Tolentino, Austin friar (1305)

Born in the march of Ancona and named after Nicholas of Myra, Nicholas joined the order of friars of St Augustine at the age of 18, being priested in

1269. He lived in various friaries before settling in Tolentino, where he became known for his tireless pastoral work among the poor, the sick and the dying and as a powerful and popular preacher. A number of spectacular conversions and miracles were attributed to him and he acquired the reputation of a wonder worker.

God of wonder, on this day we commemorate the dedicated life and work of Nicholas of Tolentino, who demonstrated the power of prayerful pastoral ministry and popular preaching. May we learn from him how to harness the power of the Holy Spirit to do your will. Amen

11 September

Deiniol, abbot and bishop (584)

Deiniol, possibly descended from a Celtic chieftain of North Britain, was the founder of the monasteries of Bangor Fawr in the Menai Strait and of Bangor Iscoed on the River Dee. These became large and famous, numbering 2,000 monks before they were desecrated by the pagan King Aethelfrith. Deiniol is best known for helping his fellow bishop Dyfrig to persuade David to speak out against the Pelagian heresy at the Synod of Brefi in 545.

God of truth and light, today we give thanks for the persuasive powers and leadership qualities of Deiniol, who played a significant role in defeating the Pelagian heresy. May the diplomacy and support for David of 'the first Bishop of Bangor' be long remembered. Amen

12 September

Eanswyth, virgin (c 640) – *see under 31 August*

Ailbhe, Irish bishop (c 526)

Ailbhe is said to have been a holy man and a powerful preacher and teacher who obtained for Enda the gift of an Aran island in County Galway from King Angus of Munster. There is a monastic rule attributed to him, though it may have been written later and dedicated to him in recognition of his leadership in doctrinal matters.

Omniscient and immanent God, we honour the memory of Ailbhe, Irish bishop, who demonstrated in his life what he wrote in his rule, by being the servant of all, humble and kind and warlike against the worldly. May his rule be our watchword too. Amen

13 September

John Chrysostom, Bishop of Constantinople, teacher of the faith (407)

Born at Antioch in 347, the son of an army officer, John was brought up by his mother, studied law and only became a monk in about 373 and then a special assistant to the bishop, being priested in 386. He became known as a powerful and practical preacher, which led to his being known as 'Chrysostom' or 'Golden Mouth'. He was elected Archbishop of Constantinople in 398 and set about reforming the Church, making enemies along the way, and was exiled twice. He is honoured as one of the four great Greek doctors of the Church. His works are still relevant and applicable today, including the *Baptismal Instructions*.

We give thanks today for the reforming zeal of John Chrysostom and his ability to communicate important Christian messages in relevant ways. Let his forthright insights and practical approach be appreciated as much in present times as they were in his day. Amen

Notburga, domestic servant (c 313)

Born about the year 1265 into a peasant family, Notburga became the kitchen maid at the castle of Count Henry. Caught giving waste food destined for the pigs to the poor of the area, she was dismissed, but continued the practice at her next place of employment. She was later recalled to the castle and became the patron saint of hired hands in Bavaria and the Tirol.

Servant and Lord of all, today we remember the service and selflessness of Notburga, who sacrificed her employment to feed the poor. As we give thanks, may we examine our hearts and be prepared to do the same. Amen

14 September

Holy Cross Day

Early in the fourth century, after the persecution era, pilgrims travelled to Jerusalem to visit and worship at the places connected with the life, death and resurrection of Jesus. This included Helena, the mother of Emperor Constantine, who in the course of overseeing excavations reputedly uncovered what was believed to be the cross on which Christ was crucified. A basilica was built on this site and dedicated on this day in 335, the holy cross gradually replacing the fish as the symbol of the Church.

On this day we commemorate the discovery of the cross of Christ by Helena, the mother of Emperor Constantine, and rejoice at this universal symbol of the Christian Church. Let it always inspire and inform our lives and our journey of faith. Amen

15 September

Cyprian, Bishop of Carthage, martyr (258) – *commemorated in some traditions on 16 or 26 September*

Born at Carthage around 200, Cyprian was an orator, a teacher of rhetoric and an advocate before his conversion to Christianity at the age of 46.

Yet only two years later, in 248, he was made Bishop of Carthage. He was a powerful advocate for church unity, while going against papal authority on returning heretics, to whom he showed compassion. When persecution returned under Valerian he refused the emperor's requirement for all to participate in pagan worship, as a result of which he was first exiled and then condemned to death and beheaded.

God of great compassion, we thank you today for the pastoral compassion and courage of Cyprian, who sought the unity of the Church and resisted pagan practices imposed by the emperor. Help us to retain pastoral sensitivities in the face of secular provocation. Amen

Catherine of Genoa, mystic (1447)

Born into a noble Ligurian family, Catherine, a serious and sensitive girl, was married at the age of 16 to a rich, carefree and spendthrift man, Julian Adorno, who was unfaithful to her and rarely at home. Catherine became a Christian and then converted her husband. Together they devoted themselves to the care of the sick in the hospital of Pammatore. After the death of her husband, who had become a Franciscan tertiary, she underwent a further deepening of her faith through visions, daily communion and long fasts, while continuing her charitable activities.

Lord of charity and change, on this day we recall with grateful thanks the life and witness of Catherine of Genoa, who turned her life round and that of her husband through following your way and developing her faith, all the while showing charity to others. Let this example be a beacon of hope to us all in a troubled world. Amen

16 September

Cyprian, Bishop of Carthage, martyr (258) –
see under 15 September

Ninian, bishop and missionary (fifth century)
– see under 26 August

Cornelius, pope and martyr (253)

Born in Rome, Cornelius was elected pope a year after Fabian's martyrdom in 250 and came up against Novatian, a Roman priest who was opposed to any practice of leniency towards wrongdoers and who set himself up as a rival pope. Although supported by Cyprian and vindicated by councils in Carthage and Rome, he was banished in the persecution to Civitavecchia, where he declined and may well have been beheaded.

Lord of justice and forgiveness, we hold up to you today your servant Cornelius, who showed clarity and mercy in his time as pope during a period of dissension and persecution for the Church. May we honour his efforts and acknowledge his martyrdom in paying our respects. Amen

Edward Bouverie Pusey, priest, tractarian (1882)

Born in 1800 and educated at Eton and Oxford, Edward Pusey was elected a fellow at Oriel College in 1823. After a period in Göttingen and Berlin he returned to Oxford as Regius Professor of Hebrew in 1828 when he was also priested. Becoming attracted to the Oxford movement by contributing a Tract in 1834, Pusey added lustre to the movement and helped to lift the Tracts from pamphlets to treatises. He was much revered by his contemporaries for his austerity, his preaching and his encouragement of the revival of the religious life within the Church of England and was a stout defender of the Athanasian Creed.

On this day we celebrate the great contribution to the life of the Church of Edward Pusey, scholar, priest and Tractarian. May we learn from his diligence in little everyday things, as well as his efforts to make holiness a concept for all. Amen

17 September

Hildegard, Abbess of Bingen, visionary (1179)

Born at Bockelheim in Germany in 1098, Hildegard had powerful visions from an early age and, influenced by her foster-mother Jutta, an abbess, became a nun herself and later succeeded Jutta as abbess. Her vision featured 'the reflection of the living light' which deepened her faith and understanding of God's creation. After twenty years she moved her sisters to Bingen and founded another house, combining her gifts as pastor, composer and teacher and writing three visionary works.

God of visions and radiance, today we commemorate the inspiring life and work of Hildegard of Bingen, abbess and visionary, who brought us pure glimpses of your creation. May we always allow you to return to the centre of our lives, however far we stray, recognising that we owe our very existence to you alone. Amen

Robert Bellarmine, theologian, Archbishop of Capua, cardinal (1621)

Born at Montepulciano in Tuscany, Robert Bellarmine was a polymath, able to debate, write verse and play the violin. He became a Jesuit in 1560 and soon became engaged in debates with Protestants at Louvain, where he studied Hebrew and engaged in preliminary work for the revision of the Vulgate, becoming Rector of the Roman College in 1592 and after being appointed cardinal in 1599, became Archbishop of Capua in 1602. His latter years were spent writing in Rome.

Lord of insight and inspiration, on this day we recall the bright star Robert Bellarmine, able critic of Protestantism but saintly in his temperate spirit towards those with whom he debated. Let us value both his words and the manner of his debating and learn from his example. Amen

Lambert of Maastricht, bishop and martyr (1095)

Born at Maastricht of a noble Christian family, Lambert was the pupil of Bishop Theodard, who was murdered on the road. Chosen to be his successor, Lambert proved to be an able bishop for some thirty years, some of which were spent in exile in Stavelot. Known as a great evangeliser in Kemenland and Brabant, Lambert was the victim of a blood feud, or possibly was killed in revenge for his opposition to the adulterous relationship of Pepin of Herstal, an East Frankish mayor, with his sister-in-law.

Today we remember the life of Lambert of Maastricht, evangeliser and martyr, whose outspokenness against sin led to his murder. Let his long ministry as bishop be a witness to his devotion to you and a model of service to the Church. Amen

18 September

Joseph of Copertino, Franciscan priest, ecstatic (1663)

Born of poor parents at Copertino, near Brindisi, Joseph was a sickly child and thought to be slow-witted. On becoming a stable boy at the Franciscan convent of Grottella he improved to such an extent that he was admitted as a friar and was ordained priest in 1628. Thereafter he practised severe austerity, experienced ecstasies and demonstrated miraculous powers of healing and levitations. Treated with severity by his superiors, he was excluded from celebrating Mass publicly for thirty-five years and moved from one friary to another, ending his years in seclusion at Osimo.

Lord of miracles and manifestations, on this day we recognise and wonder at the life and experiences of Joseph of Copertino, given special insights and powers and putting them to use in your name. Let us be grateful that he remained humble and obedient in the face of opposition and disbelief. Amen

19 September

Theodore of Tarsus, Archbishop of Canterbury (690)

Born at Tarsus around 602, Theodore was an Asiatic Greek, educated in Athens, and was appointed by Pope Vitalian to the vacant see of Canterbury on the death of the archbishop elect, Wighard, in Rome. Accompanied by Adrian, Theodore came from Rome and immediately embarked on a visitation throughout England, then called the Synod of Hertford in 673 which gave shape and order to the English Church. Theodore's legacy was the unification of the disparate elements of the English Church, forming a framework for the diocesan system which largely survives today.

> **God of order and outreach, we recall today the great enterprise of visitation and organisation which Theodore of Canterbury undertook in bringing together the English Church and giving it a lasting structure. Let us be always thankful that he was chosen and sent to undertake this great work with us. Amen**

Januarius, bishop and martyr (c 305)

Januarius was Bishop of Benevento, who was martyred with six companions at Pozzuoli, near Naples. Januarius' dried blood, preserved in the cathedral at Naples, is displayed in public three times a year and regularly liquefies, sometimes as a harbinger of important events.

> **On this day we commemorate the martyrdom of Januarius, Bishop of Benevento, and six companions. May the blood relics be a reminder of sacrifices made and unexplained events in our own faith journeys. Amen**

20 September

John Coleridge Patteson, first Bishop of Melanesia, and his companions, martyrs (1871)

Born in London in 1827, John Coleridge Patteson was educated at Eton, where he was influenced by George Augustus Selwyn. After ordination he went to work in the Pacific Islands at the age of 28, later becoming Bishop of Melanesia. He trained local evangelists to spread the gospel, a method which proved successful. Mistaken for European slave traders by the islanders of Nukapu, he was killed in his boat and two of his companions later died of tetanus.

God of hope and sacrifice, today we recall with thanks the great work of mission in the Pacific islands of John Coleridge Patteson and his companions, cruelly killed in revenge for the actions of European slave traders. May their work live on in the work of the Church in Melanesia today. Amen

Martyrs of Korea (1839)

Forbidden to practise Christianity in Korea, converted Christians from China continued to worship, despite those discovered suffering death. A bishop and two priests sent by Pope Pius 7th worked in secrecy and poverty to minister to the growing number of Christians, but violent persecution followed their discovery and martyrdom followed for the priests, including the first Korean priest to be martyred, Andrew Kim.

On this day we commemorate the dedication and bravery of the persecuted Church in Korea in the nineteenth century and the early martyrs in that country. As we learn of the persecuted Church in other countries of the world today, may we hold in our hearts those who gave their lives in the early days of the Church in Korea. Amen

21 September

Matthew, apostle and evangelist (first century)

A tax collector of Jewish race, working for the Romans, Matthew, also known as Levi, was called by Jesus from his custom house to follow him. The author of the first Gospel, it is thought that Matthew was eventually martyred in Ethiopia or Persia.

God of the Gospels, today we recall and honour Matthew, evangelist and apostle, who swapped worldly wealth for poverty at the call of Jesus, but who then captured the greatest story ever told in his gospel account. May we wonder at the miraculous way this man who was regarded as a publican and sinner was transformed through your Son's call. Amen

22 September

Maurice and companions, martyrs (c 287)

According to Eucherius of Lyons, Maurice was the commanding officer of a Roman legion of Christian soldiers from Egypt, known as the 'Theban Legion'. Ordered to take part in heathen sacrifice to the gods before going into battle to put down a Gallic rebellion by Christians, Maurice and his fellow officers refused to return from Agaunum, where they were camped, to take part in the sacrifices. The emperor ordered them to be decimated (every tenth killed) and it is said that continued refusal led to repeated decimation until all were killed, though the extent of the mutiny and killing is in doubt.

God of truth and faith, we commemorate on this day the martyrdom of Maurice and companions, cut down for refusing to take part in heathen sacrifices and dying for their faith. May we be humbled by such sacrifices and inspired by such commitment. Amen

Thomas of Villanova, Archbishop of Valencia (1555)

Born at Fuentellana in Castile in 1488, Thomas was educated at Villanova de los Infantes, where his father was a miller. After studies at Alcalá University he joined the Augustinian friars at Salamanca, was priested in 1517 and became prior in 1519. Made Bishop of Valencia, rather against his wishes, he proceeded to live an austere way of life and gave much away to the poor and needy, with special care for the position of converted Moors, and restored order among the clergy and laity with tact and discretion. He gave away all his money and possessions before his death.

God of charity and generosity, we thank you today for the selfless devotion and life of care for the sick and needy of Thomas of Villanova, who also showed himself to be a wise Archbishop of Valencia. Let his humble example be a model for leaders in our Church today. Amen

23 September

Adamnan (Eunan), Abbot of Iona (704)

Born in County Donegal about 624, Adamnan was descended from a grandfather of Columba, whose life he wrote. After a period as a monk in one of Columba's monasteries, he moved to Iona and was elected abbot there in 679. He did not endear himself to his community by espousing the Roman calculation of Easter, but did much to bridge the gulf between the Celtic and Roman traditions as he travelled widely between Scotland, England and Ireland, retiring to Iona just before his death.

We honour the memory and celebrate the life and work of Adamnan, Abbot of Iona, tireless reuniter of Celtic and Roman traditions, and biographer of Columba. Let his writings and regulations be acknowledged and remembered as important stepping stones of faith in our islands. Amen

Thecla of Iconium, virgin (first century)

Thecla, a native of Iconium in Asia Minor, was reputed to have been converted by St Paul, whereupon she broke off an engagement and dedicated her life to God. Condemned to be put to death by magistrates, first by fire, then by wild beasts, the wind and the beasts refusing to co-operate, she survived and escaped, becoming a preacher and miracle-worker in Isauria.

Lord of life, today we marvel at the conversion and miraculous escape from martyrdom of Thecla, who safeguarded her virginity through faith. Let her experiences give heart to all those women discriminated against for decisions against the cultural norm in following their faith. Amen

24 September

Gerard of Csanad (Gerard Sagredo), bishop and martyr (1046)

Born in Venice about 980, Gerard became a monk and studied at Bologna. After a period as abbot he was diverted from taking up a solitary life in the Holy Land when an abbot from Hungary persuaded him to linger there and he became tutor to King Stephen's son, Emeric, and he was made Bishop of Csanad. On Stephen's death a resurgence of paganism led to his being attacked while crossing the Danube and killed by a lance.

God of great opportunities, we remember on this day the broken journeys and seized opportunities of Gerard of Csanad, whose ministry in Hungary was special. Let his veneration as Venice's first martyr be a mark of his esteem in the eyes of fellow Christians, alongside Stephen. Amen

Robert of Knaresborough, hermit (1218)

Born in York into the family of an important townsman, Robert took holy orders early in life and was briefly a novice at the Cistercian Abbey in Newminster before choosing to live as a hermit at Knaresborough and then at Rudfarlington. After a series of temporary recluses he returned to Knaresborough, where following the destruction of his hermitage he repaired to a cave, remaining there for the rest of his life.

Lord of simplicity and solace, today let us rejoice at the life of Robert of Knaresborough, who kept close to creation and therefore close to you. In his acceptance of places to stay and to worship in commune with nature, let him be an example to us of the simple life of trust and faith. Amen

25 September

Finbarr of Cork, hermit, abbot and bishop (623)

Born at Connacht but active in Munster, Finbarr studied at Macroom under Bishop MacCuirp and then became a hermit at Gougane Barra in West Cork, gathering disciples around him. His greatest work was the establishment of the monastery at Cork, which formed the heart of the present city. He was honoured as a teacher and a loving man, and was consecrated bishop in c 600.

God of great endeavour, let us honour on this day the founding work of Finbarr in establishing the monastery at Cork and his loving ministry as hermit and bishop. May his holiness and encouragement of others be an encouragement to our discipleship. Amen

Lancelot Andrewes, Bishop of Winchester, spiritual writer (1626)

Born in 1555 in Banbury and educated at Merchant Taylors' School and Cambridge, Lancelot Andrewes was ordained priest and later appointed bishop, first of Chichester, then of Ely and, in 1619, of Winchester. He was a key figure at the Hampton Court Conference in 1604 which embarked on the reform of the Church of England, as well as in the translation of much of the Old Testament in what became known as the 'authorised version' of the Bible. His preaching, prayers and writing reflected his gentle nature and holy life.

Today we celebrate the life and works of your servant Lancelot, who through his preaching, writings, translating and pastoral ministry, brought many people closer to your kingdom. Let your light continue to shine through his example. Amen

Cadoc, abbot (sixth century)

A contemporary of David, Cadoc was a leading figure among the monks of South Wales and the traditional founder of the monastery that became known as Llancarfan, near Cardiff. Far-fetched stories of his transportation on a cloud to Benevento in Italy should not detract from his sterling work as an important missioner in Wales.

> **Lord of mission and might, on this day we celebrate and give thanks for the ministry of Cadoc, one of the leading figures of the Welsh Church, who founded Llancarfan monastery and extended the bounds of Christendom. May we remember him with gratitude. Amen**

Sergei of Radonezh, Russian monastic reformer, teacher of the faith (1392)

Born at Rostow of a noble family, Sergei and his parents were driven from home by civil war and settled near Moscow, farming the land. He and his brother Stephen became monks together and founded the monastery of the Holy Trinity, re-establishing the community life lost in Russia under the Tartars. He went on to found forty other monasteries but refused the metropolitan see of Moscow, while being consulted by Russian princes in danger of engaging in civil war. Known as a 'peasant saint', he taught humility, neighbourliness and service to his monks and is Patron of All Russia.

> **God of all creation, we commemorate on this day the great influence of a humble 'peasant saint', Sergei of Radonezh, Patron of All Russia, who founded monasteries and prevented wars amongst princes. May his example of selfless concern for his fellow humanity inform and inspire our place in the world in your creation. Amen**

26 September

Cyprian, bishop and martyr (258) – see under 15 September.
Also commemorated in some traditions on 16 September

Cosmas and Damian, martyrs (c 303)

Born in Arabia, brothers Cosmas and Damian studied the sciences in Syria and became doctors, showing great skills in healing both humans and animals without charging any fee. Known for their faith and acts of charity, they were invoked as patron saints of physicians. They were martyred at Cyrrhus during the Diocletian persecution, on the orders of Lysias, governor of Cilicia.

> **God of healing and hope, today we recall the skills and charity of Cosmas and Damian, physicians who ministered and healed without seeking recompense, and who are known as the patron saints of doctors. May we who put health and wholeness high on our list of priorities never forget that faith sustained them, even till death as martyrs. Amen**

Nilus of Rossano, abbot (c 1005)

Nilus worked in the treasury at his local town but when he lost his mistress and their child in 940, he became a monk in a Greek monastery at Palma in Campania. Known for his wisdom, holiness and austerity, he became Abbot of St Adrian's at San Demetrio Corone. Under pressure from the Saracens, he withdrew his monks to Monte Cassino in 981, moving on after fifteen years and eventually going to what became their permanent home at Grottaferrata in 1004.

> **We thank you, Lord, for the goodness and austerity of Nilus of Rossano, who was a monk for forty years and as abbot secured a permanent home for his monks, after many displacements, at Grottaferrata. Let his wisdom and single-mindedness be beacons of faith even today. Amen**

Wilson Carlile, founder of the Church Army (1942)

Born in 1847 in Brixton, Wilson Carlile, despite a spinal weakness which hampered his education, had a successful business career before he entered the London College of Divinity and was ordained priest in 1881, serving his curacy in Kensington. There he became concerned at the dislocation between the Church and the working class, leading him to begin outdoor preaching, and in 1882 he founded the Church Army, seeing it grow immediately under his leadership as Chief Secretary.

God of Christian soldiers, on this day we commemorate and celebrate the vision of Wilson Carlile, founder of the Church Army, who put evangelism at the heart of the Church. May his power of witness be an inspiration to the work of the Church today, especially in areas of both material and spiritual deprivation. Amen

27 September

Vincent de Paul, founder (1660)

The son of a peasant farmer at Pouay in the Landes, Vincent was educated by the Franciscans at Dax, and then at Toulouse University, and was ordained priest at the early age of 19. It is said that working under Peter de Bérulle and a period of ministry among galley slaves, convicts and victims of wars changed his life to one of service to the poor. He organised groups of lay people for charitable work and founded the Congregation of Mission (known as Vincentians or Lazarists) in Paris in 1625 and later, in 1633, the Daughters (or Sisters) of Charity. Vincent became a legend of selfless devotion to love of God and neighbour.

Lord of love and mercy, today we honour the selfless ministry of Vincent de Paul, whose life was transformed through his experience of helping the outcasts of society and who sought to bring this austerity into the heart of the Church's work. Let that mission continue in his tradition in present times and needs. Amen

28 September

Wenceslas, Duke of Bohemia and martyr (929)

Wenceslas was the son of Wratislaw, Duke of Bohemia, and was educated mainly by his grandmother, Ludmilla, a Christian, and at a college in Budweis. On the death of his father, his mother, Drahomira, a pagan, seized the regency and proceeded to conspire against Ludmilla, who was murdered. A few years later Wenceslas took over power and ruled in a benign, Christian way. However, his brother Boleslav contrived to have his brother killed, delivering the coup de grâce himself. Wenceslas and his grandmother were acclaimed as martyrs and Wenceslas became the Patron Saint of Czechoslovakia and then the Czech Republic.

God of standards and principles, we look on Wenceslas and give thanks for his goodness and his efforts to rule in a Christian way against great opposition, even from his own family. We acknowledge his status as Good King Wenceslas and honour his memory today. Amen

Lioba, abbess (c 700)

Born in Wessex, Lioba, a distant relative of Boniface, was educated at Minster-in-Thanet and then at Wimborne in Dorset, where she was a nun under Abbess Tetta. At the request of Boniface, she then led a group of thirty nuns to join in his evangelisation of Germany by setting up convents. They established a community at Bischofsheim where they learnt Latin and did domestic and garden manual work, but underpinned by the public prayer of the Church. Intelligent, beautiful and kind, Lioba was able to prepare many of her nuns to take up positions as abbesses in other churches.

God of great leadership, on this day we offer our heartfelt thanks for the important role of Lioba in support of Boniface's mission to Germany and the patient and kindly way she fulfilled this role, preparing and training others. Let our succession planning learn from her example. Amen

29 September

Michael and All Angels

Michael, Gabriel and Raphael are depicted in the Bible as the beloved messengers of God. Michael's name means 'Who is like God', appearing in Daniel as 'one of the chief princes' of the heavenly host and as protector of Israel, and in Revelation as the slayer of the dragon: hence his being regarded as the protector of Christians from the devil, particularly those at the point of death. Gabriel, meaning 'Strength of God', was sent by God to announce the birth of Christ to Mary, while Raphael, meaning 'The Healing of God', restored sight to Tobit.

> **God of angelic powers, we commemorate today the role of your angels Michael, Gabriel and Raphael as instruments of your will and guardians of Christians over the centuries. May we expect your angels anywhere we go, knowing they are keeping watch for you. Amen**

30 September

Jerome, doctor of the Church, translator of the Scriptures, teacher of the faith (420)

Born at Strido in Dalmatia in about 342, Jerome was brought up a Christian and studied at Rome, but was not baptised until he was over 18, coming to Christ in a conversion experience at Triers. After a period at Antioch he went to Syria as a hermit, learning Hebrew in order to study the Scriptures better. Together with his skills in rhetoric he was equipped to embark on the translation of the Bible into Latin, known as the Vulgate, for the latter part of his life settling in Bethlehem teaching, writing and studying

> **God of great communication, on this day we celebrate the learning and scholarship of Jerome, whose rhetorical and translation skills were shaped and honed in his formative years and were given expression through his translation of the Bible, used for a thousand years. May we stay the course in our own enterprises of faith and turn to Jerome for inspiration. Amen**

Honorius, Archbishop of Canterbury (653)

Sent as a missionary to the English to join Augustine by Pope Gregory in 601, Honorius succeeded Justus as the fifth Archbishop of Canterbury in 627. He was instrumental in sending Felix to evangelise East Anglia and appointed the first Englishman to be a bishop, the Kentish Ithamar of Rochester, who in turn consecrated the first English Archbishop of Canterbury, Frithona (Deusdedit) in 655.

Lord of new beginnings, today we mark the ministry and mission of Honorius, fifth Archbishop of Canterbury, who provided a link between Augustine and future English bishops. May his wisdom in overseeing change and further mission be honoured and recognised. Amen

October

1 October

Thérèse of Lisieux, Carmelite nun (1897)

Born at Alençon in 1873, into a watchmaker's family, who moved to Lisieux after her mother's early death, Thérèse followed her sisters into a Carmelite convent. She did not take full orders as a nun because of her frail health, but she carried out her duties in an exemplary fashion, making the ordinary things important. Encouraged to write, she completed her autobiography, which was only published after her death from tuberculosis at the age of 24. Known as *The Story of a Soul*, the work was hugely popular because of its message that holiness is accessible to anyone faithfully doing the small things right, her 'little way', the routine duties of daily life performed in the spirit of the love of God.

> **God of the extraordinary in the ordinary, today we cherish the memory of Thérèse of Lisieux, novice nun and advocate of 'the little way'. May her transparent holiness be a comfort and an encouragement in our daily round and common demanding task alike. Amen**

Remigius, Bishop of Rheims, Apostle of the Franks (533)

Born around 438 in Gaul, to a noble family, Remigius studied at Rheims, becoming its bishop at the age of 22. He baptised Clovis 1st, King of the Franks, following the restoration to health of his sick infant son and a spectacular victory on the battlefield, along with three thousand of his subjects. Not only did Remigius achieve success in preaching the gospel, baptising many more, creating dioceses and building churches, but the ampulla of chrism oil associated with him was used at the coronation of French monarchs.

> **Lord of great events, on this day we give thanks for the life and ministry of Remigius, Bishop of Rheims, whose notable achievements in bringing monarchs and ordinary people to you through preaching and healing inspired a nation. Let his efforts find their reward in our renewed commitment to mission. Amen**

Anthony Ashley Cooper, Earl of Shaftesbury, social reformer (1885)

Born in 1801, Anthony Ashley Cooper became a member of Parliament in 1826 and, upon succeeding his father as the seventh Earl of Shaftesbury, he entered the House of Lords, where his passion was to bring reform to social abuses, especially seeking protection for children and women in mines and factories. He also sought improvements in housing and created schools for the poor. A Christian philanthropist with strong evangelical Anglican principles, he worked tirelessly within the political system to redress and counter social evils.

God of great reforms, let us celebrate and give you thanks for the life and work of Anthony Ashley Cooper, peer and social reformer, whose spiritual energy was directed at countering evil and fostering justice. May we take heed of the principles and beliefs which drove him and renew our efforts to combat injustice in our world today. Amen

2 October

Thomas of Hereford, bishop (1282) – *commemorated in some traditions on 3 October*

Born at Hambledon in Buckinghamshire into a noble Norman family, Thomas was educated at Oxford, Paris and Orléans and probably ordained by the pope in Lyons in 1245 during the Council of Lyons. From being Chancellor of Oxford he briefly became Chancellor of England under Simon de Montfort and was elected Bishop of Hereford in 1275. Known as a man of discipline and temper, he nevertheless displayed pastoral skills and stood up for the humbler members of his flock against the wealthy, living an austere life, but generous and caring towards others.

God of might and mercy, we celebrate the life, ministry and work of Thomas, Bishop of Hereford, who contributed much in both worldly and spiritual ways to society, championing the poor and taking on the powerful. Let his fearlessness and personal austerity guide our own actions done in your name. Amen

Guardian Angels

The existence of guardian angels was supported in the Old Testament (Psalms, Judith), referred to by Christ (Matthew) and accepted by early Christians (Acts). While very different from human saints, God's angels are often celebrated and invoked in similar ways, often in the form of individual angels acting as a person's guide, protector and friend.

On this day we ask that our individual guardian angels watch over us and keep us safe. May all guardian angels be blessed with your holy insights, your grace and favour, your assurance that they will always see your face in their work of protection. Amen

Leger, Bishop of Autun, martyr (679)

Born around 616, Leger was educated at the court of King Clotaire 2nd and by a priest in Poitiers, becoming a deacon, archdeacon and, in 663, Bishop of Autun. A reforming bishop who built churches and cared for the poor, Leger fell victim of power struggles after the death of Clotaire 3rd and was pursued by the army of Elbroin, the Neustrian palace-mayor, caught and mutilated before being beheaded.

God of history and hope, today we recall with admiration the difficult challenges faced by Leger, Bishop of Autun, and the way he dealt with them, fearlessly and faithfully. May the good that he generated outweigh the strife that he experienced. Amen

3 October

Thomas of Hereford, bishop (1282) – *see under 2 October*

The two Hewalds, martyrs (695)

Anglo-Saxons, born in Northumbria, Hewald 'the dark' and Hewald 'the fair' (distinguished by their hair colour) were priests and missionaries who followed Willibrord into Frisia, preaching the gospel to continental Saxons. After a time, fearing the end of their traditional religion and customs, their hearers seized them and put them to death, Hewald 'the fair' immediately and Hewald 'the dark' after slow torture, their bodies being thrown into the Rhine.

> **Lord of courage and constancy, today we know and give thanks for the bravery of the two Hewalds, who travelled far to spread the gospel and who were met with fear and violence despite their best efforts. May we salute their mission and their martyrdom. Amen**

Josepha Rossello, foundress (1880)

Born in 1811 into the large family of a potter, Josepha showed initiative from her childhood. In 1837 she began voluntary work in Liguria amongst girls and young women with the blessing of the Bishop of Savona. This developed into the congregation of Daughters of our Lady of Mercy, offering hospitals, schools and rescue homes extending as far as Buenos Aires, and even a home for the encouragement of vocations to the priesthood authorised by the Bishop of Savona.

> **God of great vocations, we thank you for the vocation that led Josepha Rossello to set up houses, hospitals and other institutions to save principally girls and young women and later to help discern vocations for the priesthood. We rejoice at her courage and initiative in spearheading this work and ask that her qualities may be found in many today. Amen**

4 October

Francis of Assisi, friar, deacon, founder of the Friars Minor (1226)

Born at Assisi in 1181, the son of a wealthy cloth merchant, Francis, christened John but called Francesco, led an eventful and carefree youth, but experience of war and illness matured him. While at prayer in the run-down church of San Damiano, he heard a voice saying 'Go and repair my house, which you see is falling down'. Dedicating his life to both repairing the church and serving Christ through working with the poor, Francis found himself leading a growing order of friars, known as the 'Friars Minor', and later, with Clare of Assisi, he founded the community of the Poor Ladies. A man of considerable spiritual insight and strength, his deep love for Christ and redeemed creation showed in all he said and did, not least in his close rapport with animals.

We celebrate the life and works of Francis of Assisi with the awe and wonder he felt for your creation, Lord. Let his founding of the Friars Minor, the Poor Ladies and the Tertiaries be a legacy of his devotion to you and his commitment to building Christian communities. Amen

5 October

Maurus, abbot (sixth century)

Maurus grew up under the care of Benedict for his education and he became a monk, and Benedict's assistant, at the monastery at Subiaco. There his sense of obedience led him, at Benedict's command, to save the young Placidus from drowning in miraculous circumstances, Maurus apparently walking on the water to achieve the rescue. Later Benedict called him to join him at Monte Cassino, before moving on to France, where he is said to have founded the abbey at Glanfeuil, now called St Maur-sur-Loire.

God of miracle and majesty, today we give thanks for the faithful ministry of Maurus, assistant to Benedict, and founder of Glanfeuil Abbey. Let his marvellous works speak of his dedication to you and be an inspiration to us. Amen

6 October

William Tyndale, translator of the Scriptures, Reformation martyr (1536)

Born in Gloucestershire in about 1494, William Tyndale studied at Magdalen Hall, Oxford, from 1510 till 1515 and then at Cambridge.

Gifted at languages, he commenced the project of translating the Bible from Greek into contemporary English. Failing to get the support of the Bishop of London, he left England in 1524, never to return. Settling in Hamburg, he proceeded with the translation and had the New Testament published in Cologne and shipped to England in 1526. Denounced by the church hierarchy, it was banned and burnt and Thomas More led the attacks on him with obsessive ferocity. Pursued by agents, he nevertheless completed the task and wrote many powerful texts before he was tracked down, strangled and burnt at the stake in 1536. His translation has formed the basis of all Bibles in English ever since.

God of the Scriptures, on this day we honour and celebrate the groundbreaking and sacrificial achievements of William Tyndale, who made the Bible accessible to all by his masterly translation. Let his legacy be that we can understand your Word and learn your ways with a directness that brings us closer to you. Amen

Bruno, founder of the Carthusian order (1101)

Born at Cologne in about 1030, into a noble family, Bruno was educated in the cathedral school at Rheims, where he was ordained priest and where he later returned to become rector of the cathedral school, teaching, among others, the future Pope Urban 2nd. In 1084 he established, with his companions, a primitive monastic community at Chartreuse based on the model of an oratory with small cells surrounding it and an austere regime. Called by Pope Urban 2nd to be his adviser, he went to Italy but was soon allowed to set up another foundation like Chartreuse (giving the Carthusian order their name) at La Torre, where he remained, writing that only those who have experienced it can know the benefit and delight to be had from the quietness and solitude of a hermitage.

Lord of serenity and solitude, we recall today the vision of Bruno for solitary living in community that characterises Carthusian life and that developed with the help of Pope Urban 2nd. May our Christian life benefit from elements of the Carthusian emphasis on devotion, silence, austerity and solitary living. Amen

7 October

Justina of Padua, virgin and martyr (c 300)

Justina was a victim of the persecutions by the Roman Empire, probably under Maximian, leading to a church being dedicated to her in Padua, where she was greatly revered.

Today we remember one of the many victims of persecutions in the Roman Empire, Justina, whose name has long been commemorated in Padua. In honouring her, let us also recall the countless other victims whose names are known only to you, Lord. Amen

Osith, Anglo-Saxon princess (c 700)

Born at Quarendon, Osith was the daughter of Frewald, a Mercian prince, and was married young to Sighere, King of the East Saxons, perhaps to try to consolidate Christianity in Essex. Their son, Offa, became King of the East Saxons, by which time Osith had founded a convent at Chich, near Colchester, where she died a violent death at the hands of Danish pirates, because of her constancy of faith and virtue.

God who rewards faithfulness, we thank you on this day for the service of Osith who, after bearing Offa, her son, gave her life to you and resolutely met her death at the hands of Danish raiders, refusing to forswear her faith. May her steadfastness fuel our resolute love for you. Amen

8 October

Alexander Penrose Forbes, Bishop of Brechin (1875)

Born in Edinburgh, his father a judge, Alexander Penrose Forbes, after a period with the East India Company, came back to Britain for health reasons and studied at Oxford, coming under the influence of Pusey. Ordained priest in 1847, he went to serve in a deprived part of Leeds and very quickly was appointed Bishop of Brechin, a diocese which included Dundee, where he ministered to the poor and to the victims of a cholera epidemic. Known for his controversial views on the doctrine of the presence of Christ in the holy sacrament, he was supported by John Keble and the Tractarians and, in turn, he had a powerful influence on the Scottish Episcopal Church.

> **Lord of mystery and imagination, be present with us as we commemorate the life and work of Alexander Penrose Forbes, pioneer Bishop of Brechin, who ministered to the people of Dundee during a cholera epidemic and wrote powerfully of the Eucharist. May his example and his writings inform and encourage our own ministry. Amen**

Demetrius of Sirmium, soldier, martyr (fourth century)

Known as 'The Great Martyr' in the East and later in the West, Demetrius was reputed to have been a deacon who was also a warrior and who was killed without trial for preaching Christianity in the time of Maximian. Many churches in the Balkans are named after him and his name was associated with keeping away evil spirits.

> **As we recall Demetrius of Sirmium in Serbia on this day, may we honour his fearlessness in proclaiming the gospel at a time of persecution. Let us give thanks for his example in resisting evil. Amen**

Pelagia, actress of Antioch, penitent at Jerusalem (fifth century)

A beautiful and notoriously dissolute actress and dancer at Antioch, Pelagia was said to have been noticed by Bishop Nonnus of Edessa, who declared that her profession put bishops to shame in their efforts to care for their flock. Later, Pelagia was converted on hearing one of his sermons, was baptised and thereafter dedicated her life to Christ and lived as a hermit on the Mount of Olives at Jerusalem, dressed as a man known as Pelagius.

God of change and chance, we give you thanks today for the conversion and witness of the actress and dancer, Pelagia, following her providential contact with Bishop Nonnus. We rejoice at her change of heart and change of lifestyle and her dedication to you for the rest of her life, living as a hermit. Amen

9 October

Denys, Bishop of Paris, and his companions, martyrs (c 250)

Born in Italy, Denys was sent, with five other bishops, as a missionary into Gaul and preached with great success in Paris, establishing a Christian centre on an island in the Seine. Along with his companions Rusticus and Eleutherius, he was imprisoned and all three were beheaded. The abbey built over their tombs was dedicated to St Denys and became the resting place of French monarchs, Denys becoming the Patron Saint of France.

God of great callings, on this day we celebrate the life and mission of Denys and his companions, martyred in Paris. May his name be long remembered and as Patron of France may the success of his mission to Gaul be a reminder to us that his sacrifice was not in vain. Amen

Robert Grosseteste, Bishop of Lincoln, philosopher, scientist (1253)

Born into a poor family at Stradbroke in Suffolk in about 1175, Robert Grosseteste is thought to have been educated in Lincoln, Oxford and Paris. He lectured at Oxford before becoming the University's Chancellor and then, briefly, Archdeacon of Leicester, before his election as Bishop of Lincoln in 1235. His intellectual interests were very wide and included the sciences and languages, as well as theology, writing extensively in all of these areas. As bishop he carried out reforms and was known for his energy and dedication, carrying out regular and frequent visitations.

We give thanks today for the tireless ministry, extensive writing and reforming zeal of Robert Grosseteste, Bishop of Lincoln. Let his energy and dedication be a spur to the ministry of your Church in our times. Amen

John Leonardi, founder of the Clerks Regular of the Mother of God (1609)

Born at Lucca, John Leonardi was an apothecary who studied to become a priest and was ordained in 1572. He went on to found a congregation of priests living under vows dedicated to the reform of clerical life, putting this into practice himself when he was asked by Pope Clement 8th to reform the communities at Vallombrosa and Monte Vergine. He is also known for his co-founding of the Roman College called Propaganda.

God of order and reform, on this day we celebrate John Leonardi's life, ministry and inspiration as founder of the Clerks Regular of the Mother of God. May we always value the efforts of those who seek to re-order to make better rather than reform for reform's sake. Amen

10 October

Thomas Traherne, Metaphysical poet, spiritual writer (1674)

Born in Hereford about1636, Thomas Traherne was educated at Brasenose College, Oxford, and in 1657 became rector of Credenhill and then, in 1667, private chaplain to the Lord Keeper of the Seals. Only one of his writings was published before his death and his poetry, for which he is now best known, was only published at the beginning of the twentieth century, having only been in manuscript till then. His poems border on the pantheistic, concentrating on the glory of creation, and are the most celebratory and least orthodox of those of the Metaphysical poets.

Lord of creation, today we celebrate the creative inspiration of Thomas Traherne, chaplain, poet and spiritual writer, one of the group of Metaphysical poets. We recall his great gifts and wonder at the impact of his writings, even till this day. Amen

Francis Borgia, Jesuit priest (1572)

Born in 1510 into a noble family, the son of the Duke of Gandia, a descendant of a former pope (Alexander 6th) and also a king (Ferdinand 5th), Francis was appointed by Emperor Charles 5th as viceroy of Catalonia and then in 1543 inherited the title of Duke of Gandia. After his wife died in 1546 he secretly joined the Society of Jesus, renounced his dukedom in favour of his eldest son, and was ordained priest in 1551. After preaching extensively in Spain and Portugal as commissary for those countries, Francis was elected father general of the Jesuits, in which capacity he extended the work of the Order overseas, including the Americas, and won people over with his kindness and courtesy.

Holy Lord, we give thanks today for the life and ministry of Francis Borgia, model governor and enterprising and visionary father general of the Jesuits. We rejoice at his care for all and the inspiration of his leadership, which we value to this day. Amen

11 October

Canice (Kenneth), bishop and abbot (c 600)

Born around 525 in modern (London)Derry, Canice was educated by Finnian and Clonard, becoming a friend of Columba, whom he may have accompanied to Scotland and on Columba's mission to the Picts. On return to Ireland, he founded the monastery of Aghaboe in Ossory. He was known as a lover of the countryside and animal life and the medieval cathedral at Kilkenny is dedicated to him.

Lord of creation, on this day we recall the pioneering work of Canice in both Ireland and the Western Isles of Scotland, in partnership with Columba. Let his love of countryside and animal life inspire us to do the same, whether we live in town or country. Amen

Ethelburga, Abbess of Barking (675)
– commemorated in some traditions on 12 October

The sister of Erkenwald, Bishop of London, Ethelburga was probably both owner and abbess of the joint monastery of Barking and possibly of royal blood. Known for her holiness, her duty of care and various miraculous events around her, she showed herself to be a match for her brother.

Caring God, we thank you for the faith and witness of Ethelburga, Abbess of Barking, who showed in her rule and holiness her worth in your sight and in the eyes of those around her. May she be remembered alongside her brother Erkenwald, Bishop of London, as a shining example of your love. Amen

James the Deacon, companion of Paulinus of York (seventh century)

James, a deacon, accompanied Paulinus from Italy to Northumbria and assisted him in his monastery there, even staying behind to preach and baptise after the death of King Edwin at the hands of Penda, which precipitated Paulinus' journey south with Queen Ethelburga. He took part in the deliberations at the Synod of Whitby in 664 as a long-term supporter of the Roman calendar. He was also known for his love of the Roman method of chanting and for his 'nobility of soul'.

We thank you on this day for the loyalty and bravery of James the Deacon, companion to Paulinus and steadfast defender of the faith. We ask that his contribution is known, valued and built on today. Amen

John 23rd, pope (1963)

Angelo Giuseppe Roncalli was born in a small village called Sotto il Monte in Lombardy, Italy, in 1881, the fourth of fourteen children of parents who were poor sharecroppers. He entered the seminary at Bergamo at the age of 12 and went on to study for his doctorate in theology, being ordained priest in 1904. He became a bishop's secretary but was drafted into the Italian army in the First World War as a chaplain and stretcher-bearer. He served as a Vatican visitor and as an archbishop in various countries, including Bulgaria, Greece and Turkey, saving thousands of Jews during his ministry, and was made Patriarch of Venice in 1953. Appointed pope in 1958, he embarked on significant reform in the Vatican, culminating in the ecumenical council known as Vatican 2 in 1962. His papacy was characterised by an emphasis on serving the poor and apologising for the anti-Semitism of some of his predecessors.

> **Lord of challenge and change, on this day we commemorate the life and reforming ministry of Pope John 23rd, who came from humble beginnings but made a significant difference to your Church in its mission, while staying true to your purpose. May his example be an inspiration for our times. Amen**

12 October

Ethelburga, Abbess of Barking – *see under 11 October*

Wilfrid of Ripon, bishop, missionary (709)

Born into a noble family in Northumbria around 633, Wilfrid was educated at Lindisfarne, but was dissatisfied with aspects of Celtic teaching and went south to Canterbury and then to Rome, where he studied with Boniface, followed by three years at Lyons as a monk. He returned to take up the appointment of abbot at Ripon and was a leading figure at the Synod of Whitby (664), successfully arguing the case for the adoption of the Rome calendar. Spells as Bishop of York and Bishop of Hexham followed, interspersed by disputes resolved in Rome and an important period of missionary work among South Saxons and in Friesland, paving the way for the great English mission to the Germanic peoples.

> **Lord of mighty endeavours, we remember today the great and varied ministry of Wilfrid, as bishop and missionary, and the master of theological argument. May we appreciate and wonder at his impact on the Church in Britain and on the continent of Europe. Amen**

Elizabeth Fry, prison reformer (1845)

Born in 1780 at Earlham in Norfolk, Elizabeth was married at 20 to a Quaker merchant, Joseph Fry. In 1811 she was made a minister in the Society of Friends and became a noted preacher. In 1816 she began her prison work in Newgate Prison, working with female prisoners, and in 1820 helped to set up a night shelter for the homeless in London. In campaigning for prison reform she gave evidence at a House of Commons Committee. Possessing a gift of relating to people by touching their hearts through her own religious beliefs and compassion, she also travelled the country inspecting lunatic asylums.

Let us on this day give thanks for the belief and compassion of Elizabeth Fry, which led her to do great things for you, in prisons and asylums, seeking justice and reform. May we be inspired by her witness as we confront the issue of fairness in the world today. Amen

Edith Cavell, nurse (1915)

From a clergy family, Edith was born in 1865 at Swardeston. After training as a nurse she worked with the Red Cross in Belgium and at the outbreak of the Great War found herself caring for the wounded on both sides, while helping British soldiers to be smuggled out of Belgium into Holland. Arrested in 1915 and sentenced to death, she was executed by firing squad, forgiving her executioners.

God of courage and character, as we remember Edith Cavell today, we recall her dedication to nursing and her refusal to leave her post in Belgium, even with the war raging about her. Above all, let her heroic endeavours to help British soldiers to freedom, resulting in her own capture and execution, be saluted. Amen

13 October

Edward the Confessor, King of England (1066)

Born about 1004, Edward was the son of Ethelred 2nd ('The Unready') and Emma, sister of Duke Richard 2nd of Normandy. Educated first at Ely, then in Normandy, he returned to England in 1041, succeeding to the throne the following year, ending the Danish supremacy. In 1045 he married Edith, daughter of Earl Godwin, a marriage that is said to have remained unconsummated. Edward had a reputation for holiness, availability, and generosity to the poor. He was also a peace-loving man whose religious devotion led him to endow the Abbey of Westminster, where he was buried.

God of grandeur, on this day we recall with gratitude the generosity and holiness of a peace-loving monarch, Edward the Confessor, who reigned in difficult times, but left a legacy in endowing Westminster Abbey. When we enter that place, may we draw inspiration from his vision and his devotion to you, Lord. Amen

14 October

Callistus 1st, pope and martyr (c 222)

Callistus started life as a slave who, after some financial dealings that were wrong, was convicted and sentenced to hard labour in Sardinian quarries. On his release he was emancipated from slavery with the help of Marcia, a Christian and mistress of the emperor. Made a deacon, he was put in charge of the Christian cemetery on the Appian Way. In 217 he was made pope, an appointment which was opposed on doctrinal and disciplinary grounds, but he died in mysterious circumstances a few years later. Because of his background and journey from slave and convict to pope, he was known as the champion of forgiveness.

God of forgiveness, we recall on this day the miraculous prayer of Callistus' life and faith, journeying from slavery and convict to Bishop of Rome. May his witness and example show how anything is possible if we have faith. Amen

Esther John, missionary and martyr (1960)

Born Qamar Zia in India, Esther John, as she became known, attended a Christian school, which led to her quietly accepting the Christian faith and running away to work in an orphanage to avoid being married to a Muslim. She then worked in a mission hospital in the Punjab and became a missionary, teaching women to read, and ministering to them in the cotton fields. However, she was unable to be reunited with her family and was brutally murdered in her bed.

Transforming God, we give thanks for the selfless devotion and true faith of Esther John (Qamar Zia), who showed courage, gentleness and love to the Christian community she served. May we better understand from her ministry and martyrdom the courage of those who convert. Amen

15 October

Teresa of Avila, religious, foundress, mystic, teacher of the faith (1582)

Born in Avila of a good Castilian family, Teresa was brought up at home before being educated by Augustinian nuns on the death of her mother. At the age of 21 she entered the Carmelite convent in Avila, at first suffering from ill-health and from difficulties in her prayer life. Her mystical experiences brought an inner conversion and after twenty-five years under unreformed Carmelite rule she sought to establish homes based on poverty, hardship, solitude and manual work, of which seventeen in total were founded in her lifetime. Her writings included her *Life, The Way of Perfection* and *Interior Castle*, ensuring her legacy of prayerful application of spiritual growth was passed down as well as her position as one of the first two women to be declared doctors of the Church, along with Catherine of Siena, in 1970.

Lord of vision and love, today we rejoice at the insights and mystical experiences of your servant Teresa of Avila and wonder at her ability to combine them with the harsh round of work, prayer

and penance, integrating them in her writings. We praise you for the illumination they shine on our own lives of prayer and service. Amen

Tecla of England, Benedictine nun and abbess (c 790)

Tecla was a nun at Wimborne in Dorset who was sent by her abbess, Tetta, to assist Boniface in his mission to the Germanic people of continental Europe. She first served at Tauberbischofsheim and then, as abbess, at Ochsenfurt and finally at Kitzingen.

God of great callings, on this day we remember the call to Tecla to help Boniface in the evangelisation of Germany and her contribution to the life of communities there. Let her selfless service show us the way to perfect freedom through following your call. Amen

16 October

Hedwig, laywoman, Duchess of Poland (1243)

Born in Bavaria, Hedwig was the daughter of Count Berthold of Andechs and lived as a child in the monastery at Kitzingen. At a young age she married Henry, who succeeded his father as Duke of Silesia, and had six children. Henry supported her founding of religious houses, including the abbey of Cistercian nuns at Trebnitz, where she lived herself after the death of her husband, though never formally becoming a nun herself. She devoted herself to the alleviation of suffering among the poor and also acted as peacemaker and comforter of his son Henry's family on his death in battle.

Mighty Counsellor, on this day we commemorate the lifelong care of Hedwig, Duchess of Poland, for family and community, and the selfless service she offered. Let us seek to emulate her devotion and commitment in our lives. Amen

Gall, Irish monk and hermit (c 630)

From Leinster in County Down, Gall became a monk at Bangor and was one of twelve monks who accompanied Columbanus to continental Europe, where they founded monasteries in Gaul before proceeding to the shores of Lake Zurich, where, at Bregenz and Arbon, land was given for hermitages and where the Benedictine Monastery at St Gall was built later as a memorial to his pioneering work as a missionary in Switzerland. Gall lived out his days as a hermit and occasional preacher, despite efforts to make him a bishop or an abbot.

Today we thank you for the life and ministry of Gall, monk and hermit, a big man with a big heart for mission, who accompanied Columbanus to the continent of Europe and evangelised parts of present-day Switzerland which still bear his name. May we admire his faithfulness in following you far and wide in bringing the good news. Amen

Nicholas Ridley, Bishop of London, and Hugh Latimer, Bishop of Worcester, Reformation martyrs (1555) – *commemorated also, with Thomas Cranmer, on 21 March*

Born about 1500 into a prosperous family in Northumbria, Nicholas Ridley studied at Cambridge, the Sorbonne and Louvain, becoming chaplain to Thomas Cranmer and, in 1547, Bishop of Rochester, declaring himself a Protestant at the accession of Edward 6th. He assisted Cranmer in the preparation of the first Book of Common Prayer and, after supporting the claims of Lady Jane Grey on the death of Edward, he was excommunicated and burnt at the stake in 1555.

Older than Ridley, but also educated at Cambridge, Hugh Latimer was a popular preacher at university and then farther afield. Initially close to Henry 8th after the rift with the papacy, he was appointed Bishop of Worcester in 1535, but in 1540 resigned after refusing to sign the 'six articles' against the spread of Reformation doctrines. He was rehabilitated under Edward 6th, but under Queen Mary, refusing to recant his reformist views, he was burnt at the stake with Nicholas Ridley.

Lord of constant reform, we commemorate the lives, ministry, courage and reforming hearts of Nicholas Ridley and Hugh Latimer, whose steadfast faith and refusal to bow to pressures from monarchs led to their martyrdom. May we take strength from them when we need to be resolute in being true to our conscience. Amen

17 October

Ignatius, Bishop of Antioch, martyr (c 107)

Probably of Syrian origin and a disciple of St John, Ignatius became Bishop of Antioch in about 69. He is principally known for his seven letters written on his last journey, under guard, from Antioch to Rome, having been condemned to death under the persecution of Trajan. These were written at Smyrna and Troas to churches at Ephesus, Magnesia, Tralles, Rome, Philadelphia and Smyrna, and also to Polycarp. In these he showed his passionate commitment to Christ and urged his fellow Christians to maintain unity and remain loyal to their local bishop. He was thrown to the lions about 107, embracing his martyrdom with the words, 'Let me follow the example of the suffering of my God.'

God of triumph and sacrifice, on this day we recall the writings and martyrdom of Ignatius, Bishop of Antioch, in the early Church, resolute in faith and encouraging to other Christians to the last. Let his commitment to you in the face of persecution be an encouragement to us in the face of indifference. Amen

Ethelred and Ethelbricht of Kent (seventh century)

Princes of the royal house of Kent, Ethelred and Ethelbricht were grandsons of Ethelbert of Kent. Their uncle, Ercobert, ruled from 640, but when his son Egbert succeeded to the throne in 664 the princes were murdered. They were buried at Eastry on the Isle of Sheppey, where Egbert, seeking to expiate this deed, founded the monastery at Minster and the princes' sister, Ermenburga, became the first abbess.

Today we remember two Kentish Princes, Ethelred and Ethelbricht, with thanksgiving for their lives and the legacy of their martyrdom, the monastery at Minster. Let the community there be blessed with the love that the princes knew only for a short time. Amen

18 October

Luke, evangelist (first century)

Luke was a Greek physician, a disciple and friend of Paul and a companion on some of his missionary journeys and in prison. He was the author of the Gospel which bears his name and also of the Acts of the Apostles, both of which showed his artistry with words, which may have given rise to his becoming the patron of artists as well as doctors and surgeons. It is said that he wrote his Gospel in Greece, remained unmarried and died at the age of 84 in Boetia.

> God of the Gospels, we give thanks on this day for the faithful witnessing and recording of Luke in his Gospel and in the Acts of the Apostles. May we be grateful for the clarity and artistry of his writing and the generous insights into your Son's ministry that he has left for us. Amen

19 October

Henry Martyn, translator of the Scriptures, missionary in India and Persia (1812)

Henry Martyn was born in Truro in 1781 and in Cambridge became a committed Evangelical, developing an interest in missionary work through his friendship with Charles Simeon. As chaplain to the East India Company, it was expected that he would minister principally to expatriates, but he went about learning the local languages and acquainting himself with the culture, translating the New Testament into three languages, preaching and teaching in mission schools, ending his days in Armenia, a victim of tuberculosis.

Lord of communication and outreach, on this day we celebrate the gifts and the application of these gifts shown by Henry Martyn in Asia, in his role as chaplain to the East India Company. We rejoice that he formed a bond and an evangelical alliance with local people, through his missionary work and tireless translation skills. Amen

Paul of the Cross, priest, founder of the Passionist congegation (1775)

Born at Ovada, near Genoa, Paul Francis Danei was the eldest son of devout middle-class parents. Volunteering for the Venetian army, he soon realised he was not cut out to be a soldier and spent several years in prayer before experiencing spiritual enlightenment in 1720, leading him to found a congregation of missioners whose life and work revolved round the cross and Passion of Christ. Ordained with his brother in 1727, they set up the first 'Passionist' house at Monte Argentario in Tuscany. Paul himself was an inspiring preacher who had the gifts of prophecy and healing and was particularly interested in religious developments in England.

God of the cross, today we wonder at the mystical experiences of Paul of the Cross, which inspired him to found the Passionists. Let his insights and devotion fire our own spirituality. Amen

Frideswide, Abbess of Oxford (727)

Born the daughter of a Mercian king in 680, Frideswide is said to have fled from home to avoid marriage, establishing a double monastery in Oxford and becoming the first abbess, living there the rest of her days. Oxford grew up around the site of the monastery and Frideswide became the patron saint of the city and the university.

Transforming Lord, we give thanks on this day for the life and ministry of Frideswide, founder and abbess of a double monastery at Oxford, around which the city grew. May her single-minded vision show us today the value and importance of following your Way with persistent devotion. Amen

Peter of Alcantara, Franciscan priest and mystic (1562)

Born at Alcantara in Spain, Peter Garavito studied at Salamanca University and joined the Franciscan friars of the Observance and followed a strict, ascetic life akin to that of the desert fathers. Ordained priest in 1524, he showed his skill as a preacher and later wrote a book on prayer. He then established a friary at Pedrosa, dedicated to prayer and austerity, the friars living in tiny cells. He was known to Teresa of Avila, who wrote about these practices and was strongly encouraged by Peter in her Carmelite reform.

God of generosity and austerity, today let us recall and admire the determination and devotion of Peter of Alcantara, whose example is an inspiration. May we honour and learn from his mystical embrace of a life of prayer, solitude and contemplation. Amen

20 October

Acca, Benedictine monk, Bishop of Hexham (740)

Spending his early adult life in the household of Bosa, Bishop of York, Acca became the disciple and companion of Wilfrid, accompanying him on a number of journeys to the continent of Europe. While in Meaux in 705, Wilfrid became ill and on his deathbed named Acca as the next Abbot of Hexham. Acca, who duly became Abbot and Bishop of Hexham, was a noted scholar who developed the theological library and contributed material to Bede. On leaving Hexham he may have become Bishop of Withorn, though he is buried at Hexham.

Lord of companionship and enterprise, we give thanks for the life and work of Acca, whose ministry at Hexham was significant. May his tradition of scholarship and travel inspire us to do likewise. Amen

Maria Bertilla Boscardin, nun (1922)

Born into a poor family at Brendola near Vicenza in 1888, Anna Francesca Boscardin, considered a simpleton, escaped an unhappy home by joining the Sisters of Dorothy at Vicenza, becoming Sister Maria Bertilla. After a period as a scullery maid, she proved her worth when promoted to help in a children's ward at Treviso, becoming a caring and respected nurse. Banished once again to the laundry by a superior who failed to see her merits, she was subsequently restored to her role as children's nurse by the Mother-General, overseeing the children's ward at Treviso until her illness and death during an operation in 1922.

Caring and merciful Father, we celebrate on this day the unsung and devoted skills shown by Sister Maria Bertilla Boscardin, whose life resembles that of Thérèse of Lisieux. We especially give thanks for her delight in showing perseverance in doing the ordinary things well. Amen

21 October

Fintan of Taghmon, abbot (635)

Trained as a young man in monastic life under various teachers, Fintan chose to follow Columba to Iona, arriving in 597, just after the death of Columba. However, Columba's successor, Baithene, had been instructed to redirect him to Ireland so that he could become an abbot in his own right, Fintan duly founding the monastery of Taghmon. Fintan passionately supported the Ionan stance on the celebration of Easter, but Ireland subsequently fell into line with the rest of Europe on this issue.

God of leadership and obedience, we recall the discipleship and ministry of Fintan of Taghmon, follower of Columba, who obediently followed his calling and accepted the challenges of change he encountered. Give us, we pray, the serenity to cope with such challenges in our own Christian journey. Amen

Hilarion, hermit, abbot, monastic pioneer of Palestine (c 371)

The son of pagan parents from Gaza, Hilarion became a Christian in Alexandria, where he studied. He was influenced by Antony, whom he visited, returning to Gaza and becoming a hermit at Majuma in about 306 where he lived a hand-to-mouth existence, surviving on figs, vegetables and bread, with a shelter of mud and reeds. His life of austerity drew visitors and disciples and many were converted by his example and his miracles with monastic communities springing up following this model. Because of the attention he received he moved to Egypt and then to Sicily, Dalmatia, and finally Cyprus.

Today we honour the remarkable life of Hilarion, who learnt from Antony about the life of austerity and then followed his own path as hermit and monastic pioneer. We give thanks for his demonstrations of selflessness in difficult circumstances and the inspiration he gave to others. Amen

Ursula and her companions, virgins and martyrs (fourth century?)

Said to have been of British origin, Ursula reputedly came to Cologne accompanied by at least eleven (and possibly up to 11,000) virgins, on the way back from a pilgrimage to Rome. Refusing to marry the pagan chief of the Huns, Ursula and her companions were martyred for their Christian faith and buried at Cologne.

Lord of sanctity and chastity, as we recall the sacrifice and steadfastness of faith of Ursula and her companions at Cologne, may we understand better the perils faced by those professing the faith. Let her example be a reminder of our freedom to worship and the existence of persecution in parts of the world, even today. Amen

22 October

Donatus, Irish monk, Bishop of Fiesole (876)

An Irish monk who went on pilgrimage to Rome, Donatus was returning to his homeland and arrived at Fiesole, near Florence, at the time of a vacancy in the position of bishop. He was acclaimed as the new bishop and served under Lotharius and Louis the Pious, even leading troops against the Saracens. A scholar and a teacher, Donatus also founded a hospice for Irish pilgrims dedicated to St Brigid and took part in the Roman Council of 861.

God of transformation, we remember today your servant Donatus, who heeded the call to be Bishop of Fiesole, even as he journeyed home from Rome. May his deeds and writings be noted as expressions of a deep faith and dutiful discipleship. Amen

Philip of Heraclea, bishop and martyr (304)

During Diocletian's persecution Philip, who was the Bishop of Heraclea in Thrace, was confronted by the governor, Bassus, after refusing to stop worshipping the Christian God. Philip and his deacon, Hermes, refused to hand over sacred books and vessels, for which they and the goods were seized. Following failed efforts to force them to worship false gods, Justin, the new governor, had them beaten and burnt at the stake. They were followed in their martyrdom a day later by Severus.

We recall the strength of purpose and Christian defiance of Philip, Bishop of Heraclea, who passively resisted the Diocletian persecution, paying with his life and that of his deacon. Help us to understand their bravery, as we give thanks for Philip's life. Amen

John Paul 2nd, pope (2005)

Karol Wojtyla was born in Wadowice, not far from Cracow, in Poland in 1929. Following high school in his home town he studied at the Jagiellonian University in Cracow and also at drama school. During the Second World War he worked in a quarry, then in a chemical factory, but secretly began courses in the seminary, which he continued after the war. Ordained priest in 1946, he went to work in Rome and completed a doctorate in theology on John of the Cross in 1948. Returning to Poland, he served in various parishes around Cracow before being appointed Bishop of Ombi and then Bishop of Cracow. He became pope in 1978, the first non-Italian in that position for 450 years. Orthodox in his theology, he travelled widely and gave support to the Solidarity movement in his homeland of Poland. He survived an assassination attempt in 1981, later forgiving his attacker. His many writings include *Theology of the Body*, a compilation of his lectures on human sexuality.

God of transition and continuity, we give thanks for the life and ministry of John Paul 2nd, who endured the oppression of occupation in wartime and then celebrated and encouraged liberation from tyranny. As we honour his tireless ministry across the world, may we also recognise his staunch affirmation of Catholic faith and principles. Amen

23 October

John of Capistrano, missioner, Franciscan preacher (1456)

Born at Capistrano in Abruzzi, John studied at Perugia, where he married and became governor. However, parting from his wife, he became a Franciscan friar, being ordained priest in 1420 and studying under Bernardino of Siena. He then embarked on thirty years of very successful work as a mission preacher, criss-crossing Italy, as well as responding to the pope's call to undertake mission abroad. In 1451 he was sent to confront the Hussites in the Austrian Empire and then called to accompany the Hungarian general Hunyadi in a crusade, resulting in a victory at Belgrade, but also then death from the plague.

Lord of all, on this day we give thanks for the zeal of John of Capistrano as friar and missioner, giving spiritual leadership at a time of challenge and change in the religious and political map of Europe. May we honour his exploits and mourn the manner of his death. Amen

Ethelfreda, Abbess of Romsey (c 960)

The daughter of Ethelwold of Essex, who founded Romsey Abbey, Ethelfreda joined the community there at a young age, when Merewenna was abbess. Later, she herself became abbess. Known for her naked night-time swims as part of her austere life, Ethelfreda lived to a great age and was thought to have cured the queen through her intercession.

> **God of miracles, we thank you for the life, intercession and healing powers of Ethelfreda, Abbess of Romsey. May her devotions as a religious be remembered for the beneficial effects of her ministry to those who knew her and still inspire us today. Amen**

(Severinus) Boethius, scholar, statesman and martyr (524)

Ordained as a child, Boethius was brought up as the ward of Aurelius Symmacus, a noble whose daughter he later married. Renowned for his learning and scholarship, Boethius contributed greatly to the Christian West, through translations of works by Plato, Aristotle and Euclid, among others, and through his own theological writings on the Trinity and on the Incarnation, as well as through his major last work, *The Consolation of Philosophy*. A statesman and a consul, he fell foul of the Arian Emperor Theodore after he defended Albinus in court and was subsequently unjustly imprisoned and later executed.

> **God of justice and might, we recall on this day the great gifts and achievements of Boethius, writer, theologian, statesman and martyr. May his legacy be honoured among Christians everywhere who have benefited from his translations and insights. Amen**

24 October

Antony Claret, bishop and founder (1870)

Born at Sallent in northern Spain, the son of a weaver, Antony was ordained priest in 1835, went to Rome and joined the Jesuits, intent on mission work overseas. His health forced him to return to Spain, where he embarked on preaching and mission work in Catalonia, where he formed the Claretian Fathers. Then he was appointed Archbishop of Santiago in Cuba, where he carried out much needed reforms in the face of some hostility. Called back to Spain to become Queen Isabella's chaplain, he wrote some 200 books and pamphlets and established a museum and a library as well as schools of music and languages. Later he went into exile with Queen Isabella and ended his days in a Cistercian monastery near Narbonne.

> Lord of energy and innovation, today we honour the great industry and leadership shown by Antony Claret, whose ministry spread far and wide and whose preaching and writing won many hearts and minds for you. Let us rejoice that he was able to use the gifts you gave him in your service. Amen

Felix of Thibiuca, bishop and martyr (303)

Born in 247, Felix became the bishop of Thibiuca in north Africa and was one of the first martyrs of the persecution under Diocletian, who ordered all scriptural and sacred books to be surrendered and all Christian worship to cease. Felix refused and was brought to Carthage to face charges, where he stated at his trial: 'It is better to obey God rather than men.' He was condemned and beheaded, defiantly proclaiming the faith.

> Faithful Lord, we give thanks on this day for the Christian witness of Felix of Thibiuca, one of the earliest victims of the Diocletian persecution, who showed courage and resilience to the end. We pray today for all those facing persecution for their Christian faith and ask that Felix's example inspires them in their plight. Amen

25 October

Crispin and Crispinian, martyrs at Rome (c 287)

Crispin and Crispinian were shoemakers who are reputed to have preached the Christian faith in Gaul, in particular at Soissons, where they were eventually martyred in the Diocletian persecution. One English tradition is that they fled to Faversham, where there is an altar dedicated to them in the parish church. Mention is also made of 'St Crispin's Day' in Shakespeare's account of Henry 5th's famous speech before the Battle of Agincourt. Crispin and Crispinian are the patron saints of cobblers, shoemakers and leather-makers.

God of trust and tradition, we recall on this day the faithfulness of two shoemakers, Crispin and Crispinian, who brought the good news to Gaul while caring also for the soles of the feet of those they ministered to. May we in our ministry to others remember the whole person, spiritually washing the feet if need be, as your Son did. Amen

Forty martyrs of England and Wales (1535-1679)

This is a group of representative English and Welsh Roman Catholics selected from 200 already beatified by earlier popes. They suffered death for their conscience over a period of 150 years in the aftermath of the religious changes introduced by Henry 8th. They include clergy and lay people, executed for refusing to take the Oath of Supremacy or for being priests or harbouring priests, Edmund Campion, Horace Walpole and Swithun Wells amongst them.

Lord of sacrifice, today we honour all those English and Welsh Roman Catholic martyrs who refused to submit to King Henry 8th after the Reformation or to give up their priestly duties and preferred death. Let their courage show the way for all those of whatever faith or tradition, who are prepared to die for their faith, even today. Amen

John of Beverley, Bishop of York (721) – *see under 7 May*

Gaudentius, Bishop of Brescia (c 410)

A friend of Ambrose, Gaudentius was banished from his position as Bishop of Brescia in 404 for his association with John Chrysostom, but was the bearer of letters to Emperor Arcadius at Constantinople from Honorius, the Western Emperor, and Pope Innocent 1st, pleading for

Chrysostom's restoration. Although turned back, he was thanked for his efforts by Chrysostom. Gaudentius was also known as a capable teacher and preacher in his own right.

God of love and loyalty, on this day we give thanks for the life of Gaudentius and especially for his support of John Chrysostom. May we admire his loyalty and seek to emulate his willingness to help a friend. Amen

Lewis Bayley, bishop and writer (1631)

Born in 1565 in Camarthen, Lewis Bayley was educated at Exeter College, Oxford. After a number of posts in the Church he became chaplain to James 1st and treasurer of St Paul's Cathedral and then, in 1616, Bishop of Bangor. Although diplomatically his episcopate was not a success, his writing prospered and his work, *The Practice of Piety*, was very popular and went through many editions, in English, Welsh and other languages, having a great influence on John Bunyan and Howell Harris.

God of prayers and piety, we celebrate today the writings and ministry of Lewis Bayley, where his lasting legacy has been his book *The Practice of Piety*. May his wise words open our hearts and minds to your true way. Amen

26 October

Alfred the Great, King of the West Saxons and scholar (899)

Born in 849 at the royal estate of Wantage, Alfred was sent by his father, King Ethelwulf, to Rome to be anointed and confirmed by Pope Leo. Coming to the throne at the age of 22, he brought peace and stability to Church and State. He established religious houses for both education and relief of the poor, attended Mass daily and translated a number of religious texts into the vernacular. He was also known for his hospitality, his Christian mercy and compassion, and his scholarship.

Lord of mercy and might, we thank you for bringing to the throne Alfred, known as great for his sensitive leadership, his thirst for learning, and his generous hospitality to foreigners. Let us seek to do the same in our Church today. Amen

Cedd, Abbot of Lastingham, Bishop of the East Saxons (664)

A Lindisfarne monk of Irish training, under Aidan and Finnian, and the brother of Chad, Cedd was invited, along with three other priests, to assist Peada, King of Mercia, to evangelise his people. He then accepted the invitation of King Oswin of Northumbria to continue this work in Essex following the conversion of King Sigebert of the East Saxons. Cedd was consecrated Bishop of the East Saxons, building churches and monasteries including Lastingham, where he died shortly after acting as interpreter at the Synod of Whitby, accepting the Synod's decision over the timing of Easter.

Lord of great faithfulness, we remember with thanksgiving the life and service of Cedd, abbot and bishop, whose mission to the East Saxons was so fruitful. May we rejoice at the huge efforts he and his brother, Chad, made to extend your kingdom to great areas of England. Amen

Eata, Bishop of Hexham (686)

Educated by Aidan at Lindisfarne, Eata became a monk, and later abbot, at Melrose, where he trained Cuthbert. He and Cuthbert began to establish a monastery at Ripon, but could not accept the Roman calculation of Easter until the Synod of Whitby. He then became abbot at Lindisfarne, with Cuthbert as prior, and later was appointed by Theodore as Bishop of Hexham, where he died. Known as a man of peace and conciliation, he made a major contribution to church unity in Northumbria.

God of unity and purpose, on this day we recall the reconciling ministry of Eata, Bishop of Hexham, working with Cuthbert and Theodore. Let us recognise his influence in our church relationships to this day. Amen

27 October

Otteran, abbot (563)

An abbot from Meath, Otteran accompanied Columba when he sailed from Lough Foyle to Iona. He died soon after their arrival and it is said that Columba had a vision of a fight between angels and devils over Otteran's soul as it ascended to heaven.

God of great vision, we recall today the faithful journey made by Otteran as companion to Columba on his voyage to Iona. In mourning his early death, may we understand better the battles between good and evil over souls, in this life and the next. Amen

Frumentius, bishop, apostle of Ethiopia (c 380)

Frumentius and Aedesius found themselves in Ethiopia when their travelling companion, Meropius from Tyre, was murdered, along with everyone else on their ship. They were treated well in the court of the king at Axum and were educated there and given positions of trust. While Aedesius later returned to Tyre, Frumentius went to Alexandria where he asked Athanasius if a bishop could be sent to Ethiopia with new authority to finish the work he had begun and thus became known as 'apostle of Ethiopia'.

God of providence, we thank you for sending your servant Frumentius to Ethiopia and for empowering him with your Holy Spirit to minister there. Let us always look for new opportunities to do your will, whatever befalls us. Amen

28 October

Simon and Jude, apostles (first century)

Simon and Jude were both apostles. Simon was born at Cana of Galilee, giving rise to the story that it was his wedding at which the water was turned into wine. Sometimes known as 'Simon the Zealot', Jude was the brother of James, one of the 'brethren of the Lord', and was sometimes referred to as 'Thaddeus'. Jude is known as the patron saint of lost causes because interceding through him was seen as a 'last resort' in view of the similarity of his name with that of Judas Iscariot. Simon and Jude are thought to have been martyred in Persia, where they preached the gospel.

Lord of friendship and fellowship, on this day we remember the apostles Simon and Jude, faithful disciples who preached the good news in Persia and died there witnessing to the faith. Help us to understand that you are never a lost cause, even when the world says you are. Amen

Demetrius of Rostov, bishop (1709)

The son of a wealthy Cossack, Demetrius Tuptalo was a priest-monk before becoming Bishop of Rostov in 1702. A scholar, educationist and outspoken preacher, he wrote extensively, his works including religious drama, devotional and institutional works, among them the *Spiritual Alphabet* setting out clerical duties and disciplines of the saints. His style has endeared him to devotees of Russian religious literature.

God of great lives and literature, today we mark the life and works of Demetrius of Rostov, bishop and scholar, who greatly added to the Russian canon of religious literature. May we remain both inspired and instructed by such works as those by Demetrius. Amen

29 October

Colman of Kilmacduagh, bishop (c 632)

Born at Corker in Kiltartan, Colman was a monk at Aranmore and went to live at Burren in County Clare. There he was unwillingly made bishop, living on water and vegetables and with only one disciple. He founded a monastery at Kilmacduagh on land donated by King Guaire of Connaught and became its abbot-bishop. There he had a special rapport with animals and is said to have relied on a cock to wake him up for the night office, a mouse to keep him awake, and a fly became his bookmark.

God of nature and nurture, on this day we celebrate the ministry of Colman of Kilmacduagh, abbot-bishop and lover of flora and fauna. Let his affinity with animals infuse us with a love of your creation. Amen

James Hannington, Bishop of Eastern Equatorial Africa, martyr in Uganda (1885)

Born in 1847 into a Congregationalist family, James Hannington became an Anglican before studying at Oxford University. After ordination and after a five-year curacy he offered himself to the Church Missionary Society, who sent him to Zanzibar initially and later to mainland East Africa with other European and indigenous Christians. Approaching from the same direction as traditional enemies, they were seized by Mwanga, ruler of the Buganda, tortured and put to death.

We recall the pioneering missions of James Hannington, first Bishop of Eastern Equatorial Africa, who sought to extend your kingdom into Uganda and died in the process. May we always take risks for you, as your Son did for us. Amen

30 October

Richard Hooker, Anglican apologist, teacher (1600)
– see under 3 November

Marcellus the Centurion, martyr (298)

It was during celebrations to mark the birthday of Emperor Maximian that Marcellus, a centurion, considering these to be idolatrous festivities, discarded his military belt, declaring: 'I am a soldier of Jesus Christ, the eternal king. From now on I cease to serve your emperors.' Sent before Agricolanus, deputy prefect for Tangier, he admitted his actions and was sentenced to death by the sword.

Lord of courage and sacrifice, on this day we honour the bravery of Marcellus, centurion, in witnessing to his faith by refusing to take part in what he perceived to be idolatrous celebrations. We pray for all those facing difficult choices in their faith journeys, in the hope that we too would take the right course of action. Amen

Alphonsus Rodriguez, Jesuit laybrother (1617)

Born at Segovia in 1531, Alphonsus was the son of a wool merchant. He inherited the business but his wife and children died young and at the age of 40 he applied to be a lay helper with the Jesuits and was accepted. He was sent to Montesione in Majorca as a hall porter, where he remained for the rest of his life. Although largely uneducated in the formal sense, he was known and sought out for his holiness and wise counsel, notably by Peter Claver. The poet Gerard Manley Hopkins dedicated a sonnet 'in honour of Alphonsus Rodriguez'.

God of wholeness and holiness, we thank you for the quiet counsel and simple devotion of Alphonsus Rodriguez, Jesuit lay brother and hall porter at Montesione. Let his humility and service be beacons of Christian witness to us today. Amen

31 October

Foillan, Irish monk, abbot (c 655)

The brother of Fursey, Foillan came with him from Ireland to East Anglia, establishing the monastery of Cnobheresburg, also known as Burgh Castle, where Foillan succeeded Fursey as abbot, later establishing a monastery at Fosses. He was killed by robbers in a forest, returning from a visit to Nivelles, where Ita was abbess.

We recall today the missionary work amongst the East Angles carried out by Foillan, who accompanied his brother Fursey from Ireland, establishing a monastery at Fosses. May his untimely death at the hands of robbers remind us of the dangers faced by early missionaries in Britain. Amen

Martin Luther, reformer (1546)

Born in 1483 in Eisleben in Saxony, Martin Luther was educated in Magdeburg and Erfurt and ordained priest in 1507. After a spell as a lecturer at the University of Wittenberg, in 1515 he became Vicar of his Order, in charge of twelve monasteries, but became increasingly disenchanted with the Church, its worship, order and teaching. He advocated salvation by faith rather than works, citing Augustus of Hippo and opposing the teaching of the letter of James. Seeking debate by posting his 95 theses on the door of the church at Wittenberg, he sparked off the Protestant Reformation, first in Germany, then in the rest of Europe.

Lord of constant reformation, we honour the brave steps taken by Martin Luther to bring change to the Roman Catholic Church by challenging priorities and beliefs taking us away from you. Let his lasting legacy be that we now feel closer to you in our worship and in our membership of your Church. Amen

November

1 November

All Saints (All Hallows)

The Church in this festival honours all the saints together, recognising them as its foundation stories, bringing others to holiness and reflecting the communion between the Church on earth and the Church in heaven. Originally (from the fourth century) observed on the first Sunday after Pentecost, commemorating 'the martyrs of the whole world', in the eighth century Pope Gregory dedicated a chapel to All Saints at St Peter's in Rome on 1 November and this soon became the day observed as All Saints' Day.

Today we give thanks for all the heroes of the faith who have inspired others to faith and holiness. May we rejoice in the cloud of witnesses to the faith your Son taught us, seeking their intercession and your continued gift of the Holy Spirit to your Church on earth. Amen

Benignus of Dijon, martyr (third century)

Probably from Lyons, Benignus was a missionary from Lyons who was persecuted and put to death under the Emperor Aurelian. His reputation as a martyr continued and grew over the centuries at Dijon, in whose cathedral he is buried.

Lord of mercy and memory, on this day we mark the affection for Benignus in Dijon, the city where he was martyred and buried. On All Saints' Day may we be reminded that each saint has a special story, a particular legacy and a place in the Church's development. Amen

2 November

Commemoration of the Faithful Departed (All Souls' Day)

Begun as a monastic custom at the Abbey of Cluny, this commemoration became universal throughout the Western Church by the thirteenth century, affirmed in an Anglican/Roman Catholic statement, which said that, 'In Christ all the faithful, both living and departed, are bound together in a communion of prayer.' Recognising that society's approach to mourning has changed, in recent years it has become common to hold a service on or near this day for the bereaved, to allow them an opportunity to express grief within the context of a church service.

God of life in death, today we remember departed loved ones, who have joined the saints in your heavenly kingdom. May we grieve without shame, remember without embarrassment, and pray for the souls of the faithful departed. Amen

Justus of Trieste, martyr (303)

A Christian from childhood, Justus was devoted to penance and almsgiving during the rule of Diocletian and Maximian. Told that he had to obey the imperial decrees which outlawed the Christian faith, Justus refused calmly but firmly and he was condemned to death, being thrown into the sea attached to weights. His body was later found by a priest, Sebastian, and buried, later being transferred to Trieste Cathedral.

God of great commitment, may we rejoice at the witness of Justus of Trieste, who stood up to the imperial edicts on Christianity and worship and suffered death for his faith. In our admiration, let us not forget the pain inflicted as well as the glory attained. Amen

3 November

Malachy, Archbishop of Armagh (1148)

The son of a teacher, Malachy was educated at Armagh, was a monk at 20 and three years later, in 1119, was ordained priest. He began his reforms as Vicar of Armagh diocese and continued this as Bishop of Connor and Down, while restoring the Abbey of Bangor, County Down, transforming the diocese before being driven out by the local chieftain. After a period as Archbishop of Armagh he returned to his see of Down and, influenced by his meeting with Bernard of Clairvaux, he founded Mellifont Abbey in 1142 and others followed. He died at Clairvaux on his way to Rome.

Lord of reform and endeavour, on this day we celebrate the perseverance, skills and sense of order of Malachy, Archbishop of Armagh. May his impact on the Church in Ireland be recognised and marked in its lasting influence. Amen

Winifred, virgin and abbess (seventh century)

The daughter of a soldier from Flintshire and the niece of St Beuno, Winifred was a Welsh virgin who was faced with unwelcome advances from a chieftain's son, Caradoc, who, when she repulsed him, is said to have struck off her head. On that spot a spring gushed forth and Beuno restored Winifred to life. Becoming a nun, she was late appointed Abbess of Holywell, which became a pilgrimage centre.

Lord, the spring of life, we give thanks on this day for the virgin Winifred, who withstood unwelcome advances from Caradoc, was beheaded and wonderfully restored to life by Beuno. May Holywell, its well and pilgrimage centre prosper as a memorial to her miraculous restoration. Amen

Martin de Porres, friar, Dominican lay brother (1639)

The illegitimate son of a Spanish grandee and a black, Panamanian freewoman, Martin became a member of the Third Order of Dominicans at the age of 15 and, after he demonstrated his skill and compassion in caring for the poor and needy, he was invited to join the First Order as a lay brother. Known for his devotion to prayer and penance, his healing powers, his skills with animals and his wise counsel, along with a continued ministry to the poor and to African slaves, Martin was much sought after for his spiritual direction. He has been adopted as the patron saint of work for interracial justice and harmony.

Inclusive Lord, we give great thanks today for the caring and spiritual ministry of Martin de Porres, lay brother, friend and mentor to many. May he be an exemplar today of the need for prayer and patience in mending brokenness in a divided world. Amen

Richard Hooker, Anglican apologist, teacher (1600) – *commemorated in some traditions on 30 October*

Born in Heavitree, Exeter, around 1544, Richard Hooker was educated at Corpus Christi College, Oxford, and became a Fellow there. He became a parish priest and, in 1585, Master of the Temple in London and was a strong advocate of the Church of England as providing a 'middle way' between Puritanism and Roman Catholicism. Among his writings his *Of the Laws of Ecclesiastical Polity* can be accounted the greatest. He demonstrated in his writings and nature that Anglicanism can be rooted in both Scripture and tradition, ending his ministry as a parish priest in Bishopsbourne near Canterbury.

God of Scripture and tradition, on this day we recall the scholarship and reconciling ministry of Richard Hooker, who showed that different strands of Anglicanism could be held together in harmony. May his wisdom and far-sightedness be seen as part of our church life today, to honour his life and witness. Amen

4 November

Charles Borromeo, Archbishop of Milan (1584)

Born into a wealthy family near Lake Maggiore in 1538, Charles Borromeo, educated at Milan and Pavia, was able intellectually, despite a speech impediment which affected him most of his life, and proved both a hard worker and a very caring person. His uncle, Pope Pius 4th, elevated him to the position of cardinal before he was even ordained priest and gave him an important job in Milan. Then in 1563 he became a priest and was made Archbishop of Milan, having played a key role in the Council of Trent, and proceeded to set in motion important reforms, as well as adopting a humble lifestyle, taking the lead in providing assistance to those affected by famine and plague in Milan.

God of generosity of spirit, we give thanks on this day for the tireless work and inspirational leadership of Charles Borromeo, Archbishop of Milan, reformer and relief worker. May we seek to emulate his willingness to make necessary changes in the face of opposition and to set an example in our daily living. Amen

Birstan, Bishop of Winchester (tenth century)

Birstan, who was Bishop of Winchester from 931-4, was known and revered for his commitment to the poor and his assiduous prayer life, including his prayers for the departed, often said in a cemetery.

Today we recall the prayerful ministry of Birstan, Bishop of Winchester, who showed special devotion to the needs of the poor and in praying for the souls of the departed. Let his selfless dedication be remembered and emulated today. Amen

5 November

Cybi, abbot, founder (sixth century) – *see under 8 November*

Kea, monk and bishop (early sixth century)

Of noble parentage, Kea travelled to Cornwall from Glastonbury, founding Christian centres along the way. Said to have migrated to Brittany, Kea was associated there with stags, as depicted in Breton pictures of him. It became the practice to invoke his name in the cure of toothache.

Lord of all, we remember and give thanks for the journeys and legacy of Kea, in Cornwall and Brittany. May those who invoke his name share his love for you and your love for him. Amen

Bertille, Abbess of Chelles (692)

Born into a famous family in Soissons, from an early age Bertille showed a devotion to God unusual in one so young. She became a nun close to the monastery at Brie and found herself looking after strangers, the sick and children, which she did so ably that she later became the first Abbess of Chelles, in which position she served for forty-six years.

> **God of challenge and choice, on this day we give you thanks for the pioneering ministry of Bertille, Abbess of Chelles, whose dedication and devotion raised her to the role of abbess at an early age. May we rejoice that her long ministry, carried out with vigour and discretion, inspired others in their faith journey. Amen**

Zachary and Elizabeth (first century)

Zachary and Elizabeth were the parents of John the Baptist and Zachary has been immortalised in the Benedictus, Zachary's canticle. It is said that Zachary was martyred in his Temple on the orders of Herod.

> **Lord of prophecy and portent, we give thanks on this day for the parents of John the Baptist, Zachary and Elizabeth, for their faithfulness and their public support for those seeking healing and wholeness. May their selfless example be an inspiration in our own day and age. Amen**

6 November

Leonard, hermit (sixth century)

Leonard was the godson of Clovis, first Christian king of the Franks, who offered him a bishopric, which he refused, becoming a monk at Micy and then a hermit at Noblac (now known as Saint-Léonard), where he built himself a cell. When Leonard helped to deliver the baby of Clovis' wife in the forest where he lived, Clovis in gratitude gave him land on which Leonard founded the Abbey of Noblac. Because of this episode he has become the patron of pregnant women, as well as the patron of prisoners, attributed to him by grateful returning crusaders.

Today we mark the life and ministry of your humble servant, Leonard, who chose to be a hermit rather than accept preferment in the Church. Known for his practical help to those in need, including miracles of healing, may Leonard's popularity throughout Europe be remembered and celebrated. Amen

Illtud, abbot (530)

Born in Brittany and a disciple of Germanus of Auxerre, Illtud was known as one of the most learned of British scholars of Scripture and philosophy. It is said that at one stage he chose a military career, which brought him to the court of King Arthur. However, narrowly avoiding death while hunting, Illtud was drawn to the monastic life, instructed by Dyfrig, was ordained priest, and was made Abbot of Llantwit monastic school, where David, Samson and Paulinus studied, thus having a major influence on the Church in Wales.

Providential Lord, on this day we celebrate the life and ministry of Illtud, drawn to Wales from Brittany as a soldier and becoming a scholarly abbot who founded a monastery which helped to build the Church in South Wales. Let us, like Illtud, accept the changes in our lives which are presented to us through your guiding hand. Amen

William Temple, Archbishop of Canterbury, teacher of the faith (1944)

Born in Exeter in 1881, the son of Frederick Temple, then Bishop of Exeter, who went on to become Archbishop of Canterbury, William Temple had a glittering career as an academic and educationist and formed lasting interests in educational and social work, notably through the Workers' Educational Association and the Student Christian Movement. Soon after he was ordained priest he became a bishop, at the age of 40, and was Archbishop of York before he was appointed Archbishop of Canterbury in 1942. Strong on ecumenical, social and educational issues, his legacy was an important one, even though he died only two years later, in 1944.

We recall on this day the remarkable career and contribution of Archbishop William Temple, overseeing important church involvement in social and educational change in Britain. May we learn from his theological and philosophical insights and admire his practical application of these. Amen

7 November

Richard Davies, bishop and translator (1581)

Born into the family of a Welsh curate around 1501, Richard Davies was educated at New Inn Hall, Oxford, where he was influenced by Protestantism. When Queen Mary came to the throne he lost his living and went into exile with his family to Frankfurt, retiring after Mary's death to take up the bishopric of St Asaph, moving to St David's in 1561. He was a gifted writer in English and Welsh, as well as helping in the translation of some of the 'Bishop's Bible' of 1568. His legacy was to help restore in the reformed Church of Wales an early Welsh Christianity.

Transforming Lord, we remember today one of the architects of the reformed Welsh Church, Richard Davies, whose gifts of writing and translation were influential beyond the 16th century. Let us salute a pioneer who was a conscientious bishop and a scholar of note. Amen

Willibrord of York, Archbishop of Utrecht, apostle of Frisia (739)

Born in Yorkshire, Willibrord was educated in Ripon under Wilfrid, then went to Ireland, where he was ordained priest in 688, returning to England in 690. Encouraged by Egbert, he led a mission to Frisia, which prospered under the protection of Pepin of Herstal and was made Archbishop of Frisia and later of Utrecht, which he ran on similar lines to Canterbury. He was later joined in Germany by Boniface at the instigation of Pope Gregory 3rd, continuing to build churches and establish sees, despite occasional setbacks in Utrecht. Known for his energetic preaching and ministry, and always joyful, Willibrord laid the foundations for a century of English pioneering influence in continental Christianity.

God of great ambition, today we mark the energetic ministry of Willibrord, an English priest who became Patron Saint of the Netherlands by his missionary zeal and his skilful church organisation. May we celebrate his great achievements in Europe, paving the way for Boniface and others to follow. Amen

8 November

Tysilio, abbot (seventh century) – *see under 12 November*

The saints and martyrs of England/The saints of Wales

Today, in churches in England and Wales respectively, Christians from these shores are honoured and remembered, for the mission and messages of hope they shared at home and abroad. The holy, the humble, the energetic, the prayerful, the leaders and the martyrs are celebrated for their lives devoted to Christ, right across the Anglican communion and in different traditions.

Lord of love and sacrifice, may we mark today the contributions of men and women from these islands who are beacons of hope in bringing the good news to people of different lands, including our own. As we remember them collectively let us honour them individually, in your name. Amen

The four crowned martyrs (early fourth century)

The four crowned martyrs were in fact five, according to the more plausible of the two accounts of their origins and martyrdom. These were Christian Persian stonemasons, Claudius, Nicostratus, Simpronian and Castorius, joined by a fifth, more recent, convert, Simplicius, who refused to make a statue of the god Aesculapius as part of their work for the Emperor Diocletian. As a result of this, together with a refusal to offer sacrifices to the gods, exacerbated by the sudden death of the officer heading the enquiry into their actions, they were all condemned to death, by beating and drowning.

In the midst of the stonemasons' craftsmanship, we remember today an example of man's inhumanity to man, as five Christians were condemned for not using their skills to honour false gods. Help us to resist the pressures on us to worship false gods in today's world too. Amen

Cybi, abbot, founder (sixth century)

A Cornish saint and evangelist, Cybi is likely to have travelled to various places by river and sea, living as a hermit, before settling in Anglesey, where he founded a monastery at Holyhead (in Welsh, 'Cybi's fort'). The site of the monastery may have been given to him by the Welsh Prince Maelgwyn Gwynedd of Cunedda.

Lord of sea and isle, we rejoice at the founding of the monastery at Holyhead by Cybi, whose ministry was known in Cornwall and Wales. Let us celebrate this hermit turned founder, whose example of humility and perseverance is a model for mission today. Amen

9 November

Margery Kempe, mystic (c 1440)

Born at Lynn in Norfolk, Margery Kempe was a contemporary of Julian of Norwich. She experienced visions involving the Holy Family at the crucifixion, as well as having conversations with the saints. Despite being acclaimed as a visionary, she upset the Church and was imprisoned on a number of occasions. She undertook many pilgrimages, prompted by her visions, and seemed blessed with a close communion with Christ. She wrote of all these insights and experiences in her autobiography, *The Book of Margery Kempe.*

God of honesty and openness, we honour the gift of visions experienced by Margery Kempe and her willingness to share them with all who wished to hear. Let her insights encourage our exploration of a true relationship with you, loving Lord. Amen

Theodore 'the Recruit', martyr (fourth century)

A Roman soldier who refused to join his comrades in pagan worship, Theodore was facing charges when he proceeded to set on fire a temple dedicated to the Mother Goddess, which sealed his fate. He was tortured and thrown into a furnace, where he perished.

Let us today recall the horrible death of Theodore 'the recruit', after his valiant stand against pagan worship. Help us to understand fully the perils faced by Theodore and Christians like him, who took a stand against the idolatry of the times in high places. Amen

10 November

Leo the Great, pope (461)

Born at Rome into a noble Tuscan family, Leo served as Archdeacon of the Church of Rome under Pope Celestine, before being appointed Bishop of Rome in 440. His doctoral letter at the Council of Chalcedon was hugely influential as a declaration of orthodox doctrine on Christ's two natures, in the face of Monophysism. He also successfully took action to dissuade Attila the Hun from sacking Rome, though later Vandals did occupy the city for fourteen days. Leo was a wise preacher with great administrative skills who saw off a number of heretical factions, but failed to prevent the enhancement of the see of Constantinople.

Almighty God, on this day we give thanks for the life and work of Leo the Great, doctor and preserver of the faith, who faithfully protected Rome and the true faith from various assaults of the enemies. May we be equally resolute in defending the faith today, Lord. Amen

Justus of Canterbury, bishop (c 627)

Arriving in England in the second wave of missionaries following Augustine and his companions, Justus was made the first Bishop of Rochester, fleeing to Gaul following Ethelbert's death. He soon returned and became Archbishop of Canterbury in 624. He was known for his constancy and vigilance in upholding and spreading the gospel.

> We recall with thanks the mission and ministry of Justus, who came to England in support of Augustine and became Archbishop of Canterbury. Let us mark and learn from his constancy in explaining and spreading the good news, as we seek to do the same today. Amen

Andrew Avellino, priest, reformer (1608)

Born into a wealthy family in the kingdom of Naples, Andrew (who was christened Lancelot) studied both civil and canon law and after being ordained priest was employed in the ecclesiastical courts. Though initially ambitious, he joined the Theatine congregation, changed his name to Andrew and devoted himself to reforms, preaching and writing, and was much in demand as a confessor. In an act of personal charity and forgiveness he forgave the murderer of his nephew and took him into his household.

> Lord of justice and mercy, today we mark the zeal and ability of Andrew Avellino, who, instead of using his undoubted skills for his own advancement, dedicated his life to living out the gospel and showing the way to others. May we follow his example of devoted service to you, transforming Lord. Amen

11 November

Martin of Tours (c 397)

Born into an army family in Pannonia, Lower Hungary, around 316, Martin was expected to enrol in the army and he did so. Intending to become a Christian from an early age, he decided that being a soldier was not consistent with his commitment to Christ, was imprisoned and then discharged in 357. The story of his sharing his cloak with a beggar, cutting it in half with his sword, dates from this time and was followed by a vision of Christ wearing the cloak he had given away. After being baptised, he sought out Hilary of Poitiers, joined his monastery and became Bishop of Tours in 372. He later founded the monastery at Marmontier and became an active missioner and preacher, travelling widely on foot, by donkey and on water, as well as challenging the Church and emperor without fear.

God of great works, we celebrate today the fearless ministry of Martin of Tours, both his missionary zeal and his example of Christian discipleship. Give us too the courage and ambition to attempt great things for you. Amen

Theodore the Studite, abbot, monastic reformer and theologian (826)

The son of an imperial treasury official, Theodore was born in 759, was ordained priest in 787 and became abbot in succession to his uncle, Plato, at the monastery of Sakkoudion near Mount Olympus in 794. Transferring his community to Constantinople, they joined the monastery founded by the Roman Studius in the fifth century. There he embarked on far-reaching reform which greatly influenced Byzantine monasticism, in the face of great external pressures. Theodore proved himself to be a champion of the Church's independence, strong-willed and scholarly.

Lord of gifts and talents, we rejoice at the skills shown by Theodore the Studite in his ministry and reforms, pointing the way to new forms of monasticism. Let his writings and his changes speak for themselves of his love for you and his example to us. Amen

12 November

Tysilio, abbot (seventh century) – *commemorated in some traditions on 8 November*

The son of a prince of Powys, Tysilio ignored his father's advice and joined the religious community established at Meifod and succeeded Gwyddfarch, the founder, as abbot. He built up the monastery to be the most important religious community in Powys and gave hospitality there to, amongst others, Beuno. He is thought to have travelled to other parts of Wales, giving rise to a number of churches dedicated to him, and the town of Llandysilio is named after him. He became known as the saintly protector of Powys.

Faithful Lord, we thank you for the single-minded dedication of Tysilio in communities and towns across Wales. Let his mission and monastery leadership tell of his lasting reach, even till today. Amen

Machar, bishop (sixth century)

Born in Ireland of princely parentage, Machar travelled to Iona with Columba, having been baptised by Colman, and went on to evangelise Mull and then the Picts around Aberdeen, establishing a mission in the north-east of Scotland on the site on which a cathedral was built and dedicated to him. Next to this a well traditionally provided water for local baptisms and became know as St Machar's well.

Today may we celebrate the arrival of Machar in Scotland from Ireland as part of the missionary outreach from Iona. Help us to see and appreciate the lasting legacy of those like Machar who left their home to bring you to us. Amen

Josaphat of Polotsk, archbishop and martyr (1623)

Born in 1580 at Vladimir, the son of a wealthy merchant, Josaphat became a monk at Vilna in 1604. Shortly afterwards he was ordained as a priest and became a popular preacher, espousing the cause of extending the union with Rome to the province of Kiev. He was appointed Abbot of Vilna in 1614 and Archbishop of Polotsk in 1617, where he carried out reforms and embarked on a tireless round of pastoral activity and synods. Faced with a schism exacerbated by political interference and ingrained customs, his efforts at greater union with Rome resulted in his assassination by supporters of his rival to the see of Polotsk.

God of union and purpose, on this day we mark the great ecumenical endeavour of Josaphat of Polotsk, whose efforts to bridge the divide between Orthodox and Latin traditions cost him his life. May we know him as the first patron saint of ecumenism and do all we can to bring your hope for church unity to fruition. Amen

13 November

Charles Simeon, priest, evangelical divine (1836)

Born in 1759 in Reading, Charles Simeon, after attending Cambridge University, became a Fellow of King's College Cambridge in 1782, was made a priest in 1783, and was appointed vicar of Holy Trinity Church, Cambridge. An evangelical from college days, his preaching and obvious care for his parishioners won over a sceptical congregation. Famously, he carved the words from John 12:21, 'Sir, we would see Jesus', on the inside of the pulpit as a reminder that he was pointing to Jesus in his preaching. He was a founder member of the Church Missionary Society and set up the Simeon Trust to appoint evangelicals to parishes.

Loving Lord, we recall today the powerful preaching and evangelical commitment of Charles Simeon, who helped shape the Church and helped found the CMS. May his zeal to show the redeeming love of God be a lasting legacy to us all. Amen

Homobonus, layman, merchant of Cremona (1197)

Born into a merchant family in Cremona, Lombardy, Homobonus was given his name, meaning 'God man', at baptism. Brought up to succeed his father in tailoring and selling cloth, he demonstrated Christian generosity by caring for, and giving to, the hungry and the sick and was known as 'Father of the Poor'. Spending much of his time in prayer, he died at St Giles' Church during Mass, his arms stretched out.

Lord of the cross, today we remember a layman and merchant, Homobonus, who devoted his life to assisting the poor and needy, regularly praying in church and carrying out his work as a merchant with honesty and diligence. Amen

Brice, Bishop of Tours (444)

Educated at Marmontier under Martin, Brice was a troublesome character who criticised Martin, yet became his successor after seven years in exile, mending his ways and establishing a number of Christian centres. His association with Martin helped to spread his name, which is given in the Latin form, Britius, in the Book of Common Prayer.

God of amendment of life, on this day we recall the lively and challenging ministry of Brice, critic of Martin of Tours, yet becoming his worthy successor, forming Christian centres and surviving many incidents and challenges during his own long episcopate. Amen

14 November

Laurence O'Toole, abbot and Archbishop of Dublin (1180)

Born in County Kildare, the son of a rich and powerful prince in Leinster, Laurence spent part of his childhood as a hostage to Dermot, King of Leinster, until the age of 12, receiving instruction from the Bishop of Glendalough. He became a monk at Glendalough and then abbot, going on to become Archbishop of Dublin in 1162. He was known for his relief of the poor, especially during a great famine. A contemporary of Thomas Becket, he became involved as a peacemaker between the English and the Irish and between Church and State, dying in France on the way back from a peace mission.

God of peace and reconciliation, we celebrate the persuasive, prayerful powers of Laurence O'Toole, called at an early age to be Archbishop of Dublin and playing an important reconciling role during difficult times for both Church and State. Help us to approach such difficulties today in the knowledge of Laurence's example and experience. Amen

Dyfrig (Dubricius), monk and bishop (c 532)

Reputedly born at Madley (near Hereford) around 460, Dyfrig had a close connection with Romano-British Christianity. As the first bishop of an area including Llandaff, he established a number of communities and monastic schools, as did his pupils, notably Illtud and Llantwit Major. He retired in his old age to Bardsley, where he died.

> We give thanks today for your servant Dyfrig, whose pioneer ministry in Hereford and Gwent left its mark on the development of the Church in Wales, through his own foundations and those of his pupils. May we learn the art of succession planning in mission from his leadership. Amen

Samuel Seabury, first Anglican bishop in North America (1796)

Born in Connecticut in 1729, Samuel Seabury studied theology at Yale and medicine at Edinburgh and was ordained priest by the Bishop of Lincoln in 1753. He served in New Brunswick and then in New York, remaining loyal to the British Crown in the War of Independence as a chaplain in the British Army. Elected bishop in 1783, not being able to take the Oath of Allegiance now that the States were independent, he obtained his episcopal orders from the Scottish Episcopalian Church in 1784. Later he helped to unite the Scottish and English successions, securing a liturgy and structure which stood the test of time and on which he had a great influence.

> Lord of change and development, we rejoice today over the ministry of Samuel Seabury, who lived through divisive events in North America, but who with perseverance and the Holy Spirit was able to bring unity and integrity to the Episcopal Church in the new United States of America as its first bishop. Let his initiative and influence be a beacon for churches everywhere. Amen

15 November

Albert the Great, theologian (1280)

Known as 'the Universal Teacher', Albert was born into a Swabian family, was educated at Padua and joined the newly established Order of Preachers, rather against the wishes of the family. His passion was for study and teaching and after an unsuccessful time as Bishop of Regensburg he resumed his teaching and study of theology. He wrote extensively, counting Thomas Aquinas amongst his pupils. He was named by Pope Pius 11th as both a Doctor of the Church and the patron saint of the natural sciences.

God of all learning, we rejoice at the sheer love of scholarship, teaching and knowledge of the natural sciences of Albert the Great, 'the Universal Teacher'. May his rare and divine gift and scientific interests, recognised and appreciated in his day, still inspire us to continue to explore and explain your creation. Amen

Malo, missionary monk, bishop (6th-7th century)

Thought to be of Welsh origin, Malo founded the church at Aleth, with the town now called Saint-Malo as its main centre. Known as the apostle of Brittany, Malo travelled and preached widely there, often singing psalms at the top of his voice, before he was driven out by his enemies and settled in Saintes, ending his days at nearby Archingeay.

Lord of mystery and mission, may your servant Malo be remembered for his pioneering way of evangelising, his powerful singing and his roughshod manner, which sometimes caused him trouble. Help us to be pioneers in your service today, Lord, as Malo was in his time. Amen

16 November

Margaret of Scotland, Queen of Scotland, reformer of the Church (1093)

Born in 1046 in Hungary, where her parents were in exile, Margaret was the grand-daughter of Edmund Ironside, King of the English, and niece to Edward the Confessor. Following the Norman Conquest she sought refuge in the court of King Malcolm of Scotland, whom she went on to marry, bearing six sons and two daughters. Known as a woman of prayer with high standards and a commitment to charitable works, she exercised a considerable influence on Malcolm, as well as carrying out church reforms and founding monasteries.

Lord of great expectations, on this day we lift up to you the memory of Margaret of Scotland, born into royalty and into exile, but greatly influential in the affairs of State and Church in Scotland. Let us be thankful for her prayerful persistence today, Lord. Amen

Edmund Rich of Abingdon, Archbishop of Canterbury (1240)

Born in Abingdon, the son of a merchant who later became a monk, Edmund was educated at Oxford and in Paris. After being ordained priest he taught theology at Oxford and was appointed treasurer of Salisbury Cathedral in 1222. Elected Archbishop of Canterbury after three other attempts at appointing were vetoed by Pope Gregory 9th, Edmund's episcopate lasted seven years, during which he resolutely faced a number of challenges, including mediating between king and barons. In these tasks he was assisted by Richard of Chichester. A prolific writer of commentaries and guidance for clergy and laity, Edmund ended his days at Pontigny, where he was buried.

God of great opportunities, we recall today the ministry of Edmund of Abingdon, who rose up through the academic and priestly ranks to become Archbishop of Canterbury in difficult times for those who ruled England, succeeding in his peace-making

efforts and resisting interference from the monarchy. May his example of resolute and prayerful leadership inspire us in more settled times. Amen

Gertrude of Helfta, mystic (c 1302)

Born in 1256, Gertrude was entrusted at the age of 5 to the care of the nuns at Helfta in Saxony and seems never to have left the convent. She underwent a deeper conversion and at the age of 25 and thereafter had many mystical experiences, a number of her visions actually taking place during the singing of the divine office. She was one of the first exponents of devotion to the Sacred Heart and her writings include *The Herald of God's Loving Kindness*. Although never abbess, Gertrude is regarded as one of the most important medieval mystics.

Lord of vision and revelation, on this day we reach out to Gertrude of Helfta, mystic, who through prayer at the divine office reached out to you and you revealed yourself to her. May our spiritual quest be blessed with a similar response, by your grace. Amen

17 November

Hilda, Abbess of Whitby (680) – *see under 19 November*

Hugh, Bishop of Lincoln (1200)

Born at Avalon near Grenoble about 1140, Hugh became a monk at Grande Chartreuse and was invited by King Henry 2nd to become prior of a Carthusian monastery at Witham in Somerset. Under his able leadership the monastery flourished and in 1186 Hugh became the bishop of the largest diocese in England, Lincoln. There he energetically re-invigorated the life of the cathedral and diocese, through visitations and synods, embarking on repairs and enlargement of the cathedral, reviving the Lincoln schools and caring for the sick, the poor and the oppressed, often challenging successive English bishops in the process. He is regarded as one of the great spiritual leaders of the English Church.

Lord of all virtues, we thank you that Hugh, Bishop of Lincoln, came to England to revive first a monastery, then a cathedral and a diocese. May his zeal be recognised and his legacy be respected. Amen

Martyrs of Paraguay (1628)

Roque Gonzalez, Alonso Rodriguez and Juan de Castillo were Jesuits who played an important role in the 'Reduction' settlements of Paraguay for Chilean Indians run by missionaries. As guardians and trustees of the indigenous people rather than conquerors, the Jesuits found themselves in conflict with the Spanish authorities and traders, yet they extended their experiment of 'Reductions' into neighbouring areas, including present-day Uruguay and Brazil, where these three met their death when set upon by a local medicine man and his followers.

God of mission, on this day we remember the martyrs of Paraguay, Jesuits who led missions to the indigenous people and were martyred in the process. May their pioneering work, discovered hundreds of years later, be a further inspiration to missionaries today. Amen

Elizabeth of Hungary, princess, widow and philanthropist (1231) – *commemorated in some traditions on 18 November*

The daughter of King Andrew 2nd of Hungary, Elizabeth married Ludwig (or Louis) 4th of Thuringia and enjoyed a happy, but short marriage at Wartburg castle, near Eisenach, bearing three children. She was widowed when Ludwig, en route to take part in the crusades, died at Otranto and she was cast out of the castle and court by her brother-in-law Henry. She sought refuge at Marburg, becoming a Franciscan tertiary under the spiritual direction of Conrad of Marburg, who insisted on a harsh regime for her, treating her cruelly and insensitively. Despite this she proved resolute in her faith and charitable works, even going fishing to feed the poor.

God of humility and service, today we thank you for the life and ministry of your servant Elizabeth of Hungary, whose fortunes rose and fell, but whose faith was constant. Let us take heart from her continued desire to serve you though love and obedience, however harsh her circumstances. Amen

18 November

Elizabeth of Hungary, princess, widow and philanthropist (1231) – *see under 17 November*

Odo of Cluny, Benedictine monk and abbot (942)

Born at Tours, Odo's father was a knight, Abbo of Maine, and he was brought up in the household of William of Aquitaine, who later founded Cluny. He spent eighteen years as a monk at Baume before becoming the second Abbot of Cluny in 927. Odo insisted on an austere regime but was known for his sense of humour and warm heart. He transformed the life of the abbey and his reforms spread far and wide, as did his reputation for his generosity to the poor and compassion to prisoners.

On this day we mark the gifts and achievements of Odo of Cluny. Help us to catch the flame of truth and generosity which Odo showed in his life's work. Amen

Mawes, bishop in Brittany (fifth century)

Probably a companion and contemporary of Budoc, Mawes was a monk and a missionary from Wales. They founded monasteries in both Brittany and Cornwall. Better known in Brittany, Mawes has nevertheless given his name to the Cornish fishing village close to Falmouth. He is said to have become a well-known teacher (depicted in paintings as a schoolmaster) and a saint whose name was invoked in intercessions about headaches and snakebites among other things.

God of remedy and learning, we remember today the life and work of Mawes, who came to Cornwall and left his mark on Cornish life. May we honour him as a teacher and a missionary whenever we hear of the fishing village of St Mawes. Amen

19 November

Hilda, Abbess of Whitby (680) – commemorated in some traditions on 17 November

Born in Northumbria, Hilda was a grand-niece of King Edwin of Northumbria and was baptised by Paulinus with Edwin when she was 13. It was much later that she felt called to be a nun and Aidan asked her to be abbess of a convent in Hartlepool, which led to her setting up a foundation at Whitby, a double monastery of men and women, of which she became abbess, counting John of Beverley and Caedmon as members of the community. She hosted the greatly significant Synod of Whitby in 664, which decided on the adoption of the Roman calendar. She was also known for her role as educator, scholar and adviser.

Mighty Counsellor, we offer thanks and praise today for the wonderful ministry of Hilda, Abbess of Whitby, called to be a religious and to oversee the double monastery of Whitby, where she hosted the important Synod of Whitby. May we acknowledge and admire the great influence of Hilda on the Anglo-Saxon Church. Amen

Mechtild, Béguine of Magdeburg, mystic (1280)

Born around 1210, Mechtild had a revelation of the love of God when she was 12 and as a result joined a community of Béguines when she reached 18. Much later she joined the convent of Helfta, where she completed her poetic and sensitive writings, inspired by other creative personalities in the community. Her work *The Flowing Light of the Godhead* is also known as *The Revelation of Mechtild of Magdeburg*.

God of divine revelation, on this day let us rejoice at the importance you gave to Mechtild, who was called to serve you as mystic and poet in the centre of learning that was Helfta. May there be such creative forces at work today in monasteries and convents across the world. Amen

Ermenburga, abbess (c 700)

The niece of Erconbert, King of Kent, Ermenburga married Merewald, thought to have been a son of Penda, King of Mercia. Among her four children was Mildred, who became Abbess of Minster, and Milburga, who was appointed Abbess of Wenlock. On the death of her younger brother, murdered by Thunor, she received compensation in the form of land on the Isle of Thanet in Kent, where she founded a nunnery, becoming its first abbess in 670. She was succeeded by her daughter Mildred.

God of succession and dynasty, we celebrate the vocation of Ermenburga, whose loss of her brothers led to the founding of a nunnery at Minster in Thanet and to her becoming its first abbess, succeeded by her daughter. Let us honour her devotion and learn from her obedience to your will in bringing great things out of tragedy. Amen

20 November

Edmund, King of the East Angles, martyr (870)

Born in 841, Edmund was brought up a Christian and became King of the East Angles as a youth. He was known for his strong suppression of wrongdoing and for his care of the poor. When Danish forces attacked he resisted but was defeated and refused to countenance any renunciation of his faith or sharing of his kingdom and was immediately tied to a tree, killed with scores of arrows and beheaded. His body was enshrined at Bury St Edmund's (St Edmund's borough) and an abbey dedicated to his name was founded there in 1020.

Almighty God, we thank you for giving courage and resolve to Edmund, King of the East Angles, whom we commemorate today. As a martyr who died refusing to deny his faith, let us not forget his story and his contribution to the English Church. Amen

Colman of Dromore, monk and bishop (sixth century) – *see under 7 June*

Bernward, Bishop of Hildesheim (1022)

Bernward was ordained priest at Mainz, serving Otto 3rd as chaplain before his appointment as Bishop of Hildesheim in 993. Known as an encourager of the arts and a keen metal-worker and painter himself, he made his mark at Hildesheim, where his bronze doors, cross, column and candlesticks can be seen as his legacy today, along with the impressive St Michael's Church.

God of inspiration, on this day we mark the artistic and spiritual creativity of Bernward, Bishop of Hildesheim, whose patronage of the arts and his own metal-working skills have beautified Hildesheim. May we seek and find spiritual inspiration through admiring his works. Amen

Priscilla Lydia Sellon, restorer of the religious life in the Church of England (1878)

Probably born in 1821, Priscilla Sellon was a pioneer in women's ministry in the Church of England, responding to the call from the Bishop of Exeter in 1848 for workers among the poor and deprived in Plymouth. In taking up the challenge she formed the Sisters of Mercy, which later joined with the Holy Cross Sisters to form the Society of the Holy Trinity. She led the way in starting schools and orphanages, nursing the sick in the slums and caring for injured soldiers in the Crimea.

Lord of countercultures, we rejoice that Priscilla Lydia Sellon was moved to take up the call to minister to the destitute by founding the Sisters of Mercy. Let her example bring insight in inspiring our own ministry to the least, the lost and the lonely. Amen

21 November

Paulinus of Wales, abbot (sixth century)

Known principally as the tutor of Saint David, Paulinus probably spent some time as a hermit in Carmarthenshire and Brecon and taught David at Llanddeusant. A pupil of Germanus, he is credited with advising the Synod of Llanddewi Brefi to send for David to address them, to great effect.

Lord of time and place, today we commemorate the life of Paulinus of Wales, pupil of Germanus and teacher of David, whose experience as a hermit showed his self-effacing character. May his 'behind the scenes' ministry be marked, honoured and emulated today. Amen

Gelasius 1st, pope (496)

Although born in Rome, Gelasius was a Roman priest of African origin who was elected pope in 492. He served only four and a half years at a difficult time for Rome's relationship with Constantinople. Yet during that time Gelasius proved to be an energetic and effective leader, upholding the primacy of the Roman see and of spiritual power over temporal power.

God of hope, we give thanks on this day for the short but vigorous papacy of Gelasius 1st, who used his influence to safeguard the Church and especially Rome, from the challenges of the day. Set our sights high, Lord, in defending our faith, your truth. Amen

Condedus, monk and hermit (late seventh century)

Known as an English 'exile for Christ', Condedus became a monk at Fontenelle before reverting to the life of a hermit on an island called Belcinac in the middle of the Seine, near Caudebec, given as an endowment by the king. Although he built two churches on the island, the island was later submerged in the river.

God of exile and solitude, we thank you that Condedus experienced life as a monk as well as a hermit in his quest for a true relationship with you. Help us to explore new ways to experience you and know your love. Amen

22 November

Cecilia (Cecily), martyr at Rome (c 230)

A much revered Roman martyr, Cecilia is thought to have been born into a good family, who forced her to marry a young pagan, Valerian. However, she preferred to give herself to God rather than consummate the marriage. By this deed she won Valerian's respect and he and his brother Tiburtius became Christians and were arrested and martyred. She buried them and risked giving hospitality to the Christian Church at her home in Trastevere, but was herself brought before the prefect, refused to sacrifice as an act of idolatry and was ordered to be suffocated. It is said that she even converted her persecutors and for several days survived attempts to kill her before she succumbed. Her house was later turned into a church. She became the patron saint of musicians and her story is the basis of the second nun's tale in Chaucer's *Canterbury Tales*.

> **We give thanks today for the pioneering ministry of Cecilia, who showed fortitude and courage in witnessing to her faith and giving hospitality to other Christians. Let our church music remind us of her life and love for you. Amen**

Philemon and Apphia, martyrs (first century)

The recipient of Paul's short letter in the New Testament, Philemon was a Christian whose slave, Onesimus, had absconded and had met Paul, who sent him back to Philemon with the letter asking for his forgiveness for running away. Subsequently Philemon freed Onesimus, but was later martyred with his wife Apphia at Colosse.

Lord of forgiveness, we recall on this day the Christian acts of forgiveness and martyrdom of Philemon and his wife Apphia and especially for the freeing of Onesimus in response to Paul's letter. Let freedom thrive wherever the Christian faith is practised. Amen

23 November

Clement, pope, martyr (c 100)

A Roman by birth, of Jewish extraction, Clement was said to have been a disciple of the apostles, converted by Peter and Paul, and probably Peter's third successor as Bishop of Rome. He famously wrote a firm letter to the Corinthians on church ministry, probably the first time a Bishop of Rome had intervened in the affairs of another church. This hierarchical approach set the trend for future episcopal practice and ministry. Some accounts of his life suggest that he was later exiled to the Crimea and put to death there by being thrown into the sea with an anchor round his neck.

Overseeing Lord, we recall today the benign authority of Clement, the first pope to set out guidance to another church on ministry matters, which stood Corinth in good stead. We thank you for his example and good advice and mourn his martyrdom by drowning. Amen

Columbanus, bishop and abbot (615)

Born in Leinster of a noble family, Columbanus became a monk at a young age and a disciple of Comgall of Bangor, who permitted his mission to continental Europe with a number of companions. Establishing three monasteries in the Vosges and remaining true to the Irish tradition of Easter, Columbanus encountered opposition and moved on to Lombardy, where he founded the Abbey of Bobbio in 614. Known for the quality of his writing as well as the serenity of his rule of life, Columbanus' influence on monastic life was later overtaken by that of Benedict.

Lord of order and discipline, we give thanks today for the ministry of Columbanus, whose pioneering achievements and inspiration made him the greatest of Ireland's apostles to the continent of Europe. May his steadfastness of faith be a beacon to us all. **Amen**

Alexander Nevsky, Prince of Novgorod, defender and protector of Russia (1263)
– commemorated in some traditions on 23 May

Known for his victories over invading armies of Tartars, Swedes and Teutonic knights, Alexander Nevsky, who succeeded his father as Prince of Novgorod in 1236, was also said to have been a man of prayer. He took the monastic habit shortly before his death and was later invoked as a symbol of Russian resistance and nationhood, most notably during and immediately after the Second World War, helped by the popularity of Eisentein's film *Alexander Nevsky*, made in 1938.

Protector God, we celebrate today the powerful example of Alexander Nevsky, defender of Russia, whose leadership and faith were legendary. May we be inspired by Alexander and all the saints to great deeds for you. **Amen**

24 November

Colman of Cloyne, abbot, bishop (c 606)

Born in Munster about 530, Colman spent much of his life as a poet and royal bard at Cashel. Becoming a Christian partly through the inspiration of Brendan, he was ordained priest and became a bishop for Limerick and Cork, building churches at Cloyne, where there is a holy well, and Kilmaclenine.

Lord of ministry and rhyme, we commemorate on this day the life of poverty and discipleship of Colman of Cloyne. May we see his late flowering as priest and abbot-bishop as a blessing and a sign that the best is yet to come. **Amen**

Enfleda, Abbess of Whitby (c 704)

Enfleda was the daughter of Edwin, King of Northumbria, and Ethelburga, a Kentish princess. Baptised by Paulinus in 626, she grew up in Northumbria until her father was defeated and killed in 633 at the battle of Hatfield Chase. She and her mother then fled to Kent with Paulinus. She later married Oswin of Bernicia and after his death she became a nun and abbess at Whitby, having earlier helped to bring about the Synod of Whitby, which decided on a common date for Easter. Her daughter Elfleda succeeded her as abbess.

God of might and majesty, today we honour and admire the eventful life and ministry of Enfleda, in Northumbria and Kent, her contribution to the Synod of Whitby and her leadership as Abbess of Whitby. May we learn from her positive responses to tragedy and change in our faith journeys. Amen

Lucy Menzies, teacher of the faith (1954)

A child of the manse, Lucy Menzies was born in 1882 at Inchture, where her father, Allan Menzies, was parish minister. An Episcopalian but also a powerful advocate for ecumenism, she was a scholar and translator, publishing books on the saints and translating works of medieval and modern spirituality. She collaborated with Evelyn Underhill and was Warden of a retreat house at Pleshey in Essex. Known for her committed life of prayer and radiant devotion to God, she was also good at discerning and encouraging spirituality in others.

We rejoice today at the radiant spirituality of Lucy Menzies, who through her writings and prayer life had such an impact on others. Give us the energy and appetite to pursue this same path, with her ecumenical vision in our mind's eye. Amen

25 November

Catherine of Alexandria, martyr (fourth century)

Born of a noble family, this scholarly maiden of Alexandria is said to have refused the hand of marriage offered by Maxentius, professing she was a 'bride of Christ'. Faced by fifty learned philosophers trying to show her the errors of her ways, she demolished their arguments and they were burnt for their failure. She was placed on a wheel of torture (hence 'Catherine wheel'), which disintegrated, injuring bystanders, and she was finally beheaded.

> **God of faith and devotion, we remember on this day the cruel torture of Catherine on the wheel that now bears her name and also the bravery she showed during her ordeal. May we recall her martyrdom whenever we see and hear a Catherine wheel and marvel at her witness. Amen**

Isaac Watts, hymn writer (1748)

Born in 1674 at Southampton and educated locally, Isaac Watts then chose a dissenting academy at Stoke Newington to pursue his studies instead of going to university, followed by a period as pastor at a Congregationalist church at Mark Lane in London. He was opposed to the imposition of the doctrine of the Trinity and was assumed by some to be a Unitarian. He was a prolific hymn writer during the rest of his life, spent at Stoke Newington.

> **Lord of word and song, we give thanks today for the life, ministry and hymn writing of Isaac Watts, Congregational pastor. May his songs of praise lift our spirits and lift our eyes to you, gracious God. Amen**

26 November

John Berchmans, Jesuit scholar and man of prayer (1621)

A Fleming of modest social origins, John (or Jan) Berchmans benefited from a good education thanks to the initiative of Canon Froymont of Mechlin, where a Jesuit school was opened in 1615, John entering the Society as a novice in 1616. Completing his course in 1621, he successfully took part in a public disputation on philosophy and was chosen to represent the Roman College at a further disputation at the Greek College, falling ill a day or two later and dying after a week's illness. He was mourned as a man of prayer, obedience and cheerfulness.

Lord of life and death, we recall the short and prayerful life of a gifted scholar and debater, John Berchmans, who inspired others through his words and life. Let his short life be a reminder that it is the quality of our lives which matters to you. Amen

Leonard of Port Maurice, Franciscan priest and missioner (1751)

Born in 1676, the son of a master mariner, Leonard was educated by the Jesuits in Rome, but joined the Franciscan Order and was ordained priest in 1703 and restored the Florentin Friary at San Francesco del Monte based on Francis' austere teaching in 1709. He spent most of the next forty years preaching the length and breadth of Italy and even venturing to Corsica on an unsuccessful mission. He is probably best known for developing and promoting the service called *The Stations of the Cross*.

Lord of the Cross, we celebrate today the ministry and service of Leonard of Port Maurice, tireless missioner across Italy and beyond, whom we thank for the service known as the Stations of the Cross. May his inspiration be our inspiration, especially during Holy Week. Amen

Peter of Alexandria, bishop and martyr (311)

Elected Bishop of Alexandria in 300, Peter was accused by another bishop, Melitius, of being too easy-going with lapsed Christians, leading to a long-lasting schism in the Egyptian Church. He was put to death in the persecution of Maximinus and was held in high esteem as an inspired Christian teacher who was the last victim of public authority in the Alexandrian Church.

God of knowledge and inspiration, we give thanks for the life and witness of Peter of Alexandria, who faced dispute and persecution in the Church of Egypt, but left a legacy of respect and fulfilment. Let us rejoice at his example of tolerance and devotion in times of difficulty. Amen

Delphine of Provence, Franciscan tertiary (1360)

Born of royal blood, Delphine was educated by nuns under her uncle's protection. Against her will but in obedience to her family, she entered into marriage at the age of 15 for political reasons, but determined to remain a virgin. After her husband's early death she was moved to give away most of her considerable possessions and made a vow of poverty, forming a community devoted to prayer and good works. Known for her skill in expounding the Scriptures and speaking of the mystery of God, she became a mediator in disputes and lived as a recluse, devoted to a life of mystical prayer.

We offer you our thanks and praise today for the prayer life, gift of preaching the gospel and skills of mediation of Delphine of Provence. May her mystical insights help us to shine a light into our understanding of Scripture through our own prayers and practice. Amen

27 November

Catherine Labouré, visionary (1876) – commemorated in some traditions on 28 November

Catherine was a Sister of Charity of St Vincent de Paul in Paris and proved herself to be a model nun, caring and praying for the sick. In this role she experienced visions of the Virgin Mary, giving rise to the depiction on an oval medallion of an image of Mary on one side and a religious symbol on the other, which became known as a 'miraculous medallion'.

God of miracles and revelations, on this day we give thanks for Catherine Labouré, a Sister of Charity in Paris who experienced visions of the Virgin Mary. May the miraculous medals which came to be produced to commemorate them be a lasting recognition of her insights and visionary experiences. Amen

Fergus, bishop (early eighth century)

Originally from Ireland, Fergus became the apostle of large areas of Scotland, founding churches in Strogeth, Caithness and Buchan. He died at Glamis, where a well and a cave are named after him.

Lord of all, we recall on this day Fergus, the bishop who came from Ireland and was known as 'the Pict', who became the apostle of much of Scotland. Let his name live on, especially in the churches of places where he ministered. Amen

Congar, Welsh missionary and founder (sixth century)

Thought to have been born in Pembrokeshire, Congar was a missionary who founded Christian communities in Somerset and Devon, giving his name to the village of Congresbury. He reputedly returned later in his life to Wales and died on a pilgrimage to Jerusalem.

We give thanks today for the mission and ministry of Congar, who journeyed from Wales to found church communities in Somerset and Devon. Let the village of Congresbury be a lasting memorial of his life and Christian witness. Amen

28 November

Catherine Labouré, visionary (1876) – *see under 27 November*

James of the Marches, Franciscan priest and preacher (1476)

Born into a poor family in the Marches of Ancona, James became a Franciscan at Assisi, was a student of Bernadino of Siena and read law at Perugia. After ordination as a priest in 1423 he adopted an austere lifestyle, showed compassion to the poor and became well known as a preacher across a wide area. He had a reputation for being severe and ruthless in opposing heretics and worked closely with John Capistrano, succeeding him as papal legate in Hungary in 1456. Among his initiatives to alleviate poverty he set up pawnshops to enable loans to be made at reasonable rates for the needy.

Lord of charity and austerity, we remember today the life and works of James of the Marches, who used his gifts to help the poor help themselves and who fiercely opposed heresies, defending the true faith. May his clarity of purpose be an example to us in our Christian lives. Amen

Gregory 3rd, pope (741)

Born in Syria, Gregory succeeded Gregory 2nd as pope, acclaimed by the people. Known as a man of humility and wisdom, Gregory was also an eloquent preacher, protector of the poor and of widows and orphans, and a strong upholder of the faith. He found himself in dispute with Emperor

Leo 3rd over the latter's banning of sacred images. Gregory's stand against iconoclasm led to further difficulties between Church and State, but Gregory's pact with the Franks helped to ensure the papacy's independence. His backing of Boniface's missionary work led to great success in the establishment of churches and sees in central Europe. In his ten years as pope, Gregory oversaw the improvement of existing churches and monasteries in Rome and founded new ones, affirming the value of icons in the Western Church.

> **God of great works and great symbols, we recall today the tireless work of Gregory 3rd, upholder of the faith and independence of the Church as well as guardian of the poor and destitute. We give thanks for his backing of Boniface's great missionary work, as well as his stand against iconoclasm, both of which leave their legacy with us in our times. Amen**

Stephen the Younger, martyr (765)

Born at Constantinople, Stephen was a hermit monk on Mount St Auxentius and the foremost defender at Constantinople of the veneration of religious images during the Iconoclast persecution renewed by Emperor Constantius 5th. In 761 he was banished for his activities to the island of Proconnesus in the sea of Marmara. Brought before the emperor three years later, he precipitated his death by stamping on a coin with the image of the emperor on it to emphasise what it meant to do the same with images of Christ. After a period in gaol with three hundred other monks he was battered to death, resolute in his principles to the end.

> **God of principle and purpose, we recall with admiration the stand taken by Stephen the Younger during the Iconoclast persecution, for which he was put to death. May his witness inspire and strengthen our purpose. Amen**

29 November

Brendan of Birr, Irish abbot (573)

A friend and disciple of Columba, Brendan was held in high esteem by his peers and called the chief of the prophets of Ireland. His intervention at the synod at Meltown (Meath) which ended Columba's excommunication was crucial. When Brendan died, Columba's vision of angels receiving his soul led him to order a special Mass in his honour.

God of friendship, on this day we commemorate the life and loyalty of Brendan of Birr to his friend Columba, to fairness and justice and, above all, to your Truth. Let us rejoice at his ministry and the way he was welcomed into your heavenly kingdom. Amen

30 November

Andrew the Apostle (first century)

A fisherman from Bethsaida, a town in Galilee, Andrew was a disciple of John the Baptist and the first to be called to be a follower of Christ, bringing along his brother Simon (later Peter) to be a disciple too. Because of this he is known as 'the first missionary'. Andrew remained with Jesus for much of the rest of his ministry on earth, helped in the feeding of the five thousand, and famously introduced some Greeks to Jesus, who were invited by Philip to 'come and see'. He later carried out missionary work in Scythia and was martyred at Patras in Archaia, reputedly on an X-shaped cross. He is known in the East as the founder of the Patriarchal See of Constantinople and is the Patron of both Scotland and Russia.

God of great missions, we give thanks today for the missionary initiatives and zeal of the apostle Andrew, called from his nets to follow your Son and bringing with him Simon Peter, the rock on which your Church was built. May Andrew's encouragement and persistence in mission be a constant reminder of our responsibility as your followers to help others 'come and see'. Amen

December

1 December

Nicholas Ferrar, deacon, founder of the Little Gidding Community (1637) – *see under 4 December*

Eligius (Eloi), Bishop of Noyon (659)

Born into a modest Gallo-Roman family, Eligius was at first apprenticed to the master of the mint at Limoges and later secured a similar position at Marseilles. His talents for engraving and smithing were recognised by King Clotaire and his successor Dagobert, who frequently commissioned him and then made him Bishop of Noyon. In this capacity he founded monasteries at Noyon, Paris and Solignac and was a compelling preacher in his outstanding work in Tournai, Flanders and Frisia. He was known also as a distinguished craftsman and a dedicated apostolic bishop. He is patron saint of smiths, farriers and all kinds of metalwork.

God of great skills and abilities, we admire and celebrate the fine works and pastoral ministry of Eligius, Bishop of Noyon and patron of metalworkers. May his skills in parish and workshop have left their mark. Amen

Charles de Foucauld, hermit in the Sahara (1916)

Born in 1858, Charles de Foucauld became an officer in the cavalry, leading a rather dissolute life. An expedition to North Africa left its mark on him as he developed a love for that region. Reverting to the Catholic faith of his youth, he became a Trappist monk following a pilgrimage to the Holy Land and then, in search of a more austere life, became a servant to the Poor Clares in Jerusalem and Nazareth. After being ordained priest he went to live as a hermit in his beloved North Africa at Tamanrasset in Algeria, composing rules for brothers and sisters, which inspired the founding of the Little Sisters of the Sacred Heart and later the Little Brothers of Jesus. He was assassinated in 1916 in a local religious war.

God of exploration and adventure, we give thanks for the faith journey of Charles de Foucauld from dissolute soldier to austere hermit, who paved the way for brothers and sisters by his composition of rules of life. May we admire his energy and emulate his humility and interest in other cultures. Amen

2 December

Saints, martyrs and missionaries of Asia

The first missionary journeys and the first martyrdoms took place in Asia. Following the apostles, notably Thomas, early saints included Ignatius of Antioch and Polycarp and Christian communities such as West and East Syrian Orthodox Churches had a continued presence there over the centuries. Missionaries also came from the West including Francis Xavier and Henry Martyn and churches grew up in parts of India, China, Japan and Korea, often inspired by missionaries. The ancient churches of the Middle East remain a particular witness to the living truth of the gospel in the midst of tensions and persecution.

On this day let us pray for all those apostles, saints, missionaries and martyrs who served in Asia from early times, the struggles they had and the witness they showed. May the churches under pressure in these countries today be upheld by our prayers and your peace. Amen

3 December

Birinius, Bishop of Dorchester (on Thames)
– see under 4 September

Francis Xavier, missionary, apostle of the Indies (1552)

Born a Basque Spaniard at the castle of Xavier in Navarre, Francis was educated in Paris, where he met Ignatius of Loyola and was one of a group of seven who took vows as the first members of the Society of Jesus at Montmartre in 1534. Sent to Goa, Francis arrived after a journey of over a year and reformed the Portuguese Catholics there before radiating out on missionary journeys in South India, Sri Lanka (then Ceylon), Malacca, the Molucca Islands and the Malay peninsula. In 1549 he travelled to Japan with varying results and died on his way to China, having worn himself out. His impact and reputation were, and remain, considerable and his letters bear out the extent and depth of his ministry and motivation.

Lord of all good things, we commemorate today the reach and range of the missionary work of Francis Xavier, Jesuit priest and apostle of the Indies. May his fearless energy and ability to relate to high and low be a model for ministry and mission today. Amen

4 December

Clement of Alexandria, priest, teacher of the faith (c 215)

Honoured as Christianity's first religious philosopher, Clement was born in Athens into a pagan family around 153. He and others sought to explore the relation between Christian thought and Greek philosophical tradition, Clement travelling widely and learning from respected teachers of his day before arriving in Alexandria and producing an impressive body of work based on the idea of Christ as both the source of human reason and the unique interpreter of God to humanity. When persecution broke out in Alexandria he left and is presumed to have been martyred.

God of teaching and learning, we recall on this day the pioneering philosophical work of Clement of Alexandria in seeking to draw on strands of Greek philosophy in explaining and exploring the Christian story. We give thanks for his insights and understanding as we develop our own. Amen

John of Damascus, monk, teacher of the faith, hymn writer (749)

The last of the Eastern fathers, John was the son of a wealthy Damascus Christian who held the office of chief of the revenue at the court of the khalif. Educated under Cosmas, John succeeded his father in his job but in

716 became a monk and then a priest at the Abbey of St Sabas, near Jerusalem, where he wrote hymns and theological works, including *The Fount of Knowledge*, which contained an influential digest of the Christian doctrine of the Greek fathers entitled *The Orthodox Faith*. Two of his hymns, 'Come ye faithful, raise the strain' and 'The day of Resurrection! Earth, tell it out abroad', became well known in the United Kingdom.

God of knowledge and understanding, we honour today the life and works of John of Damascus, doctor of the Church and hymn-writer, whose influence was great and remains so. May we learn from his multicultural understanding and shrewd use of resources. Amen

Nicholas Ferrar, deacon, founder of the Little Gidding Community (1637) –
commemorated in some traditions on 1 December

Born in London in 1592, Nicholas Ferrar went to Clare Hall (College) in Cambridge, where he became a Fellow. After travelling in Europe for five years he entered business and then became a parliamentarian. Moving to Little Gidding in Huntingdonshire in 1625, he was joined by other members of the wider family and established a community prayer life as well as engaging in charitable works. Becoming a deacon, he was dedicated to the community life, but the community was wound up after his death by the Puritans, who feared the return of Romish practices in England.

God of community, on this day we remember with grateful thanks the commitment of Nicholas Ferrar to a life of prayer in community, based on the Book of Common Prayer. May his vision be carried on in today's Christian communities to maintain that tradition. Amen

Barbara, virgin and martyr (c 306)

A maiden of great beauty, Barbara was reputed to have been shut up in a tower by her father, Dioscorus, to discourage suitors. On learning that she had become a Christian he vowed to kill her, but she miraculously escaped his clutches and lived as a hermit in a bath-house, her father being struck by lightning and killed. In this unlikely way she became the patron saint of gunners and miners and her special emblem became a tower.

God of thunder and lightning, today we remember Barbara, beautiful virgin and martyr, who escaped death after incarceration by the lightning strike on her murderous father. May this miraculous deliverance remind us of the power of your reach in support of those who profess your name. Amen

5 December

Birinius, Bishop of Dorchester (on Thames) (c 650)
– see under 4 September

Crispina of Tagora, martyr (304)

A married woman of good standing, with several children, Crispina was brought before the proconsul Annius Anullinus for refusing to sacrifice to the gods in accordance with the laws of Diocletian and Maximian. She remained steadfast in her faith, saying 'I do observe an edict: that of my Lord Jesus Christ.' Losing patience, Anullinus ordered her death by the sword.

Lord of duty and commitment, we give thanks on this day for the faith and fortitude of Crispina, who refused to sacrifice to the gods when ordered to do so and remained steadfast in her commitment to you above all else. May her faith be our inspiration. Amen

Christina of Markyate, virgin (c 1161)

Born into a noble Anglo-Saxon family in Huntingdon, Christina vowed to remain a virgin despite the efforts of her parents and the advances of Ralph Flambard, a bishop. Forced to marry against her will, the marriage remained unconsummated and she was spirited away and put under the protection of an elderly recluse. Returning to Markyate following the annulment of her marriage and becoming a nun, she was invited to be an abbess in York, but declined and stayed at Markyate for the rest of her life, guarded by Geoffrey, Abbot of St Albans, until his death in 1147.

God of vocations and spiritual guidance, we remember today the purity of Christina of Markyate's calling and ministry, withstanding pressures to do things against her will and your calling. Let us hope for such clarity in our own vocations and ministry. Amen

Sabas, abbot (532)

Born in Cappadocia, not far from Caesarea, in 439, the son of an army officer, Sabas became a disciple of Euthymius the Great and lived as a solitary in Palestine until founding a community or 'laura' between Jerusalem and the Dead Sea. In 493 he was given oversight of all Palestinian monks living a similar life, having been ordained priest at the insistence of Sallust, Bishop of Jerusalem. Sabas' monastery, St Sabas, now called Mar Saba, is one of the oldest occupied monasteries in the world.

We celebrate on this day the life and ministry of Sabas, who chose the life of a solitary before being called by you to lead a community in the Holy Land. May this lasting legacy be a tribute to the dedication of Sabas himself. Amen

6 December
Nicholas, Bishop of Myra (fourth century)

Although little is known about his life, Nicholas has become the patron saint of many places and occupations, notably countries (including Russia), dioceses and churches, as well as sailors, children and pawnbrokers. The only certain fact is that he was Bishop of Myra in Asia Minor (southern Turkey). He is said to have loved children, saved three girls from prostitution by giving them money, and brought back to life three children murdered in a brine-tub, the latter stories giving rise to the pawnbroker sign of three balls. Among the depictions of Nicholas is the window of the Jerusalem chamber in Westminster. In some countries gifts are given to children on this day and Nicholas is the inspiration for the modern day Santa Claus, derived from the Dutch dialect form of his name.

Lord of generosity and celebration, we rejoice today at the life and legend of Nicholas, who gave generously and cared for many, especially children. As we look forward to Christmas, let us acknowledge his influence on our present-day celebrations. Amen

7 December

Ambrose, Bishop of Milan, teacher of the faith (397)

Born at Trier in 339, Ambrose was the son of a praetoriam prefect of Gaul. He practised law in the Roman courts before being appointed Governor of Aemilia and Liguria, which included Milan, where he became bishop by acclamation in 374, despite his protestations, as he was yet to be baptised, though his baptism followed within a week and he was duly consecrated. Study followed with his tutor Simplicianus and he embarked on a punishing schedule of encouraging monasticism, opposing Arianism, intervening with the emperor and writing on doctrine, including *On the Faith*. He was also involved in the conversion of Augustine and was known for his accessibility to all.

Lord of all, we offer our thanks and praise for the life and ministry of Ambrose, Bishop of Milan, whose influence spread far and wide in defending the faith and making converts, as well as setting out doctrine in his writings. May we appreciate and understand the extent of his influence in our Church today. Amen

8 December

The conception of the Blessed Virgin Mary

Dating from the seventh century, this festival honours the conception of the Mother of God and is celebrated in some traditions of the Eastern and Western Church. It marks the dawn of the New Covenant, as God prepares his people to receive our Saviour and Lord, demonstrating that mortal flesh can bring Christ into the world. This is the start of the journey with Mary on the way towards the Messiah.

God of wonder, help us today to take in the full enormity of the journey begun in the conception of Mary and taking us through to the incarnation of your Son, the Messiah. May our sense of awe combine with your many signs and signals through the prophets to give us confidence, hope and excitement at the prospect of that journey's destination. Amen

Budoc, bishop and missionary worker (sixth century)

Patron saint of Budock and Budoc Vean in Cornwall and St Budeaux in Devon, Budoc is also venerated in Brittany. Although there is a fanciful legend recording how his mother, pregnant with him, and cast into the sea in a barrel, was directed to safety by a vision of Brigid, a more significant fact is that Burdock faces St Mawes across Falmouth Harbour and Mawes had been abbot of an island monastery in Brittany close to that of Budoc.

On this day we recall the missionary monk and bishop, Budoc, who is associated with many coastal regions and islands in the west of Britain and Brittany. May his legend remind us of our dependence on the sea, whatever perils lurk there. Amen

9 December

Peter Fourier, founder (1640)

Born at Mirecourt in Lorraine in 1565, Peter Fourier became an Augustinian canon regular who, at the age of 32, was appointed parish priest at the village of Mattaincourt in the Vosges, where for thirty years he was known as 'the good priest of Mattaincourt'. Peter carried out many reforms and improvements and put into practice his ideas on education, which worked better for girls than for boys, collaborating with Alix le Clercq to form the Augustinian canonesses of our Lady. Political events forced him to go into voluntary exile in 1636.

God of innovation and change, on this day we celebrate the pioneering work of Peter Fourier in the field of education and his dutiful and pastorally sensitive work as parish priest at Mattaincourt. Amen

Hipparchus and Philotheus, martyrs (c 297)

When Emperor Maximian returned victorious from the defeat of the Persian army he commanded residents at Samosata, where the quinquennial games were being held, to engage in sacrifices to the gods. Hipparchus and Philotheus, together with five young men who had been converts by then, had absented themselves from such practices and were imprisoned. When they refused to comply they were condemned to death by crucifixion. Those who survived had nails hammered into their heads.

God of faithfulness, we give thanks today for the lives of Hipparchus and Philotheus, who resisted imperial commands to worship idols and died horrible deaths as a result. Let their sacrifice remind us of your Son's and may their witness strengthen ours. Amen

10 December

Eulalia, virgin and martyr (304)

According to Prudentius, Eulalia was a maiden in a noble family who was dedicated to an austere and strict life. It is said that as a girl of 12 she remonstrated with the judge at Merida over the requirement to sacrifice to the gods. She refused all bribes and blandishments to renounce the one true God and the judge, Dacian, had her tortured and burnt alive, her body being covered in snow before being buried.

Lord of life and death, we recall the witness of Eulalia, virgin and martyr, who stood up to the edicts of the emperor over idol worship and suffered a cruel death as a result. May we learn from the faith of young people in seeking to do the right thing in following your Way. Amen

Miltiades, pope (314)

Born in Africa, Miltiades was Bishop of Rome when Constantine decreed toleration for Christianity (alongside other religions), marking the end of persecution, having suffered much himself under Maximian. He was commended by Augustine for his moderation and peaceableness and it was to him that Constantine gave the Lateran mansion, used by popes over the centuries as their home.

> God of great milestones, we commemorate today the ministry of Miltiades, who was pope when the persecution of Christians was lifted by Emperor Constantine and was known for his moderation and peaceable nature. We ask that we learn from his approach to challenges faced by our Church today. Amen

11 December

Damasus, pope (384)

Born in Rome, the son of a priest, and possibly of Spanish descent, Damasus became a deacon under Pope Liberius and succeeded him in 366, despite the claims of the supporters of Ursinus. However, Damasus had the support of Emperor Valentinian and Ursinus was banished. Damasus had to face the challenges of Arianism and other heresies and he was aided in this struggle by the adoption of orthodox Christianity by the State. His main, lasting contribution was to encourage the biblical work of Jerome, whom he commissioned to revise the Latin text of the Bible to produce a single 'Vulgate'.

> Lord of ebb and flow, we recall on this day the foresight and courage of Damasus as pope to resist Arianism and to use the gifts of Jerome to raise the profile of the Vulgate Bible, bringing your word to many who would otherwise not hear it. Let his legacy be cherished and his role acknowledged. Amen

Daniel the Stylite, hermit (493)

Born in Maratha, near Samasota, in Mesopotamia in about 304, Daniel left home at the age of 12 and until the age of 42 he was a monk at a nearby monastery. He twice visited Simeon the Stylite on his pillar at Telanissus and, after a period at a hermitage near Constantinople, on the death of Simeon he adopted the latter's style of life, setting himself up on a shelter on two pillars, overlooking the Bosporus, where he stayed, except for a brief foray, for thirty-three years. Actively consulted by Emperors Leo 1st and Zeno, Daniel prayed for all people, gave instructions on what was necessary for salvation, offered counselling and hospitality and adopted practices 'worthy of admiration, not imitation'.

> **Today we recognise the selfless lifestyle and ministry of Daniel the Stylite, a worthy successor to Simeon the Stylite and deserving of our study and admiration. Let us be aware of his sacrifice and penitential living as a reminder of what it is that matters in life under you. Amen**

12 December

Edburga of Minster, abbess (751) – *see under 13 December*

Finnian of Clonard, abbot (c 549)

Born in Leinster, Finnian was probably educated at Idrone in County Carlow. After travelling to Wales to study traditional monasticism he returned to Ireland and founded a number of monasteries before establishing that of Clonard, County Meath, which was the culmination of his many achievements. There he gathered thousands of disciples and sought to unite study with the Welsh form of monastic life. Known as 'the teacher of the saints', those who are said to have learnt there included Ciaran, Columba and Brendan and he was perhaps the outstanding saint of Ireland after the era of Patrick.

> **God of great example, we commemorate on this day the outstanding contribution to Irish monasticism of Finnian, Abbot of Clonard, influencing among others Columba of Iona. May we celebrate his inspiration and nurturing of the faith. Amen**

Jane Frances de Chantal, founder of the Order of the Visitation (1641)

Born at Dijon in 1572, she was happily married to Baron Christophe de Rabutin-Chantal until his fatal shooting accident left her a widow with four children. In 1604 she met Francis de Sales when on a visit to her father in Dijon. This led to her combining her motherly duties with becoming a founder member of the Order of the Visitation, designed for single women and widows unable to follow the more severe way of life of other orders, taking charge of the first of the Order's convents at Annecy. She had considerable administrative ability and was a committed visitor of the sick and the poor. She was described by Vincent de Paul as 'one of the holiest people I ever met on this earth'.

God of grace and mercy, we remember on this day the remarkable life and ministry of Jane Frances de Chantal, follower of Francis de Sales and founder of the Order of the Visitation. May her example of holiness and multitasking be a beacon for our age. Amen

13 December

Odile (Odilia), Abbess of Hohenburg, Patroness of Alsace (720)
– see under 14 December

Lucy, martyr of Syracuse (304)

Born of wealthy parents in Syracuse in Sicily, Lucy is said to have committed herself to Christ when she was quite young, against her mother Eutychia's wishes, which were for her to marry a suitor, who was a pagan. Afflicted with a bleeding, her mother was cured after being brought for prayer to the tomb of St Agatha, and thereafter supported her daughter's vocation. Her faith was exposed to the authorities during the Diocletian persecution and she was allegedly consigned to a brothel, horribly injured and died of the wounds inflicted on her.

God of faith and sacrifice, we remember today the devotion of Lucy to the true faith, despite the pain and suffering she endured. Let the light of her courage shine like a beacon on those who remain faithful in the face of such forces. Amen

Edburga of Minster, abbess (751) – *commemorated in some traditions on 12 December*

A disciple of Mildred, Abbess of Minster-in-Thanet nunnery, Edburga succeeded her in that position in 716. Boniface wrote to her on a number of occasions and she sent him gifts, as well as using her skills as a scribe to produce holy scripts for him. She built a church at Minster, as well as a monastery, and was buried at Minster, where cures were claimed at her tomb.

> God of tradition and transition, we thank you on this day for the life and ministry of Edburga of Minster, who carried on the tradition of Ermenburga and Mildred and encouraged Boniface in his ministry and mission. May we acknowledge the spiritual help given to us through the faith and works of role models such as Edburga. Amen

Samuel Johnson, moralist (1784)

Born in 1709, Samuel Johnson became a serious Anglican as a young man after reading William Law's *A Serious Call to a Devout and Holy Life*. He was best known as a writer of dictionaries, conversationalist and literary editor, but was renowned also for his religious beliefs as a High Churchman and firm supporter of the practice and order of the Church of England. His twice weekly essays entitled *The Rambler* appearing between 1750 and 1752 earned him the title of 'The Great Moralist'.

> Lord of moral virtue, today we celebrate the varied life and career of Samuel Johnson, literary giant and staunch Anglican, who gave clear moral leads in his writings. May we seek your way in our own moral dilemmas and look to the likes of Samuel Johnson for insight and encouragement. Amen

14 December

John of the Cross, poet, teacher of the faith, priest (1591)

Born at Fontibere near Avila, into an impoverished noble family, Juan de Yepes was brought up by his widowed mother and went to study at the college of Jesuits. At 21 he joined the Carmelite Friars in Madeira, studied theology at Salamanca and was ordained priest in 1567. Invited to reform the Carmelite house of Duruelo by Teresa of Avila, he laboured against great opposition and was eventually confined in Toledo, where he was inspired to write some of his spiritual poetry, including *The Dark Night of the Soul.* Escaping after nine months, he acted as superior in various houses, taking the moderate line in disputes within the order and continuing his writing, before once again being banished, to Andalusia in Spain, where he died.

> **Today we recall and celebrate the tumultuous life and wonderful writings of John of the Cross, poet and theologian, whose inspiration came from difficult experiences but deep and imaginative faith. Let us take our inspiration from John in interpreting your Word in our times. Amen**

Odile (Odilia), Abbess of Hohenburg, Patroness of Alsace (720) – *commemorated in some traditions on 13 December*

The daughter of a Frankish nobleman, Adalric, Odile was reputedly born blind, brought up in the monastery of Baumes-les-Dames in Moyenmoutier and recovered her sight at her baptism. She became a nun and then abbess at Hohenburg, also known as Mont Sainte Odile. Her shrine has become a place of pilgrimage, especially for those suffering from sight impairment and eye diseases, for whom she is the patron saint.

> **God of sight and insight, on this day we recall and honour the life of Odile, begun in blindness and growing in insight as her sight was restored. May her example be a sign that miracles are possible through your Son, our Saviour, Jesus Christ. Amen**

15 December

Mary di Rosa, foundress (1855)

Born at Brescia in 1813, Mary di Rosa became involved from the age of 17 with social work for girls working in hospitals and factories and among those afflicted with hearing and speaking difficulties. Although herself physically fragile but mentally alert, she went beyond menial duties and founded the Handmaids of Charity of Brescia, in order to minister to the religious and material needs of the sick and the suffering, a much-needed ministry in the days of war in northern Italy, which were followed by a cholera epidemic.

> **Loving Lord, we offer you our thanks and praise for the work and witness of Mary di Rosa, a pioneer in developing an order for ministry to the sick and the deaf. May she inspire the continuing need for the ministry of women in war-torn areas of the world today. Amen**

Offa of Essex, king (c 709)

Offa was the son of Sighere, King of the East Saxons, became king in c 707 and was by all accounts popular among his subjects. However, he abdicated in 709 and left his family and kinsmen and went to Rome, where he became a monk, dying shortly afterwards.

> **Transforming God, on this day we remember Offa, popular Prince and King of the East Saxons, who gave up his crown and kingdom in pursuit of his calling to your service as a monk. May we all try to cope with transition and transformation in a similar way. Amen**

Nino, slave-girl (c 340)

It is said that Nino, a slave-girl, was responsible for bringing Christianity to Georgia, by her example and healing powers. She had been captured by the Georgian Prince, Bakur, who brought her back to Georgia to become

347

his slave. Impressing everyone with her obvious goodness and religious devotion, she was reputed to have cured the Georgian queen and encouraged the king to call on Christ for help. Led by the king, the people were keen to become Christians too and the king requested Emperor Constantine to send clergy to Georgia.

God of service, we thank you for the example of the slave-girl Nino, who brought the good news to the great and the good in Georgia and through them to the ordinary people. Let our ministry be inclusive, as hers was. Amen

16 December

Adelaide, empress (999)

Adelaide became the second wife of Otto the Great, whose first, Edith, sister of Athelstan of England, had died. On his death in 973 she endured family strife and was forced to leave the court not once, but twice, by her son, Otto 2nd, and later by her grandson, Otto 3rd, before she found a more peaceful life under the guidance of Adalbert of Magdeburg, among others. She was called 'a marvel of beauty and goodness' in a memoir about her and died in the convent she had founded, at Setz in Alsace.

Today we honour the memory of Adelaide, wife of Otto the Great, who, following his death, suffered misfortune at the hands of her family, but radiated beauty and goodness in the midst of strife. Help us to bear turmoil with the equanimity she showed, Lord. Amen

17 December

Olympias, widow and deaconess (c 408)

Born about 368, Olympias was left an orphan and brought up by, among others, Theodosia. At the age of 18 she married Nebridus, treasurer of Theodosius the Great, but in less than two years she became a widow. Despite being rich and charming, she vowed to remain single in the face of pressures to marry and eventually was free to give over large sums for charitable purposes. Under the guidance of John Chrysostom until his banishment she became discriminating in her benefactions, but suffered for her loyalty to Chrysostom after his exile. She showed exemplary patience and dignity in the face of adversity and oppression.

> **God of steadfastness, we remember on this day the loyalty and dignity of Olympias, left a rich widow, but determined to share her riches with the poor. In today's world of inequality, may we seek to do the same. Amen**

Eglantyne Jebb, social reformer, founder of *Save the Children Fund* (1928)

Born in 1876, Eglantyne Jebb studied at Oxford, becoming a lecturer before ill-health curtailed that career. Turning to charitable works, in 1913 she went to help refugees in the Balkan Wars. She founded the Save the Children Fund with her sister Dorothy Buxton after the First World War, in order to help suffering children during the famine in Europe and lobbied the League of Nations to set out the rights of children, which led to the 'Children's Charter' in 1924.

> **God of great movements, we give thanks for the life and work of Eglantyne Jebb, tireless worker and advocate for the rights of children and co-founder of the Save the Children Fund. Let her inspiration move our hearts and direct our charitable giving and our prayers. Amen**

Sturm, abbot (779)

The son of Christian Bavarian parents, Sturm, at the instigation of Boniface, was trained at Fritzlar and after being made a priest was sent as a missionary in Hesse, where he stayed for three years. Later, directed by Boniface, he found a suitable site for a monastery, at Fulda, and in 744 became its first abbot. The later part of his ministry was interrupted by an intervention by King Pepin, who removed him temporarily, and then by Charlemagne's approach to mission, which differed from that of Sturm and Boniface.

Lord of initiative and outreach, on this day we rejoice at the ministry of Sturm, faithful disciple of Boniface, who ventured out on his behalf and became the first Abbot of Fulda. May we be faithful advocates for your Church and followers of your Way. Amen

Lazarus of Bethany (first century)

Lazarus was the brother of Martha and Mary who was raised from the dead by Jesus, the cause of his veneration, especially in Jerusalem. He regularly went with his sisters to Cyprus, where he lived for thirty years and where he became a bishop. Vincent de Paul took the name of the Order of Lazarus he founded from the Parisian church dedicated to him, Saint-Lazare.

God of resurrection, we celebrate the life, raising from the dead and ministry of Lazarus, brother to Martha and Mary. May he always be a reminder and affirmation of your power, through your Son, to bring life out of death. Amen

18 December

Flannan, missionary and pilgrim (c 640)

Flannan was the disciple and successor of Molua, founder of Killaloe monastery and cathedral in County Clare on the River Shannon. A wanderer and a preacher, Flannan was, like many Irish saints, a traveller who embarked on long journeys, by water and over land, as both pilgrim and missionary. On one of the Scottish Flannan Islands there are the remnants of a monastery called the chapel of Flannan.

God of enterprise, we give thanks today for the wandering preacher, Flannan, who founded Killaloe monastery, with its cathedral and oratory. May we be appreciative of the achievements and outreach of the Irish saints, including Flannan. Amen

Winnibald (Winebald), Abbot of Heidenheim (761)

Along with his brother Willibald and sister Walburga, Winnibald went on a pilgrimage to Rome,where he stayed for seven years before returning to England. He then took with him some companions and went to join Boniface in Thuringia in 739, undertaking missionary work and being ordained priest. He then teamed up with his brother Willibald to found the new monastery at Heidenheim, which followed the Rule of Benedict. This became a centre of evangelism and was often threatened by local pagans. A double monastery, Heidenheim was run by his sister Walburga after his death.

> **Lord of brotherhood and sisterhood, on this day we mark the life, mission and ministry of Winnibald who, with his brother Willibald and sister Walburga, gave so much to your Church in its outreach, prayer and purpose. May his name be a source of inspiration and comfort. Amen**

Samthann, Irish nun (739)

This Irish saint was the founder of a convent at Clonbroney in County Longford. Probably fostered by Cridan, King of Cairbre Gabhra, she became a nun under Cognat at Ernaide in Donegal after a miraculous occurrence which prevented her marrying. Known for her skill and devotion in prayer, a monk enquired of her the best position to pray, to which she answered that standing, sitting or lying were all acceptable. She had a ready answer to any question on study, prayer and pilgrimage and preferred to live in poverty rather than accept gifts, except the six cows to start the community herd.

> **God of community, we rejoice today as we mark the life and wise ministry of Samthann, who devoted her gifts to her community and to prayer. May we seek to make the most of being a member of any community of which we feel a part and develop our prayer life accordingly. Amen**

19 December

Nemesion, martyr and others (250)

An Egyptian falsely accused of theft at Alexandria at the time of the persecutions of Decius, Nemesion cleared himself of that charge but was immediately accused of being a Christian. Confessing his faith before the prefect, he was scourged and condemned to be burnt, alongside criminals and robbers. At the same time others, including soldiers, were condemned as Christians and beheaded. Others were torn limb from limb before being burnt, but a youth, Dioscorus, was discharged to be given time to repent.

On this day we mark the terrible persecution of Decius in Egypt, resulting in the deaths of many professing the true faith, including Nemesion. May these deaths remind us that faith can be costly but that your commitment to us is total, for which we give you thanks. Amen

20 December

Dominic of Silos, abbot (1073)

Born into a peasant family in Rioja, Navarre, Dominic worked on the family farm before becoming a monk and then being ordained at the Benedictine monastery of San Millan de la Congola, rising to novice-master and then prior. Exiled over property issues, he and two companions were invited to revive and rebuild the monastery of St Sebastian at Silos, near Burgos. As abbot he rebuilt the church, planned the cloisters and established an impressive scriptorium. Known for his learning, his healing and his holiness, Dominic's fame spread and the monastery flourished, with over fifty monks in residence at his death, and the monastery is still known today for its Gregorian chants.

God of great opportunities, today we celebrate the ministry of Dominic of Silos, who from humble origins took steps to pursue his vocation, which opened up a pathway to great challenges for your sake, bringing life to a moribund monastery and learning,

healing and holiness to those around him. May his holistic ministry be an encouragement to our own efforts in ministering to others. Amen

21 December

Thomas, apostle (first century) – *see under 3 July*

Peter Canisius, Jesuit priest, writer and educator (1597)

Born at Nijmegen in Holland, the son of a burgomaster, Peter Canisius attended Cologne University and Louvain, where he studied canon law. Back in Cologne he was drawn to the Society of Jesus through Peter Favre and became a Jesuit in 1543. He became known as a preacher, spent time with Ignatius Loyola and taught at the Jesuit school in Messina at the University of Ingoldstadt, becoming its rector, then vice-chancellor. Next he turned his attention to strengthening the faith of Catholics faced by Protestantism, publishing his famous *Catechism* as a Catholic response to Luther, going on to preach, write, travel, and, in between, founding schools, colleges and seminaries as provincial superior of the Jesuits. Later he helped found Fribourg University.

Lord of insight and understanding, we celebrate and give thanks for the extraordinary energy and enterprise of Peter Canisius, a man of courtesy amidst controversy and learning in the midst of ignorance. Let his writings and his example be recognised and emulated in today's Church. Amen

22 December

Frances Xavier Cabrini, nun and foundress (1917)

Brought up the youngest of a family of thirteen children on an Italian farm near Pavia, Frances lost her parents when she was 20. Refused on health grounds by convents in her quest to be a nun, she worked as a teacher and with her parish priest reorganised an orphanage, but she was thwarted in her efforts by an incompetent foundress and the orphanage was closed. She became a missionary and then a prioress, forming the 'Missionary Sisters of the Sacred Heart', and went to work with Italian immigrants in New York, running an orphanage and establishing a novitiate. Foundations followed in other parts of the USA, as well as in Buenos Aires and in Bromley, Kent. Known to be strict, just and loving, though occasionally lacking in sensitivity to the culture around her, she was tireless in carrying through her vision, which resulted in sixty-seven houses and 1,500 nuns in her congregations, in eight countries.

God of plenty, we thank you today that you gave Frances Cabrini the vision of her calling and the means to carry through your plans for orphanages, convents and other foundations across the world. Let her legacy be prized and valued even – and especially – in our secular age. Amen

23 December

Thorlac of Skalholt, bishop in Iceland (1193)

As a young priest, Theodore left Iceland to study in Paris and Lincoln over a ten-year period. Returning to Iceland, he embarked on a life of prayer, devotion and pastoral ministry. He founded a community of Austin canons, of which he was abbot, and in 1178 became Bishop of Skalholt and started a programme of radical reform, which was partially successful. He became a spiritual guide and worked with Eystein to draw up a code of law for both clergy and laity, as well as writing *The Lives of the Saints*.

Almighty God, on this day we commemorate the great contribution to the Icelandic Church of Thorlac of Skalholt, his reforming zeal, his pastoral ministry and his writing. May all those who seek change and development in your Church also set out the way to do it, as Thorlac did. Amen

John of Kanti, priest (1473)

Born at Kanti in Poland, John was educated at the University of Cracow and ordained priest soon after completion of his course. Appointed as a lecturer, he combined this with preaching until he was removed from his post and appointed as a parish priest, which did not prove a great success. He was recalled to the University and later took the Chair of Theology. Extolling the virtues of mediation and good manners in controversy, he was held in high esteem by his students, as well as living austerely and giving generously to those in need. This was remembered in the University's use of his gown in conferring doctorates.

We acknowledge today the academic excellence and humble lifestyle of John of Kanti, especially in his work at the University of Cracow. May academics today learn from his example and the esteem of students for him as lecturer and pastor. Amen

24 December

Sharbel the Maronite (Charbal Maklouf), monk and hermit (1898)

Born in the village of Beka-Kafra in the Lebanon in 1828, Sharbel Maklouf was orphaned in childhood and brought up by an uncle. He joined the Maronite Baladite order and was ordained priest in 1859. He delighted in singing the office and was an avid follower of *The Imitation of Christ*. He was a model monk and then, in 1866, he became a hermit in the hermitage of St Peter and St Paul, living an austere life devoted to prayer and fasting. People sought him out for counsel, prayers and blessing.

God of great blessings, we rejoice at the life and selfless ministry of Sharbel the Maronite, who embraced austerity, chanting the office and prayer. Help us to understand and appreciate such a sacrificial life and be grateful. Amen

25 December – Christmas Day

Anastasia, martyr (c 304)

Anastasia was martyred at Sirmium (now Sremska Mitrovica) in Serbia. An alternative legend suggests that she was a Roman matron associated with Chrysogonus, also martyred in 304. There was a church dedicated to her in Rome where the pope was used to singing the second Mass on Christmas Day.

Lord of love, on this Christmas Day, as we celebrate the birth of your Son, we recall also the life of Anastasia, martyred for her faith in the story of the Nativity of Christ, the Son of God. May we all freely rejoice and remember all those who died professing your name and spreading the good news. Amen

26 December

Stephen, deacon and first martyr (c 35)

Described in the Acts of the Apostles as 'a man full of faith and power', Stephen, a Greek-speaking Jew, was one of the seven deacons with the task of caring for widows in the early Church in Jerusalem. He was also a zealous preacher, well versed in the Scriptures and the history of Judaism. Brought before the Sanhedrin accused of blasphemy, he argued eloquently and passionately that all might hear the good news of Jesus. He was taken out of the city and stoned to death without a full trial, the first martyr, with Saul of Tarsus standing by.

On this day we give thanks for the life and martyrdom of Stephen, whose wisdom and spirit in preaching the gospel led to his stoning. We pray that his example of selfless courage shines as a beacon to us all. Amen

27 December

John, apostle and evangelist (c100)

Also called 'the Divine', John was a Galilean fisherman, the son of Zebedee and the brother of James. He and James were known as 'the sons of thunder' who, with Peter, were present at the momentous events of the transfiguration, the last Supper and the crucifixion. Known as 'the disciple whom Jesus loved', John was entrusted by Jesus to care for his mother just before his death on the cross and was among the first to see and believe in the resurrection. The author of the fourth Gospel and three epistles, in later years John was exiled to the Island of Patmos, where he is said to have written the Book of Revelation. He died at Ephesus in advanced old age.

We pray for the memory of John, evangelist and apostle, who was present at the Transfiguration, experienced the Last Supper, witnessed the Crucifixion, stood by Mary in her grief, and saw and believed the Resurrection. We give thanks for John's loyalty and devotion, his deep and rich faith, and the ability to communicate it, to your glory. We ask this through your Son, Jesus Christ. Amen

28 December

The Holy Innocents

Told by the Magi of the birth of the new king, and a possible rival, King Herod gave orders for all the children of Bethlehem who were two years old or under to be killed. These 'holy innocents' were venerated as martyrs from early times, though the numbers have sometimes been exaggerated beyond the likely twenty who suffered this fate.

We give thanks today for those innocent young ones who died at Herod's whim. Mistaken for a threat to the world, they died for the Saviour of the world. May they be thanked and thanked again, in heaven and on earth, and never forgotten, through the grace of the one whom Herod did not reach, the one who would have reached out to him, your Son, Jesus Christ. Amen

29 December

Thomas Becket, Archbishop of Canterbury and martyr (1170) – *commemorated in some traditions on 7 July*

Born in Cheapside, London, into a wealthy Norman family of merchants, Thomas received a good education before entering the service of

Theobald, Archbishop of Canterbury, who made him Archdeacon of Canterbury, demonstrating both administrative and diplomatic skills. Appointed Chancellor of England by Henry 2nd in 1155, Thomas became Archbishop of Canterbury in 1162 and adopted an austere lifestyle, jealously guarding the independence of the Church and becoming a shepherd of souls. After six years of exile in France, Thomas returned after an apparent reconciliation with the king, but Henry's angry words led to his martyrdom at the hands of four knights in Canterbury Cathedral, his shrine becoming one of the main pilgrim attractions of Europe.

> God of peace, we commend and celebrate the life of Thomas Becket, cut short in Canterbury Cathedral, for which act Henry made due penitence. We draw courage and comfort from Thomas' openness and vulnerability; from the pilgrimages made over the ages to mark his martyrdom: and from the inspiration of your Son in all that Thomas did in your name. Amen

30 December

Tathan, abbot (sixth or seventh century)

The son of an Irish king, Tathalius, Tathan travelled to Gwent, where he was given some land at Caerwent by King Caradog. Here Tathan set up a famous Welsh monastic school where, among others, Cadoc studied under him. He was well known in the neighbourhood for his generosity of spirit, his hospitality and his defence of the woodland country and is said to have been a miracle-worker.

> May the love of education and the knowledge of your love for us show forth in the fruits of Tathan's life so that, from generation to generation, his good works and prayerful commitment may inspire and influence, through school and college, through baptism and hospitality, and through the love of your Son, Jesus Christ. Amen

31 December

John Wyclif, reformer (1384)

Probably born into a family owning property in Richmond in Yorkshire around 1330, John Wyclif became a Fellow of Merton College, Master of Balliol and Warden of Canterbury Hall. He was expelled from Canterbury Hall by Archbishop Simon Langham, who wanted the college to become a monastic foundation and which led to a lawsuit and John's lifelong hatred of monasticism. Protected by royalty, he continued to speak out, but his denial of the Church's teaching of the presence of Christ at the Eucharist was a step too far and his opinions were formally condemned in 1381. Believing that the Bible was the sole criterion of doctrine, he put his weight behind the project of translating the Bible into contemporary English and was a considerable influence on future reformers.

On this day we give thanks for the life and witness of your servant, John Wyclif, who showed, by using his gifts of preaching and translating, a true discipleship. Just as he brought us closer to you through knowing your Son, so may we be equipped to know and share your word through strengthening our understanding of the faith. Amen

Bibliography

Celebrating the Saints, Robert Atwell (SCM Press)

Celtic Daily Prayer, Andy Raine and the Northumbria Community (Collins)

Common Worship (Church House Publishing)

Exciting Holiness, Brother Tristram SSF and Simon Kershaw (Canterbury Press)

Lives of the Saints, Alban Butler (Studio Editions)

Saints of the Isles, Ray Simpson (Kevin Mayhew)

The New Mass Book (C.B.C. Distributors)

The Oxford Dictionary of Saints, David Farmer (Oxford University Press)

The Oxford Dictionary of the Christian Church, F. L. Cross and E. A. Livingstone Eds. (Oxford University Press)

The Penguin Dictionary of Saints, Donald Attwater with Catherine Rachel John (Penguin Press)

The Revised Common Lectionary

Walking with the Saints, Jenny Child (The Columba Press)

Index of Saints in Alphabetical Order

(with page numbers)